Memphis
Hoodoo Murders

Donation 2/18/16

Memphis Hoodoo Murders

Kathryn Rogers

Mojo Triangle Books™

An Imprint Of

SARTORIS LITERARY GROUP

A traditional publisher
with a non-traditional approach to publishing

SARTORIS LITERARY GROUP
Metro-Jackson, Mississippi
www.sartorisliterary.com

Dedicated to my grandparents whom I adore
and whose influence is ever present in my life

Memphis
Hoodoo Murders

Chapter 1

If I told you that people had been trying to kill my family and me my entire life, you would probably just think I was being paranoid, but it's not paranoia if it's real.

Sometimes healthy people run for exercise, and oftentimes energetic individuals run for fun. In my neck of the woods, you run just to stay alive. Today I only hoped that the gang members didn't murder me so I could make it home in one piece. My legs were pumping so hard I thought they might fall off.

Grandma and Pop would tell you I'm petite and pretty when really I'm short and perfectly ordinary. I don't look anything like them except that we are all small in stature, though I'm so little I look like a shrimp by comparison. I have straight, brown hair with no bangs, smooth skin, and sharp, green eyes. I've never dressed fancy as I've never had much to begin with. Besides, in my neck of the woods, when you get something shiny, folks try to take it or talk about you for having it, so the more you blend in, the better off you're bound to be.

"Hey, short stuff! You with the ponytail! I told you to get over here!"

It was my favorite neighborhood thug heckling me.

Just don't trip. Whatever you do, don't trip, Addie.

The limb from the fallen tree did not hear my inner monologue, because my foot caught on the log and slung me onto the sidewalk.

"I told you there was no point in running from us," he said coldly. "We always get what we want."

I winced in pain and grabbed my right knee, which was running red. I felt like a bleeding fish in the middle of a shark tank.

Show no fear. Don't cry.

I forced myself to stand and face my antagonists. Their clothes and tattoos were clearly reflective of the Memphis gang, the Skullbangerz—not that I would be privy to any admission from them about this.

"Ouch! Looks like you got a boo-boo," said a slim, jumpy guy, eyeing me from the stems up. "Want me to kiss on you to make it all better?"

"No, thanks—you're really not my type," I said thankful I had enough spirit to sound snarky.

"Oohh, she's a feisty one. I like that in a lady," he toyed dangerously with me.

"Enough with your mouth. You're wasting my time." The tall, muscular gang leader cut him off as he stepped towards me. "Yeah, you got to be her," he remarked as he studied my face.

"Got to be whom?" I asked sullenly.

"June Jackson's granddaughter," Jaydon Swisher announced.

I was surprised that he knew who I was. Everyone around here knew him. Just thinking about his cruel reputation made me shudder.

"How do you know her?" I asked to try to pump information out of him.

"So, you is Mrs. Jackson's girl?" he quizzed me clearly not wanting to give anything away.

"What's it to you?"

"You ain't in the position to be asking questions of me. You give me what I want, and I might let you go in one piece...might. You act uncooperative, and I'll butcher you up while you're still alive. Then I'll mail individual pieces of you wrapped up as Christmas presents to your Grandma. Do you understand what I'm telling you right now?"

He was close enough for me to feel his hot breath on my neck.

I knew most people made idle threats. However, I could tell from the way the other gang members kept their distance from him, Jaydon was telling the Gospel truth.

The waterfall of blood continued to rain down my leg. Every fiber in my being told me to get as far away from them as possible. Unfortunately though, as history had indicated, I was too clumsy to outrun them. So, I stalled for time and willed myself to exhibit grace under fire.

The leader of the pack misinterpreted my silence for newfound cooperation and continued to press me, "So, where is it?"

"Where's what?"

I winced to try to hide my pain.

"Your Grandma's ring." he stated as if it should be obvious to me.

"Come again?"

"Don't test me," he said, raising his voice. "You better show me quick, or I'll be forced to strip it off of you."

"I seriously don't know what you're talking about."

My head was spinning. I thought this was the truth, but I wasn't 100 percent sure. My Grandma wore her blue starred ring a lot, which she had never allowed me to touch. I didn't know if this was the ring he was referring to or if this was any of the mounds of rings she kept locked up in her jewelry box.

Before I had time to figure out how to respond, he slapped me hard right across my face. I was stunned. I had never been hit by a guy before. Growing up, my Dad had broken everything in the house, including my Mom's nose a time or two. Yet even in his drunken rages, he had never once laid a hand on me.

I guess there's a first time for everything, I thought.

"I told you. I always get what I want. Now I'm going to ask you one more time to give it to me. I'm trying to be nice about this. I'm warning you. Don't make me be a bad guy, Addie."

I had never told Jaydon my name, so as the reality of being under his radar hit me, my fear intensified, and a lump began to fill my throat. All of the gang members positioned themselves around me as if braced to attack me at his command.

I couldn't decide which way to go. He didn't like the truth, and I hadn't come up with a lie big enough to save me yet. So, I decided to stall a bit more.

"I know you're not a bad guy," I said smoothly. "You go after what you want, and I respect that. Now why don't you tell me what you want with the ring so I can better help you?"

He sneered, and the other hoodlums howled.

"You think you're going to charm me? Wasting my time isn't going to save you. Listen, honey, everybody wants that ring, and I mean everybody. I don't care if it's today or tomorrow or next week or ten years from now, but eventually, I'm going to have it. I've already spelled it out for you loud and clear. If you help me get it, I'll let you live, but if you don't, the first thing I'll do after I get it is kill you ... slowly ... painfully ... So, which way are you going to have it, Miss Jackson?"

Jaydon cracked his knuckles fully prepared to make good on his promises.

There was no story I could concoct that I thought he would buy. He wouldn't accept the truth, and he was not about to be charmed. So, I did the only thing I could think of. I took off running, zig-zagged as fast as the pain in my knee would allow, as I hollered for help at the top of my lungs.

Unfortunately, I did not see any neighbors out on my street. My neighborhood had gotten extremely dangerous in recent years, and I had been the only non-gang member stupid enough to go for a run this morning—a mistake I did not plan on repeating if I were lucky enough to survive the day.

I darted, screamed, and prayed for safety. Maybe I could make it home alive. Maybe I could get inside, call 911, and get the cops over there before the gang broke in my house. Maybe I was dreaming to think I'd survive any of this.

I heard an army of footsteps behind me. When they caught me, they'd murder me quickly at best, or they'd rape and torture me before killing me slowly at worst. Either way I was totally and completely screwed.

I could see the top of my Grandma's oak tree in the distance. The sight of that beacon of hope gave me the adrenaline rush I needed to push through the searing pain and the horrifying fear to make it into my yard.

Just as I stepped foot into my grandparents' grass and let out one final cry for help, a strong, heavy hand came down on my back and pushed me into the dirt. The gang leader flipped me onto my back and pulled his fist back to punch my face when I heard gun shots right beside us. To my surprise he jumped off of me immediately.

"It's really you," he stammered. "Wow. I was just talking to your granddaughter about you."

Coward, I mentally swore at him.

"You get off my girl, and you and all of your filthy dogs stay away from my family and off of my property!"

My Grandma's thundering voice made her sound like my personal arch angel, who had arrived just in time to pull me up from the gates of hell.

"If I ever smell your stench again, I'll send you straight to Hades for a permanent visit. Then I'll bury you in my backyard myself, and your people will hunt your remains for the rest of their lives. Seeing as how your thug friends and you seem to be so close, I'll make sure they get a spot in the backyard beside you, because I'm just sweet like that."

Well, maybe she was no angel, but she was my unconventional, heaven-sent guardian. Normal senior citizens called the cops when they were threatened by criminals; my grandparents just pulled out bigger weapons to intimidate the convicts and "took care of things themselves."

The leader of the pack turned, terrified. He recognized that she had meant her threats just as much as he had meant his. However, the tables had turned on him, because she was the one holding the weapon, ready and willing to gun him down.

"I understand, Mrs. Jackson," he stuttered before calling off the dogs and running away with his tail between his legs.

After Grandma was sure that they were out of her sight, she hollered into the house for my grandfather. "Louie! Get yourself out here!"

"What is your problem, woman? I was just sitting down trying to read the paper. Can't a man get some personal time around here?"

"Addie's hurt—get out," and before Grandma could finish saying "here," Pop flew out the door and ran over to me.

"Oh, no, sweetheart!" he groaned. "What's done happened to you?"

The adrenaline had worn off, but now the trauma was kicking in.

"They chased me down and threatened to butcher me if I didn't cooperate with them. They wanted ..." I tried to explain, but Grandma cut me off.

"This is too much talking and not enough resting," she ordered abruptly. "We've got to get you inside."

Pop scooped me up, which intensified the pain in my knee, so I began to cry.

"I'm sorry, sweetie, but it ain't safe for you to sit out

here no more." Pop said by way of an apology. "I got to doctor you up in the house."

"Don't you think maybe I need to go to a hospital?"

"We ain't going nowhere today," Grandma said soberly as her blue eyes gleamed intensely.

I had often thought that my Grandma could extract confessions from the most hardened of criminals with just one somber stare. I noticed for the hundredth time how much thinner she had gotten in the last year with her fading health; however, despite her sunken shoulders, her permed, white hair was as stiff as ever.

Pop carried me inside and laid me on my bed. Despite Pop's physical infirmaries, he still carried himself well. My grandparents both have wiry, gray hair. Pop's hair is almost gone now, but Grandma's stays stiff and curly on account of her weekly beauty shop appointments with a lady named Erlene. Both of them have piercing blue eyes and wrinkled faces, and they are significantly stronger than one would expect from individuals their age. Their good looks have withered and faded with time, but they are still beautiful, old souls to me.

As I watched, Pop began mixing all manner of herbs and powders together to form a strange smelling concoction.

"Oh man, what are you whipping up for me now?" I whined.

"Something that will get that knee as good as new by morning."

Pop spoke much more cheerfully than any of us actually felt.

"Why can't y'all just give me some pain medication?"

"Fiddlesticks! This here is a motion potion; you'll be moving around just as right as rain in the morning once I get you fixed up with some of this."

I waited for Pop to pour an eye of newt into his brew and cackle wildly, but he disappointed me by leaving his broom stick by the back door and stirring the paste with a boring wooden spoon instead.

He nursed my knee with the weird hoodoo goo as Grandma assessed the damage.

"Grandma, that guy said he knew who we were. He said he wanted your ring and that that was why he was giving me such a hard time."

"Child, there ain't no need in worrying about people like him. That man's crazy, and if I ever see him again, I'll shoot him dead, so he ain't nothing to concern yourself with."

"But he knew who I was and who you were! What ring was he talking about? Was he talking about your blue-starred ring?"

"How am I supposed to know what that lunatic was saying?" she snorted in disgust. "People these days are all mad or drunkards anyways. You can't listen to nobody about nothing anymore. Why, just the other day I was watching the news about King Kristoff. Would you believe he thinks a lot of our black birds are monsters, so he's recruiting his band of rednecks to hunt them down? Now have you ever heard of such a thing? Hunting blackbirds in the city limits!"

I was much smarter than she was giving me credit

for. Her subtle attempt to avoid the real issue by broaching an irrelevant subject was not new to me. Our local "celebrity," King Kristoff had no more to do with what had happened just now than the man in the moon.

"Grandma, I'm not talking about King Kristoff or blackbirds. I'm telling you this guy recognized me. He knew you, too, and he said he was going to kill me if I didn't give him the ring. You've got to tell me what he's talking about!"

"I done told you I don't know! Now you're just going to have to put all of this out of your mind. You got too much good going on in your life to let somebody like him mess it up. We're Jacksons, sugar, and Jacksons don't let nobody get them down. Do you understand me?"

She stared me down and silently compelled me to drop the subject.

Pop finished pasting my knee and bandaged me up as he quietly hummed to himself in a less than subtle attempt to stay out of the conversation.

"Pop ..." I turned to him for support, but he began humming even louder to will me to shut up.

I knew Grandma was lying to me again. She was slick though, and I was very aware that she would do whatever she had to to protect me, even if that meant being dishonest. I felt disappointed knowing that I would not be getting the information I wanted from her today. So, I gave up and fell silently and angrily into the bed.

"There now," Grandma coaxed me kindly. "You're plumb worn out from all of this craziness. I'm going to bring you some hot breakfast. I just got the grits done, and

I made some fresh buttermilk biscuits, too. I'll even bring you a cup of hot black coffee just like you like it. I'll let Shelby College know you'll be absent today, but when you go back tomorrow, just remember that it won't do you no good to be talking about this little incident with none of your classmates, professors, or friends. It'd just get them all worked up and stressed out for no reason, so let's just keep it between the three of us. You go ahead and lay down there like a good girl, and I'll be back with some grub for you."

There was never any point in arguing with Grandma, because it was like trying to win an argument with a four year old. She could wear me down to the point where I would finally just give up. Then just like a kid, she would be happy and energized by the outcome, and I would be mentally exhausted.

Before long Pop and she came back in with an overflowing plate of unhealthy foods.

After she set the food down, she lit up a cigarette and started wheezing that hacking cough, which came from a lifetime of smoking like a chimney. I swallowed a bite of biscuit, which was covered in buttery, syrupy goodness.

"Your Pop was over at the church working on the grounds this morning while you were running." Grandma changed the subject after she cleared her throat. "He said parts of the church got vandalized again last night."

I turned to Pop, feeling alarmed.

"What's all that about?"

"I don't know. This whole country's just gone to hell."

19

With that they both went off ranting on their soap box.

"So, who's been messing around over at the church?" I asked once they had quieted down. "What did the minister say about it?"

"Oh, probably these hoodlums in the neighborhood. I tell you what, when Pop and I moved here, this was a fine neighborhood. A fine neighborhood, I tell you! But over the years, it's just gone down, down, down...And now these yahoo's are trying to mess with you! They just don't know who they're playing with."

Grandma and Pop exchanged a knowing look.

I shuddered thinking about the Skullbangerz and winced at the pain in my leg. My Pop must have picked up on my discomfort, because he surprised me by handing me some pain pills.

"Wow, it feels like Christmas! You gave me medicine that didn't come from a bush or a dirt pile."

"Quit all that fussing! I know you're hurting a lot more than you're letting on. Go on now, and take them."

I swallowed the drugs, as my Grandma picked up on her rant right where she'd left off.

"I tell you what … I'm going to be paying special attention to these kids now. I'm sorry you got hurt today, but I'm kind of glad I got a chance to formally introduce myself to them this morning. Bunch of hoodlums, all of them! Now that they know I got my pistol loaded for whoever hurts my family and disrespects my church, maybe they'll think twice before they come back again!"

"Grandma, you are seventy five years old, and you

have a health history longer than a serial killer's rap sheet. You have no business provoking 'hoodlums' or packing heat!"

Pop snickered at me from behind Grandma's head, so I could see that he would be of no help in this discussion.

"Listen, I know you're tough stuff, and nobody has any business messing with your family or your church, but I don't want to read about you in the news," I continued. "If you mess around and get yourself thrown in the slammer, I don't have enough money in the bank to bail you out! Why don't you just call Nosy Rosy next door and gossip about this like you usually do instead of acting like a cowgirl in an old, Western movie?"

"You know that's like the pot calling the kettle black!"

She pointed at me, poking fun as she wagged her tongue and her index finger at me.

"Little Miss I'll just go for a run and play chicken with our local drug dealers!"

"I swear you about give me a heart attack sometimes. I don't know what I'm going to do with you!"

I sulked as Grandma started patting down her hard hair helmet.

"Don't say 'swear!'" she retorted defensively as she lifted her chin. "It ain't Christian to swear!"

Resorting to violence and pulling weapons on the neighbors? Totally acceptable in my Grandma's world. Gossiping with Nosy Rosy? Her most favorite hobby. Turning the other cheek? Not likely in spite of her regular church attendance. Dropping the word "swear" around my Grandma? Completely horrifying and "vulgar language" that would certainly result in a severe lecture from her. She was the only woman I had ever met, who substituted the word "swanie" for "swear."

I couldn't help but shake my head in disbelief at Pop, who was smiling mischievously. I scowled at him as Grandma pulled her old pocket watch out of her robe to check the time before she gave me a critical look. Inspecting that watch was one of her many nervous habits, and after today I couldn't help but wonder if it, too, held any value to the gang leader.

As soon as I had finished my breakfast, the pain pills really started kicking in, and I began fighting the urge to drift off to sleep.

"Go on to sleep now, child," said Grandma. "You need to rest."

"I don't want to go to sleep if you're going to act like a vigilante while I'm out."

Without explanation, she kissed the top of my head.

"Oh, phooey! I survived the Great Depression and World War II before you ever came along, girly!"

Pop and she talked a good game, but everyone knew that they needed me just like I needed them, and that was how it had always been. I might be a full time student, but every since I had moved in with them in elementary school, I had considered taking care of them to be my most important role. Over the years I had passed up a lot of fun opportunities and withdrawn from many a college class to tend to them when their health was poor. I didn't mind the sacrifices most of the time, because I felt like when the lives of the people I loved stopped, my life stopped with them. Besides, no matter what they went through, they always survived like they were cats with nine lives. As tough as they were, sometimes I actually believed that they could never die.

"Pop, keep your wife from doing anything too illegal while I sleep." I did my best to give him a stern look. "And Grandma, I'm calling Rosy on you later today to tell her how riled up you are. I'm putting her in charge of keeping you in line, so you two had better behave yourselves!"

They howled at that and then turned the television to a martial arts show. They were talking about how they were going to learn some new moves to take down the hoodlums as I curled up under the warm pile of quilts they had tucked around me. I looked out my window to find a black bird perched on my ledge peering curiously at me. It was strange how many animals had been popping up around our house lately.

I became vaguely aware that my grandparents had never explained what had happened with the church break-in's. Then not long after Grandma and Pop thought I had gone to sleep, I overheard them whispering in their room.

"Their warning couldn't have been clearer." Grandma murmured.

"Yeah, no question about it—them intruders at the church know hoodoo," Pop muttered back.

"Why else would they all break in dressed up like the Man?" Grandma whispered anxiously. "Them doing that means we is at a crossroads. We got something they want, and they is dressing up like the trickster to try to get us out in the open to take it, but it ain't going to work."

"Them leaving that mojo sack at the scene was intentional, no doubt about it. The cops didn't know what to make of it. They never seen no mojo sack before. They didn't think a red flannel sack with nails and dirt in it meant anything significant for their investigation."

"But anybody familiar with hoodoo would know that them nails and that dirt wasn't ordinary nails and dirt," Grandma replied solemnly. "Them was coffin nails and graveyard dirt."

I could almost feel her shiver as she soberly added, "And that means death for whoever they is after…"

It was the last thing I heard before the pain pills took me down for the count, and I fell into a slumber. My sleep is usually stressful and filled with dreams so vivid that upon waking I have to remind myself what is real and what was imagined. Sometimes I revisit the past, sometimes I stop in the present, but more often than I would like to, I visit the future.

The biggest problem for me with my dreams is that they are predictive and tend to come true with freakish, detailed accuracy. Even awareness of the bad things to come thus far has given me no capability to stop what's ahead. The feeling of powerlessness as a result of this has always been a very depressing aspect of my life.

Today I'm dreaming that I'm alone in my house when I hear an uninvited visitor in my grandparents' attic. Naturally I am alarmed, so I carefully slip up the ladder to find out who is there. My heart is pounding, and beads of perspiration are creeping down my neck. I sense him before I see him, and as usual I am both immediately elated and utterly terrified.

Gavin's tall frame is leaned over, rummaging through my Grandma's cardboard boxes, all 6'3" of him. I would have thought he was a god if I weren't so convinced he was the devil. His dark expression twists into a wry smile as he turns his head to glance back at me mischievously. As usual his blue eyes are covered in gray clouds, keeping his thoughts and soul a mystery to me.

"I should have known you wouldn't stay downstairs like I told you to. You're too much like your Grandma."

I sauntered in feigning cockiness I didn't feel and retorted: "I take that as a great compliment. Besides, I don't take orders from anybody, least of all you, and whatever you're doing in my house is more my business than yours anyways. What makes you think you have the right to just go digging through other people's stuff like this anyhow?"

I was too proud to tell him that my grandparents had never actually allowed me up here before. Going into secured areas of their house had always been strictly forbidden, and as far as locked perimeters went, they had more rooms vaulted and sealed up than the Federal Reserve.

He tilted his head to the side as the light peeking through the attic window made his disheveled black hair shine as darkly as a raven's wing. Nobody this dangerous should be that attractive. It made him more lethal than necessary, which was just an unfair advantage to all of the other questionable men in the world. I noticed a lucky rabbit's foot clipped to his jeans, peeking out from under his black leather jacket, and something about it made me wonder if he was involved in any of the hoodoo my grandparents had whispered about.

"You know I struck a deal with your grandparents, so I'm here to fulfill my end of the bargain. Besides, with all of your family's skeletons hidden around here, you would think you'd want somebody with you when they're found."

"What do you think I need? Moral support from you?"

"No, of course not," he said, speaking calmly, as if he had just said the sky was blue. "You're going to need someone to help you bury the bodies."

"You do mean metaphorical skeletons and not actual corpses, I hope?"

"I guess we'll just have to keep digging around up here until we find out, now won't we? Besides, if there's anything I understand in this life, it's that all people, even your grandparents, have something they want. I am here to help fulfill their request—and naturally I have a lot to gain also."

"So, you keep that poor rabbit's foot on you to provide good luck so you can just steal whatever you please from all of the vulnerable, unsuspecting, old people?"

"Oh, Addie, your naivety makes me laugh. I am neither a thief nor a pirate."

Considering I had never actually met Gavin in real life before, I was certainly not in any position to tell him what he was or wasn't. I might be sassy, but even I had a personal standard of boundaries.

I pulled my eyes away from his olive complexion and noticed the banjo on the floor beside him as I swallowed nervously. I made an effort to change the conversation as I said, "I didn't know my grandparents were musical."

"They aren't—the banjo is mine now."

"What did you do ... trade someone for it?"

"Of course." he remarked.

"It looks very old and well cared for—like it was really important to whoever owned it."

He moved towards me stealthily and murmured quietly, "It was."

"So, why would you take something that important from someone else?"

"I don't take anything that isn't freely given to me. Those are the rules."

"The rules?" I suddenly realized exactly how close he had gotten to me.

His eyes drank me in, and the fight or flight in me screamed I should run from him. However, the curiosity Grandma said would be the death of me keeps me standing firmly planted close enough to appreciate his scent. Being this close to him made me feel all warm and heady, and it was clouding my judgment.

"Yes, we've talked about this before." He smirked as he gently reached over to slowly run his fingers through my brown ponytail.

I gasped, and my fair skin flushed as I retreated from him. I became vaguely aware that I was dreaming and that this wasn't happening yet. I didn't know what the nature of my relationship was supposed to be with him, and despite all of the years I have dreamed of him, he had never actually touched me until now.

He cautiously approached me again as carefully as if he were trying not to spook a wounded animal. How strange that he should look as if he were scared of me when he terrified me to my core. For once in my life I forced myself to keep quiet to hear what he was going to say next.

"Have you thought anymore about my proposal?"

He quizzed me carefully as he continually eased closer to me. He asked the question as if anticipating a negative reaction.

"Proposal?! I'm not ready to get married!"

He burst into laughter, but even that was tinged with darkness.

"Addie, you know that's not what I meant."

"You can't buy my soul, if that's what you're after. It's out of season and not on the market this time of year. Unfortunately for you, I don't have any banjo's you would be interested in purchasing either."

"You know we're talking about trading, not buying. Besides, I think you should seriously consider what I have suggested."

He looked me up and down as he tempted me by saying, "Trust me. I'll make it worth your while..."

"You look like Trouble with a capital 'T,' and if my Grandma knew you were up here, she'd get her broom and chase you out of her house like a cat."

The normally dangerous expression he wore as comfortably as his dark clothes softened as he looked deeply into my eyes.

"Addie, you have bewitched me body and soul."

"Gavin, I think you would win the award for being the witchier of the two of us," I said, smarting back, but I could feel that I was starting to lose my ground.

"Your green eyes are truly magnificent."

"Yeah, well, you can't trade me for them either, big shot." I was talking a good game, but my knees and my heart were weakening by the second.

"I'm not interested in only having your eyes. They wouldn't be enough. I couldn't be satisfied until I had all of you ... always." He pulled me to him and kissed me. His mouth was gentle at first, but then he pressed me against him with forced intensity. My bottom lip tingled, and I was surprised by how well my smaller stature fit perfectly into his embrace. I forgot to breathe and became light headed until he forcefully pulled himself away from me.

He gripped my shoulders as he implored me, "Say yes to our deal. Just say yes. Please don't torture me anymore."

Even though I had no idea what deal he had been trying to coerce me into, looking into his eyes made me think there wasn't anything I could tell him no to. So, as if I was moved by a force outside of my control, I nodded my head and whispered, "Yes."

All of the darkness in the energy surrounding him cleared for the first time as the clouds in his eyes lifted. He broke out into a bright smile before enveloping me in his jacket and kissing me deeply again.

It would have been nice to have relished my hot fantasy a bit longer. If only it hadn't been disturbed by

Grandma screaming as Pop attacked an intruder trying to break into his garage.

Chapter 2

Some neighborhoods had the ambiance of tweeting birds and Sunday drivers. Ours had routine drive-by shootings and the ever pleasant wail of police sirens. I tried to shake off the haze of my dream as I followed the sound of my grandparents' voices. They were hollering in the kitchen loudly enough to raise the dead. I was grateful for the hoodoo goo Pop had put on my knee because I didn't think I would have been able to walk today without it. For the five billionth time this week I mentally cursed myself for not knowing how to use a gun.

I found Grandma in her bathrobe with her electric blue rollers in her hair and her tattered, old pink bunny slippers on her feet. The rascally rabbits on her footwear looked as irritated at being up at this hour as I was.

"What in the world is going on? It's three o'clock in the morning!"

I rubbed my eyes.

"Y'all had better get over here quick!" Grandma yelled over the phone. "The old man's done lost his mind. Tell your men to come fast before things get ugly!"

"Woman! I'm the man of this house, and I got a right to protect my family!"

Pop paced the room, ranting and raving.

"I'm trying to tell y'all—I can't hold him back no more!" Grandma continued fussing at the person on the other end of the phone. "He's done gone crazy!"

"Mama, you better get back and let me do what I'm supposed to do!" Pop hollered back in equal amounts. "I don't need no cops out here—I can take care of this myself!"

He angrily slapped on his baseball cap and grabbed his gun.

"Pop, where are you going with your rifle?" I screamed. "What are you loading that gun for?"

"Somebody's breaking into Pop's garage, and I'm trying to get the law over here after them," Grandma shouted back. "This dang fool's wanting to go outside to confront the burglar and shoot him himself, and I can't talk no sense into him!"

It was strange to me that tonight Grandma was okay with involving law enforcement in our lives. This made me even more alarmed that the situation was serious enough for her to admit they might actually need back-up this time.

Perhaps the attack against me from the Skullbangerz yesterday had scared her more than she would acknowledge. Either way, the idea of police involvement did not provide me with any comfort.

"Pop, put the gun down!" I cried out. "The cops will be here soon enough. What on earth is wrong with you?"

"Sweetie, a man's got to do what a man's got to do," he said firmly through a set jaw, as he cocked his gun and headed out the back door.

"Pop!" I shrieked.

"Louie!" Grandma wailed, but he was halfway to the garage by now.

Without thinking, I grabbed the first object I saw—Pop's gardening shovel, before I trailed along behind him. The cold air nearly knocked me down, and it was so dark outside that it took me a moment or two before my eyes could adjust. Pop had already disappeared behind the garage, and I could hear him arguing with the burglar.

"You get on out of here! There ain't nothing here for you! We already done called the cops, and I got a loaded gun with your name on it if you don't get off my property right now!"

Pop pointed the gun at someone I couldn't see yet.

"Addie!" Grandma screeched as I rounded the corner. "You come back into this house right now!"

Pop bossed me when he noticed my presence. "You go inside immediately!"

I ignored them both and rounded the corner to find myself face to face with the prowler. He was a dark skinned African American man with two gold front teeth, and one of his teeth had a star in it. His gilded fangs gleamed in the moonlight, and the amulet around his neck glowed even brighter than his teeth.

"Well, well now," he hissed, sizing me up. "What do we have here?"

Pop cocked his weapon and raised it up higher and closer to the man's head as he threatened, "*We* ain't got nothing here. *You* got a gun pointed at your skull. And *you* got about sixty seconds before you get arrested or shot if you don't leave!"

The man turned his head to the side and checked me out from top to bottom. It was then that I noticed the pit bull he had on a leash, and the dog was lunging towards Pop just itching for a bite.

"Well, Mr. Jackson, you never told me you had such a good looking house guest," the intruder said, taunting my Pop. "I would've been here sooner to have made her acquaintance."

"She ain't got nothing to do with this! And that there amulet ain't going to give you enough luck to protect you from one of these here bullets!" Pop lifted his chin and his piece. "I don't know what you're after, man, but I ain't got nothing, and I ain't got nothing to lose, and I'd just as soon shoot you as look at you."

"You know exactly what I'm after, and I ain't leaving until I get it."

The man growled and glared at Pop through dark, narrowed eyes.

"All I know is that the last two men who tried to break into my property had a rough time of it after they left. One wrapped his car around a tree and left the crash scene in a coffin. The other wound up at the bottom of Pickwick Lake. So, how do you expect things to turn out for you?"

The man cackled a sinister laugh, as he sized up my grandfather to decide how much of a threat he really was.

"Now, Mr. Jackson, you look geriatric enough that I believe I could take you. Besides, you know if anything were to happen to me, they'd just send somebody else." The intruder lowered his cold voice. "They're going to keep sending somebody until they get what's theirs, and they don't care if I end up round a tree or in some lake."

Pop frowned at him in sadness.

"You're a young man. You got your whole life ahead

34

of you. Why do you want to run with people, who don't care nothing for you when you know they're using you like a dog?"

"Look, man, everybody got a job to do," the man angrily said. "They pay me plenty, and that's all that matters to me. I got a family to feed just like everybody else. They powerful people, too, and they say they're going to bring justice to the people, who's been wronged. So, what's so bad about working for them?"

"Look, son, them people ain't looking for justice. They're looking for revenge against people who ain't done nothing to them. They ain't no good, and you're going to get hurt staying mixed up with them."

"Who do you think you are?" The guy asked, and all of the alarm bells in my head started going off. "You ain't my family! You don't know what I've been through! You don't know nothing about my life, man, and it ain't been easy. So, don't tell me what I ought to do, because what I ought to do is sic my dog on you to teach you a lesson for talking about things you don't know nothing about!"

In his fury, the intruder distractedly lifted his fist to shake it at Pop when his dog lunged free. The canine bit hard into Pop's leg, and Pop let out a painful scream and fell to the ground. I wailed and brought my shovel down squarely on the mutt's skull.

The burglar cursed at me before dropping a small object into the grass. He then sprinted off and cleared the fence just as the blue lights and police sirens pulled up in our driveway. I don't know if I killed that mutt with the first swipe of my shovel or not, but I kept beating the fleabag and yelling like a mad woman until the law enforcement pulled me off of it.

By the time I got done, the pit was a limp pile of flesh, and I was shaking like a leaf. My grandparents were very distracted with all the excitement, and I was surprised to see that I was the only one who noticed the intruder left something behind before he escaped. I walked over to where it had fallen and found a small coin with the head of an Indian on its face. The penny had a small hole through it, which made it even more unusual. I looked over my shoulder to insure no one had seen what I had found before I slipped it into my pocket.

The straggling cops certainly took their time getting out of their patrol cars and poking around the crime scene.

Their lead officer scratched his head before introducing himself. "I'm Officer Stringer, and I'm afraid I don't quite know what to make of y'all."

"What do you mean?" I nonchalantly inquired, trying to look as innocent as possible.

"Well, half the boys on my team go to church with y'all, and all of them are telling me y'all are right good peaceful people," Officer Stringer remarked as he wiped his brow. "None of y'all have any kind of a police record, as far as we can tell."

"That's right, Officer!" Grandma spoke up proudly. "Hallelujah! Jesus saves! We're a God fearing family..."

"Ma'am, I wasn't finished yet," Officer Stringer interrupted.

Grandma shut up (temporarily, at least).

"I was saying, the boys here are all telling me y'all are faithful members of their church. However, Mr. Louie is over here holding a gun, and he's threatening to blow some man's brains out—a man, who is not here and who only your family were actual witnesses to." Officer Stringer continued thoughtfully. "And Mrs. June, you've been carrying on like a wild ruffian every since we got here."

"Now hold on there just a cotton picking minute," said Grandma, raising her voice.

"One more outburst out of you, lady, and I'll drag you down to the poky, and I don't care how many of my men you've made pecan pies for and attended church socials with!"

Officer Stringer spoke authoritatively as he adjusted his belt buckle for effect.

To Grandma's credit, she finally had the good sense to close her mouth.

"Your granddaughter, Addie, here just pulverized a pit bull with a shovel, when you all must be aware it ain't legal to kill domesticated animals," Officer Stringer said, continuing his unfavorable assessment of my family.

"Now officer, I would never try to hurt anyone's pet, but we were under extreme duress," I interjected as I attempted to make our tale even more dramatic than it already was. "That monster of a dog charged my grandfather trying to kill him! I mean, what would you have done if some rabid mongrel was trying to kill your kin? And don't we have the right to bear arms to protect ourselves?"

The officer eyeballed me and admitted, "Um ... Miss

Addie, we officers of the law realize that you have the constitutional right to bear arms. We've just never seen anyone kill a mutt with a garden tool as an example of it."

"So, what should I have done? Just stood there and let my Pop get hurt even more than he already has? Just look at him! You need to be helping him get some medical attention instead of standing around here lecturing me for defending him!"

Pop came to my aid and on cue made an afflicted expression and howled in pain.

"Miss Jackson, the emergency medical techs will be tending to your grandfather shortly, so I'd appreciate it if you'd refrain from telling me how to do my job."

Officer Stringer rubbed his temples and sighed.

"Officer, you ought to be labeling this child a hero instead of demonizing her," Grandma admon-ished him as she approached me and put her arms around my shoulders proudly. "Why, y'all should be ashamed of yourselves. An eye for an eye and a tooth for a tooth—that's in the Bible, in case you haven't read it."

"Ma'am, I'm a member of the First United Missionary Baptist Church of the Bluff City." The officer defended himself through narrowed eyes. "While my family does not attend your particular church, we are all firm believers in the Bible."

"Well then, you understand the Golden Rule, so you need to just go on now and chase that bad guy," Grandma ordered as she poked her finger in his face. "You should do under others as you would want them to do under you."

"Do under others?" Our officer inquired looking

extremely confused. "Ma'am, I don't think that's what that verse says …"

"See there! Now that's why you need to go to church more. You don't even know what the Golden Rule says. If you was to be getting ravaged by a super strong bully breed we'd be all up under that dog to protect you, so you should be all up under helping us, too."

"Amen and hallelujah!" my Pop chimed in. "Preach it, June!"

Officer Stringer shook his head in exasperation.

"Mrs. Jackson, you do realize that the Golden Rule isn't even in the Bible."

"I feel right sorry for you, what with not getting a real Bible school education and all, but we'll just excuse that and turn the other cheek since that's what Jesus would do. Asking yourself 'WWJD?' is how you make good decisions in life—you need to write that one down now, son."

Grandma patronized him as she clicked her tongue and patted his shoulder.

All of the cops looked some combination of amused and pleasantly confused by this point. So at last, after two hours of questioning, standing around scratching their heads, and searching the neighborhood for a burglar they never found, they eventually wrote up their report, hauled off the mutt, and went on back to their station.

I could have sworn I overheard Grandma grumbling about how she remembered now why she never calls the cops when this sort of thing happens to us, but she would never own up to saying it.

After Pop was all bandaged up and had been plenty pampered, I couldn't resist grilling him. "What were you and that burglar talking about? How did he know who you were? What was he after anyway?"

However, of course in true Jackson form, he wouldn't tell me anything.

"Sweetie, I think you must have misunderstood the conversation we were having," Pop lied smoothly.

"Pop, I was there, and I didn't misunderstand a thing, and I want to know what that whole cryptic conversation was about!"

"Now darling, that man was a sick individual, and there's no way of knowing why he was acting the way he was," Pop crooned. "Lord knows everybody's got their own set of troubles, and we can't help everybody as much as we wish we could."

"Pop, in spite of your country upbringing, you are one persuasive son of a gun. If you had had the right education, you would have made a darn good lawyer," I admitted after I could see he wouldn't budge.

"You got that right," Grandma concurred. "I've always said your Pop was so good at talking, he could convince people an egg was blue if he wanted to."

Pop smiled back at me full of secrets he was clearly not willing to share today.

"This world is just full of evil," Grandma muttered as she walked off. "Dr. Martin Luther King, Jr. getting murdered here was just a sign of more bad things to come ..."

"Has she always been like that?" I asked Pop as we

watched her walk away.

"Like what, sugar?"

"Good at changing the conversation from one bad situation and connecting it to a completely unrelated one."

"Your Grandma is like an onion with a lot of layers," Pop waved his hand to dismiss me. "Why don't you get on back to bed and try to get some rest?"

It was too late to get any rest, and even if it hadn't been, I was way too wired to sleep. I slipped the Indian head coin into a pair of jeans I rarely wore before I made myself get ready for class. I didn't want to think about who I associated it with, and I didn't want to invite any more trouble onto my head by finding out more about it. I hated to leave my grandparents after an incident like this, but I had missed more than my fair share of lectures on account of unexplained events like this.

I certainly didn't want to push my luck with my mostly understanding professors. Besides, I needed time with some sane members of society for a change. It was all that kept me from strangling my grand-parents most days.

Unfortunately for me by the time I had driven my old car onto campus, I walked into my psychology class late, which made my professor mad. Professor Parrot always had this crazed look in her eyes as if she would fit in much better in a psychiatric ward than teaching psychological theories at Shelby College. She accused me of assuming I knew everything I needed to know about counseling since I had missed part of her class.

To my credit, I was smart enough not to tell her I didn't actually believe in her profession anyway. In retaliation for my tardiness she assigned me to videotape myself providing therapy to a couple of folks.

"It shouldn't be too hard for you since you have clearly learned everything there is to know on the subject already," she noted smartly.

By the grace of God I survived the rest of her class and refrained from stabbing my eye out with a pencil.

Fortunately my best friend, Keisha, was meeting up with me for lunch after class today. She was my rock and my most trusted confidant. It was a good thing too, because I needed to talk to somebody, who had her head screwed on right, unlike Grandma, who I was starting to think was certifiably insane.

Shelby Diner was a casual local favorite that provided a welcome change in environment for me today. While Keisha wasn't likely to consume much besides the diet sodas she chugged like they were going out of style, even she was a sucker for their fries. I found her at a corner table surrounded by walls covered with graffiti from its regular neighborhood patrons.

"Hi, Ad! I went ahead and ordered for us – I hope that's okay. How's it going?" She smiled her broad, beautiful grin and greeted me. I smiled back and immediately felt more relaxed just by seeing her sweet face. Her smile could stop traffic. It was so bright that it got noticed before her caramel complexion, almond eyes and straight, dark hair. There were no bones about it. Keisha was gorgeous.

"Oh, good, thanks! I'm starving. It's going okay. My grandparents are on a tear again, so you know ... same stuff—different day."

Keisha's eyes lit up as she encouraged me to keep talking. "Well, you know how much I enjoy hearing you talk about their wild antics."

Grandma loved Keisha, who had always been her favorite of all of my friends. However, Keisha's dad was Mr. Kane—a high profile official in the City of Memphis. While he had always been kind to me and gotten me out of more than my fair share of parking tickets through the years, Grandma had always been wary of him. It wasn't that he was a bad person; it was that he was power hungry and had made no apologies about his plans to advance within the ranks. Grandma had never said it in so many words, but I had always suspected she was afraid that if he knew too much about my family and me, he would use it for self gain when the opportunity to benefit his career presented itself.

Keisha and I had been buddies since we met in my grandparents' neighborhood. Her family had lived there too, but unlike my nutty grandparents, her folks had been smart enough to move away years ago while the getting was good.

The day that we became friends I was four years old and running around Grandma's front yard. Keisha was playing hopscotch and jump rope with some other kids down the street. We always waved when we saw each other, but we had never exactly been chummy. However all of that changed the day an unfamiliar car pulled up in front of Grandma's house. Two white men came out and headed toward me. I didn't know who they were, but they called me by my first name, which made me trust them.

Then they asked me if I was June Jackson's grandchild. I told them yes, because I figured they must be friends of hers. However, the situation headed south fast. The man with dark hair instructed the younger, muscular guy to grab me, and I started screaming and trying to run away. Keisha saw what was happening, left her jump rope behind, and ran towards me. She began hollering and chunking rocks at the two men.

They hesitated at the unexpected attack from a four year old black child. Keisha's beads and braids were flying with every thrown rock she could get a hold of. I took the lead from her and got a hold of some rocks myself, as I screamed bloody murder while causing as much of a raucous as I could manage. Keisha's Daddy came out and took the situation a step further by picking up the stack of bricks off of his porch which were left over from his latest home repair. Mr. Kane chunked those bricks at them while telling Keisha's Mama to call the law straight away. Pop ran out with his shotgun, and Grandma bolted towards them with an iron skillet full of scalding grits.

After it was clear that our neighborhood watch had just turned into an army unified against them, the would-be abductors abandoned their intended kidnapping, jumped into their vehicle, and sped out of there as fast as greased lightning.

Unfortunately, there was no license plate on their car for the cops to trace. However, even though the police eventually concluded the case could not be solved, I've always believed my grandparents took steps to make sure those men never got a second shot at stealing me. I never saw that car or those men again.

The local newspaper ran an article about us. Most of the story talked about Keisha's heroism since she was the brave daughter of the high ranking city official. The most significant part of that terrifying situation for me was that she and I had been inseparable ever since. I had gained a lot of scary material for my future nightmares from the experience, but I had also gained an invaluable best friend. From that day forward, there wasn't much my grandparents wouldn't do for Keisha. Her courage had set the events in motion to save me, and for that, they felt indebted to her for life.

"Tell me what they've gotten themselves into now," Keisha coaxed me.

"I swear my grandparents are going to get themselves killed one of these days if they don't watch out!"

I frowned and fussed as she giggled. I hesitated to continue. As usual I had been instructed not to talk about everything that had happened this week, but keeping all of my family's secrets ate me up inside. In the Jackson household, there was really only one cardinal rule; what happened within the family stayed within the family.

"Addie, come on! You know I won't say anything, "Keisha implored me.

I knew she wouldn't ever break my confidentiality intentionally, but I had always worried about accidentally endangering her by telling her too much. Ignorance had always been bliss for a reason.

"I know that. I do. I just don't like burdening you with

this mess all the time."

She rolled her eyes at me, as I knew she would. "Puh-lease! This is my weekly entertainment. I've been studying the history of the Civil War all week. Please make my life worth living again and give me something interesting to focus on for a change!"

I decided to succumb to temptation a little and tell Keisha just part of the story. There had been far more questions than answers for me in the last 48 hours. So, I chose to only to tell her the parts that would result in the fewest number of questions. I was feeling lost enough for the both of us, and there was no point in stressing Keisha unnecessarily with problems I didn't have solutions to.

So, I took a deep breath and recounted, "Well, our church has been getting broken into. And you know how my Grandma is … she's convinced she knows who did it."

"Uh-oh." She chuckled.

"'Uh-oh' is right," I chuckled back. "She went down to the 'hoodlums' house. She drove her big, old car right up into the middle of their yard!"

"Oh, no, she didn't!" Keisha's dark almond eyes widened with shock.

"Oh, yes, she did. She got out smoking up a storm and went around to all of them shaking their hand and introducing herself before she started to grill them."

"What in the world did she say to them?" She whispered.

"She said she knew after meeting them that a couple of them were involved in the church break-in's," I answered.

"Addie, where is her head at?"

"Who knows? Grandma is so nuts."

"Where does she get off thinking that it's okay to approach people like that?" Keisha stared at me wide eyed.

"You know how she is—she's always saying stuff like that," I said with a shrug. As long as I could remember, Grandma had been meeting people and claiming to have knowledge about really dramatic descriptions of their personal lives and what's important to them.

"What'd she say about the 'hoodlums?'" Keisha hissed after the waitress had brought us our cheeseburgers, fries, and soft drinks.

"She rambled on about how they were motivated by power and control. She even discussed events that had helped shape who they are today. You know, I'm ashamed to admit that I used to take her seriously and think that she had some kind of psychic powers."

"Addie, your grandmother is hilarious…." Keisha laughed.

"You only think she's hilarious, because she's not existing for the sole purpose of embarrassing you all the time." I argued wryly.

A few years ago, Grandma had figured out I was actually starting to believe her wild claims, so she told me she was full of bull. She said she liked to keep me on my toes and not to pay her any mind. Still, it raised too many questions for me as to why she would go to all that trouble to maintain a pack of lies … unless she was lying about lying … good Lord, that woman made my head hurt.

I continued to vent, "What kind of a person goes

around making this stuff up just for the heck of it? You would think she would try to make things easier on me with all the stress I'm under instead of making things intentionally harder just to get a rise out of me! Why can't she just play Bingo and bake cookies like all the other grandma's in the world?!"

Keisha bit her lip to hold back her amusement and mused, "I don't have much doubt that school age kids, who hang out on lawn chairs smoking pot all day long are not going to be winning the Best Neighbor award. But that doesn't mean they broke into her church …"

"I know it, but Grandma was on a roll. She called the cops, who probably know our number by heart after this week, I might add. She told them they needed to keep a special eye on these kids, because she thought they were up to some suspicious activity, and she thought it was her duty to warn them."

I held up my hands as if to surrender.

"Addie, you have got to be kidding me." Keisha's mouth dropped open.

"Oh, I only wish I was. That's my Grandma—a self-appointed detective." I said as I raised an eyebrow.

Keisha sipped on her diet soda and nibbled at her food while she waited for me to go on. She knew me well enough to know I wasn't telling her everything.

"Well, there's only one more, tiny, little thing I guess I should tell you, which ..."

"Doesn't leave this table like everything else ..." she finished my sentence and pressed, "Go on."

"Some gang members chased me to my house and

threatened to kill me. Then some scary guy broke into our garage and got into it with my Pop, so I used a garden shovel to kill his dog. Mind if I have a fry?"

I rushed through my announcements.

"What in the world? Don't you dare change the subject now, Addie Marie Jackson!"

"What? They look good," I remarked, as I stole a handful off of her plate and dipped them into her ketchup. As little as she ate, I figured she wouldn't miss them. No wonder she stayed so thin.

Our waitress came by to check on us; I made mindless small talk with her about the muggy weather and some recent local events just to irk Keisha, who tapped her foot and scowled at me until the waitress finally walked off.

"How can you just drop lines like that into conversations with me?" Keisha fussed.

"Um, how else am I supposed to drop lines like that?"

"You announce people are trying to kill your family like you are casually mentioning you just picked up milk and eggs from the store" she raised an eyebrow at me.

"What am I going to do with you?"

"Shhh! Lower your voice. What do you want me to do? I've tried for years to get them to move out of their scary, old neighborhood, and we both know they won't budge. They need me too much for me to leave them over there by themselves. So, that puts me living in the projects until they kick the bucket. Do you think I actually like living on the edge and playing chicken with my life every day?"

"Sometimes I wonder," she remarked as she gave me the evil eye.

"Oh, that's complete crap, and you know it. The minute they give me the green light, we're taking the first one-way trolley ticket available to East Memphis," I said more confidently than I felt.

"But what if they never agree to relocate? Addie, I know you love your grandparents, but sooner rather than later you're going to die on account of their insanity. You're not getting to have a normal college experience. You haven't even dated anyone in years."

I sidestepped her concerns about my impending doom. I couldn't argue against them, and talking about my imminent demise only stressed me out. So, naturally I focused on the aspect of the conversation I actually had an argument against.

"How exactly am I supposed to date someone? I'm like a single parent to two dependent senior citizens; any self respecting guy would want to be a significant priority in the life of whomever he's dating. If I were seeing someone, he couldn't come first or even second. At best, he would come third after Grandma and Pop, and that would only be when school, Amber, or you didn't need me. No normal guy is going to understand that, and I wouldn't blame him for it either,"

"You've put Will on the back burner for years, and he's still stuck on you," she argued.

"Will who?" I played stupid just to give her a hard time.

"Oh, Addie, you're as infuriating as your Grandma!"

"No, I'm less so actually. She would be insulted to hear you say that—you aren't giving her enough credit about how difficult she actually is."

"I told Will you'd go out with him Friday. He's taking you to the Destination."

"You told him what?!"

I raised my voice aghast.

"You heard me. You need to do something fun with someone under the age of 70 for a change."

"Listen, I know you want to play matchmaker and all, and as much as it pains me to admit it ... there's nothing wrong with Will," I confessed to her surprise.

"That's your argument against dating him?! So, if he were hopelessly flawed, you'd be all about it? Come on, Addie. What's the problem?"

"Keisha, did you not just listen to my eloquent rant from five minutes ago? I've got people trying to kill me now. Going downtown with Will isn't exactly on my bucket list."

I grabbed more of her fries and popped them into my mouth.

"You have promised him a date for years. It is just one night. If you go and don't like him, I'll never bother you about it again. I just want you to have some fun for a change—you deserve a good night."

"And you deserve a kick in the head for trifling with my lacking love life."

Keisha didn't get the satisfaction of responding to my stubborn stance, because right there in Shelby Diner before our very eyes, one of my predictive dreams started coming true. Unfortunately for me though, this time there was nothing dreamy about it.

Chapter 3

I had gone to Shelby Diner with Keisha with every intention of having a normal, peaceful lunch with meaningful conversation. I had not ordered a side of Hoodoo Helen, but apparently the kitchen messed up my order, because the hoodoo conjurer was staring me down from across the room.

If it wasn't so scary, it could have been funny, because it would have made much more sense for me to have run into her in Hoodoo Hollow. One of the many problems with getting stared down by Professor Helen Harrison, AKA Hoodoo Helen, was the fact that I didn't actually know her yet.

"Earth to Addie! What's going on?"

Keisha snapped her fingers in front of my eyes to attempt to grab my attention.

I stared back and forth between Keisha and Helen. The witch doctor held her menu, but my gaze met with her eyes. She watched me as if she recognized me and was waiting for me to acknowledge her, which I had no intention of doing.

How can she look at me like she knows me when we've never met?

"Didn't your Grandma ever tell you it's rude to stare? Come on! I've got an afternoon class. I'm ready to get out of here."

Keisha tugged at me.

"Okay, okay, I'm going." I stammered nervously to Keisha before casting one last glance back at Hoodoo

Helen.

Helen had no food or drink on her table, and she was alone. Could it be that she was at the restaurant not to eat but to see me? She was even scarier looking in person than she had been in my dreams. The animal bones she wore around her neck and in her ears did nothing to make her appear more approachable.

Keisha seemed oblivious to the significance of who I was staring at, and this seemed unfathomable to me since in that moment, Hoodoo Helen was the only person I could see in the room. I supposed it was possible Keisha didn't notice the bones the conjurer was wearing, but the even more disturbing thought crept in that maybe Keisha didn't notice her, because she wasn't actually there.

Keisha dragged me out of the restaurant into the parking lot, where I sat down, put my head in between my knees, and started gasping for air.

"Oh my word, what is the matter with you?" Keisha asked.

"How could you not see her?"

"See who?" she asked in exasperation.

"The hoodoo guru!" I wailed.

"The what?"

"The witch doctor!"

"What the heck are you talking about?"

"It was the conjurer!"

"What the heck is a conjurer anyway?"

Keisha tried not to look at me like I was crazy.

"No, no, no, this isn't happening. She can't be real. It's all coming true, and just like before, I can't stop it. I can't do anything to change it. I'm going to die just like Amy did."

"Addie, get in the car with me. I'm driving you home."

Keisha stuck me in her ride and peeled out of the parking lot.

"Noooo, you can't. My car's still there. You have to go to class!"

"Um, you having a nervous breakdown versus a routine math class?" asked Keisha. "Obviously I'm making sure you aren't about to go to the mental institution as opposed to doing college algebra today."

I was too freaked out to argue with her and almost too freaked out to be embarrassed about my outburst ... almost. For a split second I caught a glimpse of Hoodoo Helen watching us out of the restaurant window before Keisha's car thankfully took us away from her line of sight.

"Addie, what are you talking about with thinking you're going to die? What aren't you telling me today?"

"It's nothing. I'm sorry. I just need to get some air. I felt like I was suffocating in there."

I rolled down the window to take deep breaths, even though this did nothing to alleviate the pressure in my chest.

"That's it. I've had it," Keisha said tersely as she pulled over and parked.

"What are you doing?"

"Demanding answers. You think you're tired of waiting around for your grandparents to explain things to you? Think about how I feel for a minute. We've been best friends since Pre-K. I tell you everything about my life, and all you give me are crumbs to follow, all the flipping time. I have never given you any reason not to trust me. Why on God's green earth won't you just talk to me?"

"I do talk to you ... all the time. You're my best friend."

"Yeah? Well, in my world, being best friends with someone means you're supposed to tell that person what's actually going on in your life instead of just making jokes and changing the subject when things get uncomfortable. You hate the way your Grandma won't open up with you, but you do the same exact thing with me, and you're too hypocritically blind to admit it. Addie, I love you, and I'd do anything in this world for you, but I can't help you with anything you don't tell me about. So, please—for once— just let me in."

Tears rained down my cheeks, and I wished I had a jar big enough to collect them all in. I hated feeling so exposed, because it made me feel vulnerable, and that was dangerous in my world.

Keisha reached over immediately and held me while I sobbed. I selfishly wanted to tell her everything so I could have someone I trusted to share my burden with, yet simultaneously I unselfishly wanted to protect her by hiding it from her, too. I knew if I didn't tell her what was going on, she would be mad as blazes, but she would probably be a lot safer. Yet if I didn't let her in, she might be mad enough to walk away from me for good this time, and I didn't think my heart could take that. She waited patiently while I calmed down enough to speak.

I wiped my eyes and asked, "How much do you want to know?"

Without hesitation she responded firmly, "Everything."

I waited a few seconds before asking two final questions. "What if you get hurt as a result of what I tell you? How in the world could I live with myself if I lost you?"

She considered the question thoughtfully for a while before she spoke again and said, "Addie, you're the family I would have chosen for myself. You're never going to lose me, and it hurts me every time you lie to me. It would hurt me far less if you would just tell me the truth."

So, with that confident encouragement from Keisha, I told her everything. For the first time in our friendship I didn't withhold any part of the story from her. She impressed me as she sat calmly through everything I shared. I was relieved that she didn't run away screaming even though she would have been insulted to have known I was afraid she would do that to me. Then she asked me about the huge area of guilt I really didn't want to discuss.

"Addie, you said you were afraid what happened to your sister, Amy, would happen to you. You said something about not being able to stop it. What did you mean by that?"

Amy was my autistic sister, who died in a hit and run when I was in elementary school. After her unsolved "accident," as it was labeled by local authorities, my parents divorced and moved to different states, and I moved in with my grandparents in spite of both of my parents kicking and screaming in opposition. Dad was an alcoholic, who was married to his beer, and Mom was a workaholic, who was in a 24/7 relationship with her job. So after Amy passed, Grandma's house felt more like home than my own, and I started living with them. Because of my parents' neglect toward my sister and myself, I overcompensated for their lack of involvement and felt extremely responsible for Amy's wellbeing.

Right before she died, I dreamed about her passing in vivid detail and tried to warn my parents, but they wouldn't listen to me. So, after her death, I had equal helpings of blame for them as well as for myself. It was the worst prediction I had ever watched come true, and fifteen years later the guilt and pain were still as raw for me as the day it happened.

I forced myself to speak as calmly as possible.

"My grandparents and you are the only people, who know about my weird dream quirk. You know I dreamed about Amy passing before it happened, but I wasn't able to save her. Well, I dreamed about this scary hoodoo doctor, too, but she was so bizarre that I had almost convinced myself she couldn't really exist. Yet she's sitting right there inside Shelby Diner, and I think she was waiting to talk to me."

"Addie, you were no more responsible for your sister dying than the rain we had here yesterday," she said. "I saw you staring off into space earlier, but I thought you were just looking at one of the waiters, who had been checking us out. I didn't see any hoodoo doctor in there. Are you sure you saw her?"

"Yes, of course I'm sure. She was larger than life, but now I'm worried since you didn't see her, too. What if I'm losing my mind? Maybe I'm hallucinating!"

"Have you ever had delusions before?"

"No, not that I know of. But maybe that's because I'm delusional, so I wouldn't know any differently!"

"Have you ever considered therapy?" she asked.

"I have to do a therapy assignment for Professor Parrot. That'll be enough psychoanalysis for me."

"Addie, you know that's not what I meant ..."

"Oh, no!" I buried my face in my hands. "You really do think I'm crazy!"

"Of course you're crazy—we're all a little nuts, but I don't think you're crazy because of this. I do think your stress level is through the roof though. Maybe talking to somebody about it would help."

"Keisha, I'm a Jackson. We don't do therapy. There is no way I'm going to lay down on some hippie's couch."

Keisha rolled her eyes and said, "Fine. Suit yourself. Drive yourself up the wall. But the next time you complain about your grandparents and how stuck in their backward ways they are, remember this conversation, and take a look in the mirror. If you don't get some perspective soon, you're going to end up just like them someday."

"Keisha, I'm sorry I haven't been honest with you. I thought I was protecting you, and I had no idea that was hurting you."

Then just like that I was in un-treaded water. I had promised her to be honest about everything in my life going forward, a deal I had never extended to anyone else.

Would she still be there when all of my walls were down? Only time would tell. I knew one thing for certain: if she left me after I finally exposed my soul, no one would ever see it again.

She drove me home and was quieter than usual; I knew her brain was probably on overload from all of the bombs I had dropped on her today. We whizzed down I-240 before hitting Poplar and heading down to my neighborhood. While my shoulders felt lighter now that I was sharing my burden with someone else, I also felt worried for Keisha's safety. If anything bad ever happened to her, I didn't know how I could ever come back from that or if I would even want to.

Keisha dropped me off, and she waited until I had walked past Grandma's bottle trees and had made it to the front porch before she pulled out and drove off. A black cat sauntered up the steps and purred as he rubbed against my legs. I didn't know where he had come from or who he belonged to, but I scratched him for a minute before I went inside.

Grandma was home and was far too observant to miss my red eyes.

"Doll, what's the matter with you?" she asked.

"Oh, um, I got reprimanded in Professor Parrot's class. Pop and you get to do the honor of being my guinea pigs for a pretend therapy session with me tomorrow."

"Okay ... but I know you, and you would not look like somebody had just run over your favorite puppy about something as petty as that. Where's your car?"

"I left it at Shelby Diner. Keisha took me home."

"How come?" she asked. Well, come on out with it—spit it out."

"Talking about it wouldn't do any good."

"What makes you say that?" she asked in concern.

"Because no matter what questions I ask, you won't give me any answers."

At this accusation, Grandma started patting down her bathrobe looking for her cigarettes, so I knew I had struck a nerve. She found a cancer stick, stuck it in between her lips, and lit it up before remarking: "All people think they want to know what's down the rabbit hole. But then after they get down there and get stuck, there ain't nobody to pull them back up out of the madness."

"Grandma, I don't care about a rabbit hole." I exhaled in frustration. "I want to know your story."

She spun her ring around her finger a few times before answered hesitantly, "Doll, my story's already been written. Let's just focus on yours now because that's the one I really care about."

"Am I ever going to be able to understand things with Pop and you? Do you plan on ever letting me in?"

She lit up another smoke and sucked in a big breath of nicotine before she responded thoughtfully and said, "Give me a minute. Let me just get more of my yoga on."

Only Grandma would think breathing in toxic doses of nicotine was as healthy as practicing breathing exercises in yoga class. I waited attentively as she got her fix before she continued on.

"Someday you'll understand me more, but that don't mean I'm happy about it. When I am grayer and have

61

finally kicked the bucket, before you make any decisions, before you call the family … before you call the preacher man ... before you call the police ... before you do anything at all … you make sure you call John Hamilton."

My eyes widened at the mention of the guy I had dreamed about the other night, so I asked, "Who's John Hamilton?"

"Don't be asking no questions about him today." She shook her head firmly. "You just get in touch with him, and you tell him you need to get my safe deposit box. You don't let nobody else enter this house until that happens, and I mean nobody. I don't care who they are or what they say it's about ... Addie, you're the only one mature enough to handle this."

Her face spoke volumes about the seriousness behind her words as she went on to talk about my first cousin and surrogate sister, Amber. "Listen, you and I both know that Amber's a good kid, but she's so young and fragile, and you're the one I've got to count on. I hate to put this on you, child. If there was any other way I wouldn't, you understand? There just ain't no other way ... I've done figured it and figured it, and I can't see no other way."

I realized then that she had been talking to herself more than me. It was surreal to feel like I knew my grandparents so well most of the time, but at other times I felt like I didn't know them at all.

I spoke bluntly without thinking. "I'm just so tired of y'all keeping secrets from me. You want everything to be so hush-hush all of the time. For crying out loud, I think I'm mature enough and trustworthy enough to be confided in for a change."

Grandma's eyes snapped at me as she interrupted, "Child, I've always been trusting you. It's the rest of the world I'm trying to protect you from."

"Grandma, I'm just so curious about you," I confessed.

"Well, you know what they say about curiosity."

"What's that?" I asked.

"It killed that there cat, so it makes me afraid for you."

"Grandma, I am not a cat, and nothing is going to happen to me as long as you're alive—isn't that what you're always telling me?"

"It's not the 'while I'm alive' part that I'm worried about," she said behind a shaky voice. "It's the 'after I'm gone' part that keeps me shaking in my boots … I'm just trying to hold on for as long as I can."

She pulled her pocket watch out, flipped it open, and stared at its face for a few somber seconds before slipping it back into the pocket of her bathrobe.

"And then what? What comes after that?"

"And then all of my hope will be in you, sugar," she said softly.

"I'm not sure I deserve that much trust."

"Oh, my child, you deserve so much more than that." She leaned over and gently cupped my chin and kissed my forehead in a rare show of affection. "I will always wish I had more to give you than this."

"Well, let's just start with you giving me a therapy session to remember tomorrow. I don't want to fail a course I don't even believe in."

"Oh honey, you know that if I'm in it, it's bound to be memorable."

Only tomorrow would tell which would be more stressful in my life—hoodooed henchmen or senior citizens on the loose.

Chapter 4

Giving two cranky senior citizens medication every day and making sure they take it? Check.

Surviving life in a neighborhood most sane people wouldn't even drive through? Check.

Cohabitating with grandparents, who are living double lives for most of my existence? Check.

Providing legitimate looking marital therapy for the two of them so I could pass my class? Highly doubtful.

Now it was official. Professor Parrot was in on the conspiracy to try to kill me, but fortunately for me, I was used to troubles like that. The only factor in my favor today was that as usual Grandma and Pop were off the chain, so it would require no acting on their parts to make them look like they needed professional help.

My cousin, Amber, had come to watch; she wasn't big as a minute and had hair as red as her mama's. Her eyes were blue like Grandma and Pop, but her complexion was covered in a cute smattering of freckles. Anytime she complained about her red hair, Pop was quick to chime in that redheads were good energy, so she was our family's good luck charm. Amber was her high school's most talented soccer star, and she was everybody's friend. She was as boy crazy as teenage girls can be. Like most of her friends, she had developed an affection for coffees with elaborate names and loads of sugar and whipped cream. Her coffee orders took longer to make than any food order anybody had ever placed. Today she had brought popcorn to watch the show, and I didn't really blame her. If she had been taking on this tumultuous task, I would have taken a front row seat, too.

"Don't laugh!" I lectured her. "Grandma and Pop are distracting enough as it is!"

"Well, good luck with them, because you're going to need it," Amber responded with a giggle.

Grandma walked into Pop's study, which had been converted into a faux therapy office; Amber immediately ignored my demands to be serious when she burst into laughter.

"Grandma, why are you getting so dressed up? This is a pretend therapy session—not the prom!"

"Now Addie, this here session is going on tape for the world to see, so I've got to look my best," Grandma announced in a serious tone, which contradicted her ridiculous outfit.

"Grandma, pearls are completely unnecessary."

I planted my face in my hands.

"Oh, you hush now before you spoil all my fun."

"Just please give up the bunny ear house shoes during the recording—that's all I ask," I begged.

"I did more than give them up. Check this out!"

"Grandma! Where on earth did you get cheetah print high heels?!" Amber asked giggling.

"I can hang with you young folks," she said proudly as she raised an eyebrow and showed off her stems. "Your whipper snapper college friends ain't got nothing on these legs, child."

Amber howled and said, "This is great. We should do this more often!" which resulted in a scowl from me as I covered my face and moaned. "I am completely mortified. Maybe we should just call this whole thing off."

"And ruin the highlight of my week? Oh no, sugar plum. I'm counting on you to get me a brand new husband out of this marital session. And after Pop's a new man, he's going to see what a good woman he's had and wish he'd treated me better."

"Um, okay, I think we need to discuss reasonable expectations for therapy." I stammered before Pop walked in and interrupted me by saying, "Hey there, gals."

"Hey, Pop," we said in unison.

"What in the world do you have on, June?" he guffawed.

"Them are my high fashion heels."

"Looks like somebody put road kill on your feet. You need to get that looked at by a doctor."

"Oh, Louie, you hush!" Grandma shot him a look that could kill.

Pop turned on his best acting abilities, which really wasn't saying much. "Miss Therapist, I sure am glad you're going to give us some couples' counseling, because June don't cook for me enough, and I'm about to trade her for a hot, young blonde. Can you help me with that?"

"Pop, you better be serious about this, because my grade depends on it," I lectured him.

"If you were so worried about your grade, you should have thought about that before you asked this here crazy woman to be on your tape!"

Grandma set a mature example and flipped him off as Amber grinned in amusement and threw some more kernels into her mouth.

"I bet all of my classmates are having an easier time with this class than I am. Let's just get this project over with."

"Yeah, let's get this party started," Grandma said as she reapplied her lipstick and smacked kisses at Pop, who feigned disgust back at her. I set up the videotape to start rolling while Grandma and Pop bickered about who got to sit in which recliner. They had agreed to convert Pop's office into a faux therapy office on the condition that they got to sit in their recliners during the session.

"Grandma and Pop, you two are ridiculous; your recliners are identical! I can't believe I conceded to you two sitting in those. This is really going to look unprofessional with y'all sitting in those giant, overstuffed dumpy chairs."

"Child, we are old enough to do whatever we want to do!"

"I can't argue with you about that." I threw up my hands in frustration and reluctantly admitted. "Just please try to behave, and please don't embarrass me any more than you already have over the last twenty years." Their facial expressions told me I needed to have more realistic expectations for their behavior.

"Okay, here we go now." I sighed as I started the tape. "We are officially recording."

Amber quietly sat out of the video camera's line of sight but was positioned close enough to watch the show.

I wheeled myself in their squeaky office chair over to their recliners to give my pretend introduction as I said,

"Hello, Mr. Louie and Mrs. June. I'm Addie Jackson, your new therapist, and I'm going to be working with both of you to help you improve your marriage."

"Well, how do you do there, Miss Therapist?" Pop grinned and shook my hand. "I sure hope you can help me, because I'm about to kill my wife."

"Louie, I told you you're supposed to be serious." Grandma snapped at him. "That's what's wrong with this man. He ain't never serious with me!"

"Mr. Louie, are you having true homicidal ideations about your wife? If so, we need to do a safety contract."

"A what contract? Listen, I been wanting this heifer to keel over since the day I married her, but I ain't about to do her in. It'd be too risky about me getting caught, and if I got caught, I couldn't get no insurance money, and that just wouldn't suit me at all."

Oh. My. Word.

"Well, um, I'm glad to hear that you have no intent or plan to harm her. Hmm ... so Mrs. June, you were saying that you feel like your husband doesn't take you seriously, and that makes you feel frustrated?"

"Of course I'm frustrated!" Grandma rolled her eyes in disgust. "Wouldn't you be frustrated listening to him yap all day long and living his whole life just to irritate you? I expect you would!"

"I can't take you serious, because you're about the craziest, old lady I ever saw," Pop smarted back.

"You see? You see what I got to live with?" Grandma implored me.

"Why don't you just go ahead and kick the bucket, so

I can finally get me some peace?" he asked her with a twinkle in his eye.

Grandma fussed, "You got to help me, Miss Therapist Lady, because this man's making my blood pressure go sky high!"

I tried my best to keep a straight face.

"Well, Mr. Louie, why don't we start off with you telling me what you'd like to improve about your marriage?"

I attempted to keep the session therapeutic.

"Well, I'd like to get this here gal a muzzle," Pop said, pointing his thumb in Grandma's general direction. "Do you think you can help me with that?"

"So, would it be fair to say that the two of you are having a hard time communicating?"

"Communicating? Communicating?" Pop raised his voice. "Listen, lady, the only person here doing any kind of communicating is her. I have to just sit here and look like I'm listening, so she don't get mad and not cook for me and so she keep washing my clothes."

"Okay, so you would like for your wife to listen to you more. Is that right?"

"Yeah, I guess you could say that," Pop conceded after some consideration.

Grandma huffed and puffed and crossed her arms while wearing the world's biggest scowl.

I turned to Grandma and inquired, "So, what would you like to improve in your marriage?"

"All I do all day long is cook for him, wash his underwear, make his bed, and iron his clothes. He ain't took me out on no date nowhere romantic in years. He gives me cash every year to go pick out my own birthday present. Then if I want to open something up, I got to wrap what I buy myself. He goes shopping at the drug store every Christmas Eve to get my presents, and half of the time, I know he sends you to pick them out for him," she said pointing an accusing finger at me. "Last year I got panty hose and a can of mixed nuts. Now how you think that make me feel? And I don't get no respect and no appreciation from him for all the things I do for him neither!"

"Now you see what I'm talking about? Talk, talk, talk ... yap, yap, yap ... I might as well just take a nap."

Pop goggled his eyebrows at me in a knowing way before he slumped down into his chair and pulled his hat over his eyes.

I counted to ten and exhaled.

"Mr. Louie, I think what your wife is trying to say is that she would like to spend more quality time with you. She wants to feel special and cherished, and she would like to go on more dates with you. It also sounds like she wants you to put more thought into the gifts you give her."

Grandma jerked up out of her seat with her eyes wide open nodding furiously at me.

"You're good, Miss Therapist Lady! You're real good! You're going to save a lot of marriages from DEE-vorce."

"Now look here, Mama, I been married to you for almost fifty-five years, and all of a sudden you're telling me you need me to wine and dine you?" Pop responded indignantly. "You been with me for this long, so why I

71

need to go do all of that stuff now? And besides, I thought you liked panty hose and mixed nuts!"

"'Of course I like mixed nuts, Louie, but I like them for a snack—I don't like them as my only Christmas present!" Grandma snorted. "And of course I want to go out on dates with you. But please don't buy me no more panty hose. You always get me size B, and I wear a Queen in pantyhose, because I'm the Queen of this house!"

"Now look here, woman, you know I love you. I been married to you for fifty-five years. I never cheated on you, and I never hit you." Pop raised his voice at her. "What else you want from me?"

"So, that's all I get, huh?" Grandma yelled back. "A lifetime of not getting knocked in the head and run around on, and I'm supposed to kiss your feet. Well, you can kiss my grits, for all I care. I deserve better than this, you ugly, old bald headed man!"

I was really thinking my therapy session had taken a permanent nose dive south by this point.

"Mr. Louie, do you think you could manage to take your wife out on a date somewhere you both like to go?" I intervened. "It might be fun for the two of you to spend some quality time together."

"Quality time? With her? Now if that ain't the most conflictual thing I ever heard. I can't have no quality time with that woman over there!"

"Lord, I don't know why I still put up with this man!" Grandma groaned while fanning herself. "I must be a martyr. God's going to give me a big crown someday when I get to His Kingdom for all my troubles with him! He

72

don't know nothing! All the trouble I went through raising his kids—not to mention the birthing of them! They were the biggest babies any woman ever had to deliver!"

"You hear this, Miss Therapist? She's over here talking about things she did at least two hundred years ago!"

"Two hundred years—what're you talking about two hundred years?" Grandma asked with a puzzled expression.

"As old as you look, woman, it got to be at least that long since you was popping out babies!"

"Okay, everybody just calm down." I interjected before an all out war started. "Now, Mr. Louie, you must be happy with some things in your marriage to have been married to your wife for fifty-five years. Why don't we talk about the positive aspects of your relationship?"

"Positive aspect of what? What the devil you talking about?"

"Louie! Don't say 'devil!' It ain't Christian! Lord, how you make me end up with a man who ain't Christian? What lesson you trying to teach me, Jesus? You might as well just take me on to Heaven, because I've about had all I can take down here." she cried as she folded her hands and started rocking in prayer.

"Well, look here now, Miss Therapist, you done got my wife so riled up that she's gone off talking to Jesus. She'll be talking to Him for a long time. She always does that when she's mad at me. You want to go grab a bite to eat until she calms down? I'll treat you to a sausage biscuit—on me."

"This session has turned into a runaway train…" I muttered.

"What you say, doll?" Pop inquired. "Did you say it was going to rain? We better get a move on. I left my umbrella in the car…"

"No, Mr. Louie," I interrupted impatiently. "I did not say it was going to rain. I appreciate your offer about breakfast, but I'm much more concerned about your marriage than eating right now. Don't you want to stay and talk this out with your wife?"

"Look, lady. After fifty five years, we ain't got nothing left to talk about. You're a cute, pretty, little thing, and I've been looking for some fun. So, let's get out of here before my wife drags us both to church!"

"Now Mr. Louie, I'm very disappointed in you. You're putting fast food before your marriage! Does your marriage really rank that low on your priority list?"

I resorted to using guilt as a desperate therapy tactic.

"Priority smiority! Lady, you're too smart. You way over my head. The only thing wrong with my marriage is that my wife's got trouble with commitment. The problem being she's certifiable, and I need you to commit her. So, why don't you take care of that while she's calmly praying, and then we can go out to eat?"

Pop grinned.

"Mr. Louie, I'm not interested in going out to breakfast with you. I'm focused on helping you improve your marriage, but since you don't seem to be worried about that at all, and your wife is talking to the Lord right now, maybe we should just reschedule."

"Aww ... come on now, darling. I didn't mean to mess up the therapy for you. I'm just having a little fun with my honey over here."

"Sir, don't you think you're upsetting your wife? Don't you see how she's rocking back and forth praying, because she's distraught?"

"Heck, no ... she rocks back and forth, because she's loony – that's the only reason she do that. I don't believe for one minute she that upset with me. She'd be bored stiff around here without me, and I'd be lost without her, too. I just like seeing her get all riled up, because it keeps things interesting."

"Louie, you think I make your life interesting?" Grandma exclaimed with tears in her eyes as she abruptly came out of her rocking prayer. "You think you'd be lost without me? Well, Lord, if you don't beat all..."

"Now, now don't go getting all excited!" Pop began backpaddling and sputtering. "I'm just saying that there are worse things than being married to you...like Chinese water torture....that'd have to be at least a little worse than living with you."

Grandma reached over, grabbed his face, and kissed his cheek. She patted his knee and then grinned with pride before she announced, "You see? I've still got it after all these years. Now I can write a therapy book on marriage! I've been married a long time, and I've been through therapy. So, now I'm qualified ... I'm an expert!"

"Qualified ...certified ... take your pick," Pop muttered under his breath.

"Louie, I heard that!" Grandma snapped.

My head was spinning, but I jumped in before they started bickering again,

"Well, um, I'm glad to see that we made some head way today. How about I check in with you next week to see how you are progressing?"

"Follow-up what?" Pop jerked his head up and stammered. "What you mean next week? I thought we done graduated from this mess."

"Why you need to talk to us about our marriage next week? Didn't you just hear me say that I'm going to write a book now since we done so good today?"

I was completely out of responses at this point, so I surrendered.

"Okay, if you feel content with your marriage, and you think you've met your treatment goals for now, you could just follow-up with me at your leisure."

"Leisure ... leisure ...." Pop puckered his mouth up and repeated the word, obviously trying to figure out what it meant. "What that? That French? I'm American, and you know, we don't like the French."

"No, no!" I interrupted in frustration and said, "All I was saying is that if you are happy with your marriage right now, then we don't have to follow-up next week."

"Who said we wanted to talk next week?"

"What're you talking about, Miss Therapist?" Grandma scrunched up her face. "I do declare, I think you're real sweet and all, but maybe you need to work on your listening skills a bit. I don't think you understood about my book and my desire (pronounced DEE-sire) to be Arthur now."

I squinted my eyes and leaned forward.

"You desire to be Arthur?"

"Now you've got it!" She sat back and smiled in satisfaction. "That's right. An Arthur."

"Excuse me, but what is an Arthur?" I asked after I counted to ten to try to compose myself.

Grandma and Pop looked at each other dumbfounded before looking back at me.

"Lord, child, how you get through all that school and not learn about no Arthur's? I swanie, these schools nowadays ain't what they used to be. When I was in school I had to learn about all them Arthur's."

"Oh, authors!" I laughed hysterically. "You want to be an author! I've got it now."

"Yes, Miss Therapist Lady," Grandma said bobbing her head up and down. "That's exactly what I said ten minutes ago. I think you need a hearing aid. I got mine down at the drug store. I'll take you down there if you need to go and get you one, too. You've been real helpful, but we've got to go now. My hubby's got to take me out on a date."

"I've got to do what?" Pop snapped up his head with a frown. "Hold on now—you're supposed to go write your book, so I can take the cute therapist out to eat. What're you talking about a date?"

"Louie, I swanie I get worried about you. Maybe you're catching the Old Timers. You just told me you're taking me out to eat barbecue, don't you remember? Come on now. We got to go."

"Did I just tell her I'd do that?"

Pop looked perplexed, and I bit my lip.

"Well, I can't exactly say, seeing as how I need a hearing aid and all, but I think it sounds like a wonderful idea. Y'all have fun."

Pop scratched his head the whole way out the door, as Grandma smiled at me mischievously and dragged him by the hand. I shut off the tape, thankful to have that assignment behind me. I said a prayer hoping I would never have to do that again. Amber cracked up, and she and I cut up for a bit before she headed home.

With Grandma and Pop out of the house for a bit and no one tugging at me for anything, fatigue set in. I laid down in my room for a matter of minutes before the toll of all the stress I had been under took a hit on me, and I drifted off to sleep.

In my dream I'm restlessly pacing the house, and no one else is home, which is very unusual. I assume that Pop must be helping out with security over at the church grounds with all the break-in's, and Grandma is probably getting her hair done. Either way, the house is deathly quiet, and I don't like it one bit.

I head to my room feeling like the energy here is far too cold for comfort when I open the door to find Gavin. He's in my room sitting on my bed as if he belongs there. I immediately remember I'm dreaming, but I'm too interested in this scenario to will myself to wake up.

"What is up with you? Don't you ever knock?" I ask.

"Of course. Well, sometimes at least. Besides, you told me to come in, so I just made myself at home."

"In my room," I remarked.

"Naturally." he teased.

"On my bed?"

"Obviously," he said with a smirk.

"Is there any particular reason why every time I see you you're always wearing black?"

"Of course. It suits my style, don't you think?"

"Is your fashion goal to look like a gothic country singer? Because then yeah—you nailed it."

I gave him a burn instead.

"I like dark colors. They're very comfortable on me. Besides you're bright enough for the both of us. You're the only sunshine I need."

His stare did more for me than any man ever had.

I tapped my fingers on the door frame as my eyes swept the room. I noticed wildflowers and four leaf clovers in a vintage bottle on my window ledge.

"Wildflowers ... my favorite."

"I know. I remembered," he said softly.

"How in the world did you find all of those four leaf clovers? I've never even found one."

He looked at me quizzically with his cloudy blue eyes and responded gently, "I know, Addie. We talked about that. It's why I brought them. I found thirteen for you."

"Are you trying to bring me bad luck?"

"Never," he said seriously. "Besides, I think of you as a very lucky lady actually."

"Oh yeah? So, how exactly do you figure that?" I questioned him.

"Because you've got me. In the flesh. On your bed. Right now," he flirted. He stretched and laid down on top of Grandma's hand stitched quilt and propped his head up to look at me. I shook my head at him.

"You think a lot of yourself now, don't you?"

"I think about you a lot more than myself, all teasing aside," he said sincerely.

My head got all fuzzy again. I had almost sat down on the bed beside him, but then I nervously stood up and paced the room. I had to remind myself that this wasn't real and that I didn't know anything about him. I should make him leave. Pop would shoot him when he came home and found him here. As far as he was concerned, any uninvited visitor at the Jackson household was safer dead than alive.

I noticed a box from Saucy Shirley's on my nightstand and asked, "What is that?"

"Banana pudding," he answered as if I should know the answer already.

"I love their banana pudding ..." and my voice trailed off as he looked at me knowingly. It occurred to me he was already aware of this, and that's why he had brought it for me. "It's Pop's favorite. We'll have to let him have some when he gets here. He'd be fit to be tied if we didn't," I mused.

To my surprise, Gavin reached over and stroked my cheek softly as he said, "Oh, Addie," in the saddest tone of voice. Something was wrong, but I couldn't put my finger on it. He was looking at me sympathetically as if somebody had just messed me over, and I didn't know it, but he didn't have the heart to tell me yet.

I looked into his face, and a sudden awareness began

to sink into my subconscious as his eyes gave away the deep feelings he had been hiding for me. The desire I had always interpreted as dangerous lust for me was only a mask, and for the first time I was seeing his soul behind it. Even though I knew this was just a dream with no repercussions attached to it, I still swallowed and hesitated in what I was about to ask.

"Gavin, there has always been so much darkness surrounding you, but no matter what, you've always been there and looked out for me. Why are you so nice to me?"

The intensity of his facial expression and his gaze took my breath away, as he said, "Why do you think I'm so nice to you?"

And right then I saw it. I knew. He loved me. He had loved me for years. I had just been too blinded by fear to see it. He might be tinged with darkness, but his affection for me was flooded with light. In his eyes the clouds parted, and I saw all of the memories we had shared together, our present, and our future which was yet to come. My eyes welled up with tears as he pulled me into his arms and kissed me like it was the most important thing he would ever do. I lost myself in him.

I was tangled up in every inch of his magnificence, and I don't know how long he kissed me, but it felt like it would never be long enough, as he clung to me like I was the last hope for water in an endless desert. I could have rolled around in that quilt with him forever if we hadn't been interrupted by fists pounding on the front door. Immediately, all of my defenses went up, and I scrambled to my feet. Gavin, not surprisingly, was quite cool and collected.

"Come back to bed," he tempted me. "Whoever it is will get tired of knocking eventually and go away." The knocking grew louder, and I seized his hand and dragged his reluctant self out of the room, down the hall, and towards the front door. There wasn't much that scared Gavin, and today was no exception.

"Who is it?" he asked playfully in a sing song voice through the door.

"It's me. Open up," an unrecognizable male voice replied.

"Are you a Jehovah's Witness?" Gavin asked, which resulted in an arm slap from me.

"Would you just open the door already?" the annoyed man's voice replied.

"You're not smooth enough to be a Jehovah's Witness. You must be a Bible salesman. Oohh...or maybe you're a Mormon."

"If I asked you if you had found Jesus, would that make you open the door?" the voice inquired dryly.

"Found Him? How strange. I had no idea He was missing. Perhaps you should put His face on a milk carton?"

"Oh, for crying out loud! I'll open the door," I said rolling my eyes as I slung the door open.

A young African American guy stood on my porch. It wasn't every day that I had two good looking men unexpectedly show up at my house. The only trouble was that I had no idea who my second visitor was. He was tall, dark, and handsome, and his voice boomed when he spoke. He was attractive enough that in a suit he could fly under the radar at a fancy charity event. However, with the right street clothes on the wrong side of the tracks, he appeared tough enough that I would probably steer clear of him if I happened to pass him alone.

"Addie, what's going on?"

Unfortunately for me, he knew exactly who I was, and I was expected to know him, although naturally I didn't. So, I decided to stall and play along.

"What are you talking about?" I asked, attempting to play it cool.

"Yes, John, why don't you tell Addie exactly why you're acting like I'm a terrorist holding a bomb you intend to deactivate?" Gavin said casually behind a yawn. To my extreme embarrassment he made no attempt to hide his halfway un-tucked shirt.

John turned to Gavin angrily and said, "You can call me Mr. Hamilton seeing as how you and I ain't exactly on a first name basis." He then pointed his finger in my face in an accusatory way as he fumed, "I thought we talked about this. You can't afford to be taking no risks. I told your Grandma and Pop I would look after you, and this," he thumbed towards Gavin "ain't no part of what I promised them for you." I suddenly realized that he was the guy I had heard about in my dreams, and he was who my Grandma had told me to get in touch with if anything ever happened to her. I thought about how strange it was for him to be at my house today.

"Why should I listen to you?"

He ran his hand over his head in a very frustrated

manner and then spoke to me as if he were completely exasperated. "Addie, we've been over this and over this. I made a vow before God. I've dedicated my life to keeping you safe. And that right there ain't nothing but trouble."

He pointed at Gavin.

Gavin leaned towards him steadily and spoke so quietly it concerned me. "Don't talk about me like I'm not here. I can't help what I am anymore than you can change the color of your skin. Prejudice comes in many forms, my man. Don't judge me for the things I can't change. I don't judge you for yours."

John narrowed his eyes and hissed, "Being black and being evil is two very different things. Besides, I ain't got no vested interest in your feelings; my concern is keeping this here girl alive. Your presence is too dangerous and presents far too great a risk. I'm afraid I'm going to have to ask you to leave."

I stepped in. "Whoa! Where do you get off telling other people to leave my house?"

"By the authority your grandparents gave me—that's how."

Gavin stood up feigning nonchalance, but the tightness around his eyes told me better. He went on to announce sardonically, "Don't worry about me. I'll be leaving now. I have evil plans to concoct and worlds to destroy, so I best be on my way."

Yet just before he walked out the door, he planted a firm kiss squarely on my mouth before giving John a look that told him to go somewhere hot...permanently. I had no sooner closed the door behind him before John scolded me fearfully, "What the heck are you thinking? I told you that you best stay far away from that man!"

"Hey, first of all, you had better get your facts straight; he's the one who's seeking me out—not the other way around. Besides, what's the big deal? You act like he's the devil himself!"

John's face implored me and begged me to see reason as he defended his disapproval with a response that terrified me to my core.

"Addie, that's because he is ..."

Chapter 5

It's not every day that you find out that the love of your life is Satan incarnate, but today just happened to be that day. My head was swimming, and I could not reconcile in my mind the intensity of Gavin's care and concern for me with anything intrinsically evil.

"John, are you telling me that my Prince Charming is really the Prince of Darkness? If so, you really owe me a lot of frogs to kiss."

"Addie, he's not 'the' devil per se, but he is 'a' devil."

"Get out of town!" I stated in shock.

"No can do," said John. "You're stuck with me here in the Bluff City on your Grandma's orders."

"John, you can't make me believe he's a bad apple—you just can't."

"Addie, you can't tell me you haven't smelled the fruit."

"Say what?"

He sighed and sat down on Grandma's couch as he inquired, "Can't you smell it on him?"

"I don't know what you're talking about. He smells pretty darn good to me."

"Exactly. That's the problem."

"So, I should run for the hills on your lame theory that my boyfriend is an evil mastermind based on the evidence that his scent is intoxicating?"

"You made him your boyfriend while I was out?! I was only gone for the afternoon!"

"Okay, so he's not exactly my boyfriend. I don't really

know what he is to me."

"But surely when you've been around him, you've notice the aroma of apples."

Something in my head clicked. Gavin intoxicated me, and I had always subconsciously attributed this to his naturally sensual pheromones. But John was right; the scent of fresh, warm apples followed him wherever he went. I buried my head into my shirt sleeve and inhaled the lingering essence of him; I had the same warm, heady feeling in reaction to it today that I always did.

I decided to reluctantly concede the point. "Okay, so yes, he smells like apples. Since when does that make him Hitler's clone?"

"Addie, he's forbidden fruit." John exhaled sadly. "You're not supposed to have him."

"Forbidden..." Suddenly it dawned on me. "Like the tree of knowledge..."

"Of good and evil in the garden of Eden," he finished for me. "And just like Adam and Eve, anyone who partakes of it."

"Will surely die," I completed the thought with a whisper. I had always believed that the truth would set people free, except apparently if it was presented in the form of my personal evil human temptation, in which case it would certainly be the death of me. "But John, how could he be so appealing to me if he's so terribly wrong for me?"

"The most dangerous evils are always seductive. Even sociopaths can be charming."

I started shaking like an earthquake. Then I realized

that actually someone else was shaking me, because Pop was waking me up.

"Addie? You got a phone call. Can you take it?" he asked. I shivered more from my dream than the cold air that hit me when I pulled my covers back. I was on fire from Gavin and more in fear of him than I had ever been.

"S-sure," I stammered as I picked up the land line.

"Addie?" a guy inquired. "It's Will. I was checking to see if we were still on for our date tonight."

His voice was light and warm. I mentally cursed myself for forgetting what I had promised Keisha.

"Oh...umm...yes...the Destination at 7 p.m. right?"

"Yeah...if that's okay with you, of course," he remarked politely.

It was considerate of him; he wasn't a devil as far as I knew. There was no point in pushing him away for some guy who probably didn't even exist and who was apparently hopelessly evil. I supposed when you found out your imaginary boyfriend was a devil, you could only upgrade from there by default.

"Yes, that sounds great."

"Okay, I'll pick you up at your place. See you soon."

I hung up to find Grandma and Pop with eyebrows raised in amusement and arms crossed as they watched me curiously.

"Do you have a 'date' tonight?" Pop asked the question and pronounced the word "date" as if it was an unfamiliar one for him to articulate.

"Yes, Keisha is making me go. But if you guys need me and want me to stay home, it's no problem – I can

88

cancel..." I stammered.

Grandma cut me off by saying, "No way, Jose. You never go out. I'm just flabbergasted you're going out at all and that I didn't know anything about it."

"Yeah, well, that's because I kind of forgot."

"Addie Marie Jackson, that's just plain rude!" Grandma lectured me.

"Look, he doesn't know I forgot. Nothing against him, but I've had a lot on my mind. It's no big deal—we're just having dinner, and then I'm coming straight home." I said clearly indicating that they needed to back off a bit.

Pop shrugged and handed me a $100 bill, my cell phone, and some pepper spray and announced, "I want you to have as much fun as possible. But if that yahoo gives you a hard time, you call me, and I'll bury him where the sun doesn't shine. And between the time that you call me and I get to you, you mace him real good, and use the money I gave you to catch a cab home. If he's a nice young man and he's good to you, then he's okay in my book. But if he hurts my girl, well, I'm gonna hurt him."

"Pop, you know you're actually pretty scary for an old man."

"You don't know the half of it," he snickered as Grandma and he exchanged a knowing look. They left me alone to get ready for my date, and I called Amber and Keisha to get clothing advice. I eventually decided on some dark washed jeans, my favorite linen shirt, and some dressy sandals to help combat the Memphis heat.

Will arrived to pick me up but found Pop sitting on our porch instead. Unbeknown to me, Pop had found some hunting gear, despite the fact that I had never known him to hunt. He was covered from head to toe in camo. Naturally he was polishing his shot gun surrounded by boxes of shells, so I felt certain my first date with Will would be my last.

Will was white as a ghost but complimented me on my outfit, shook hands with my grandparents, and then quickly escorted me to his ride. I apologized profusely for Pop, but to his credit Will was good natured enough to blow him off. While we zipped along towards the Destination, Will jabbered on about college, his family, our friends, and all of the other mindless, mundane topics people normally talk about. He was attractive, attentive, and obviously crazy about me. When I told Keisha there was absolutely nothing wrong with him, I wasn't kidding; he was gosh darn perfect.

Despite all of these wonderful traits, there was only one problem. He wasn't Gavin. I mentally cursed Gavin for ruining my love life. It was easy to blame him since I didn't exactly know him, and it was highly unlikely he would ever get his feelings hurt by my mental angst. Dreams of him pervaded my nights. Thoughts of him invaded my days. There was nowhere I could go to escape from the awareness of him, and no matter what Will did, I knew he couldn't be him.

Maybe I was officially crazy; it was entirely possible. Most girls would have killed to have had a nice guy like Will to take them out. But me? I was fantasizing about the devil. In an instance I could recall Gavin's hot breath on my neck, the way his eyes darted mischievously towards me, the gentleness with which he caressed my face, and the steady way in which he was always there waiting for me in the background, quietly tempting me, almost as if he had seen all of my options and knew eventually all of my choices would lead me back to him.

"Addie, are you ready to get out?"

Will interrupted my daydream. I started suddenly as I realized his car had stopped, and he was waiting on me.

"Absolutely," I said as confidently as I could as I flashed a bright smile at him; I secretly prayed he was oblivious to my mental fantasy and was relieved when he seemed completely unaware.

We walked to the Destination together as the sound of blues wafted up through the muggy, Memphis air. Memphians were usually divided over whether they liked Saucy Shirley's or the Destination better. I didn't think you could get bad barbecue in Memphis; Grandma thought my nonchalance about barbecue was borderline sacrilegious, but of course she was funny like that. My only issue with the Destination was the occasional rude service. The wait staff was not particularly patient, but then they had never had to be. Because for every patron sitting down inside, there was a long line of hungry people in the alleyway chomping at the bit to get in. In my opinion, in spite of the less than stellar service, the dry ribs and Memphis slaw still made the trip worth it.

"The Destination will be good if I can find it," Will said lightly.

"What are you ... chicken about walking there?" I teased.

"No, but I don't really like having to drive all the way downtown, wandering past the Peabody Hotel, and taking some long, dark alley with no street signs to get there."

"If you're scared, we can always go somewhere else," I said.

"I ain't no chicken, but the walk there is enough to make you feel like you're going to get shanked before you ever arrive!" he said.

"Good thing the food is worth the trip," I remarked.

"That we can agree on." he conceded. For the first time I wondered if the reason he selected the Destination was because Keisha told him I liked it and that possibly he didn't normally come down to Beale Street.

"Will you protect me from any attacks?"

"Of course, ma'am," Will laughed and gave me a gentlemanly bow.

Fortunately we made it to the Destination in one piece. After being seated and ordering, we were quickly provided with dry ribs, baked beans, sweet tea, and cole slaw. I enjoyed the ribs and would have licked my fingers if I hadn't been on a date.

Our irritable waiter walked towards us and handed us our check with no conversation. Will picked it up and refused to let me help pay for it. We talked about how hot the weather had been this summer while the server ran Will's credit card. Our waiter returned to our table carrying Will's receipt and a red gift bag.

The server handed the gift bag to me and said, "This is a present from an individual, who wishes to remain anonymous."

I looked at Will quizzically, and he confessed, "I didn't do that. I wish I had, but it wasn't me."

The bag was a deep blood red, and there were hearts and glitter all over the tissue paper inside. But when I pulled out the paper, it was all I could do not to scream at what was inside. For while I had never seen a hoodoo bag in person, I remembered quite clearly the conversation I had overheard my grandparents having recently. They had said that a hoodoo bag with coffin nails and graveyard dirt meant death for the recipient, and that was exactly what lay before me. It felt like an elephant was sitting on my chest, and I could feel a panic attack coming on.

"Addie, what is it?" Will inquired looking confused.

I forced myself to breathe and willed myself to maintain my composure in this public place and in front of Will. I did not know him well enough to confide in him about what was going on. I wanted to throw the bag out the window, but that would attract too much attention. Despite my repulsion, the logical part of my brain knew I would need the bag when I talked to my grandparents about it.

"It's nothing important really," I lied as calmly as I could while my chest heaved in and out. I continued, "Let's get out of here—I've got an early morning class tomorrow."

He looked uncertainly at me before conceding, "Okay, whatever you wanna do."

We got up and walked out of the restaurant.

I grabbed his hand because I was suddenly feeling

extremely vulnerable; he mistook my gesture for impulsive affection as he put his other arm around me and kissed my cheek. At that point in time I didn't much care what he kissed as long as he got me back to Grandma's in one piece.

I felt like easy pickings for whoever felt like jumping me for kicks tonight, and I immediately realized I had no confidence in Will's ability to keep me safe. He was too vanilla, and he had no idea what he was up against, because his world consisted of white picket fences and suburbia. While this was a nice place for me to visit, and we lived in the same city, our experiences and perspectives of living in Memphis were worlds apart.

My mind raced wondering who could have sent the bag. We made it back to his car where he opened the door and waited for me to put my seatbelt on with shaky hands. I was just about to breathe a sigh of relief as we were driving down the alleyway when the shadow of someone stepped out in front of us in the middle of the road.

I panicked and screamed, because suddenly I was staring into the face of the Skullbangerz gang leader. Will's car screeched to a halt, and the man zoomed in on my face before he started heading right towards me.

"What are you...crazy? Drive for heaven's sake!"

I hit Will in the shoulder.

"Ow! What's your problem? I can't exactly run him over!"

"The heck you can't!"

I slipped my leg over the console into his floor board, pressed down on the gas pedal, and grabbed the wheel. He hollered a stream of profanities at me, but I didn't hear anything he said as I barreled right towards the Skullbangerz leader. The gang leader's eyes widened as the realization hit him that I wasn't going to stop, and at the very last second, he got out of the way before I screeched out of that alley. We had driven all the way past the river before I would give the wheel back to Will. He looked furious, and considering he didn't have a clue about the back story, I couldn't exactly blame him.

"What the heck was that?" he demanded flashing his eyes at me as he yanked the steering wheel back from me. "You can't drive around trying to run over homeless people. It's insane."

The only way to get out of this situation without him telling half the campus I was certifiable would be to tell him at least part of the truth, so I did.

"Will, I know that guy. He attacked me in my neighborhood recently. He's dangerous. He's not home-less—he lives around the corner from my house. He is stocked full of bad intentions. I have never tried to run over anybody before tonight. I honestly believe he would have killed me just then if he could have gotten to me. There wasn't time to explain. By the time I would have, we would have both been dead."

Then as bluntly as I had relayed that information to him, I reclined the passenger seat and laid back willing my heart to stop beating out of my chest.

"What in the world? Addie, you should call the police instead of trying to run him over!"

"Will, Memphis has more criminals than churches.

Do you really think the cops would have gotten here in time?"

He considered the question before reluctantly conceding, "Well, no, but you still scared the heck out of me. Don't ever do that again."

"I hope I never have to."

We drove back without any of the cheerful banter we had enjoyed at the start of the evening. I figured he had chalked me up as being crazy with a capital "C," so I didn't expect a repeat date with him ever again.

So, I was surprised when he walked me to the front door and kissed me on the cheek. He told me to try not to die between now and the next several days, because he would like to take me out again next weekend. I couldn't hold back my grin, and I even hummed a little when I strolled inside the house.

Nothing prepared me for what I found there. As soon as I entered, I could tell that my grandparents were still up, because I could smell coffee brewing when I pushed open their squeaky, back door. Yet, no one was in the kitchen, and while the television had the evening news on as usual, neither one of them was sitting in their recliners.

"Grandma! Pop!" I called as I wandered into the back of the house. I entered the living room and was startled by what I saw. "What is that? When did you two get a trap door? What is that safe for, and why are you keeping it underneath our house?"

They looked alarmed, and their eyes widened dramatically. "Child, this is none of your business right now. Now go on into the kitchen, and we'll be right along behind you," Grandma ordered through a shaky, tense voice.

"Grandma, what are you talking about? Everything with you two is my business."

"Not this...this here ain't," Grandma said. "Now you get on up out of here. This ain't your concern."

"What is going on? I know you two can be secretive and elusive about things sometimes, but now you are completely shutting me out!"

I was stunned. For one moment I had caught the glimpse of a safe between them before Grandma shut the door in my face while Pop stared apologetically after me. I had never had this feeling of complete rejection by them before. The strangest thing was that that was no ordinary safe. The safe had a chain attached to it that went underneath the floor. There was some kind of trap door compartment hiding the safe, but I didn't get to see enough of it to understand exactly what I was looking at.

"Why on earth are you two still keeping secrets from me?" I yelled through the door at them. "I am so sick of this!"

"I told you to get on out of here!" Pop bellowed. "This ain't none of your business!"

"I knew that senior citizens had their quirks and all, but you two have gone completely mad! This is ridiculous!" I screamed angrily even though I knew it was a low blow. I glared at the door and rattled the door knob loudly.

"Addie Marie Jackson, you had better get yourself back into the kitchen right now or else!" Grandma hollered

97

back. When Grandma resorted to calling me by my full name, I knew she meant what she said.

I stormed off into the kitchen, pacing the floor trying, to make sense of all of this. I racked my brain trying to figure out how to approach them, but I didn't have long to think before Grandma and Pop returned. Grandma sauntered in smoothly fixing her hair and patting down her apron; her casual demeanor clearly indicated she intended to act as if all of that didn't just happen.

"Well, there's my sweetie! How's my girl doing?" Pop recited his usual greeting as he kissed me on the cheek. I stiffened at the affection and angrily pulled away.

"I'll be just fine, Pop, when you two kindly tell me what on earth is going on. Since when do we have a trap door under our living room couch? How far down does that hole go? What was in that?"

Grandma straightened her shoulders, looked me squarely in the eyes, and pointed her finger at me. "Addie, I don't want to talk about it now, you hear? There ain't nothing to talk about neither! Some things you don't need to know, and that's just all there is to it!"

I stormed back past Grandma into the living room where the couch had been pushed back to its original spot keeping the trapdoor hidden underneath it perfectly. I whirled back into the kitchen and confronted her.

"Grandma, the Skullbangerz leader showed up on my date tonight, and an 'anonymous friend' left this threatening hoodoo bag for me at the Destination. I've got more than enough right to know what's really going on, and you and I both know it ain't right to keep leaving me in the dark!'"

My Southern accent was sounding stronger than a body builder in a wrestling match. When I get really upset, all of the country just spills right out of me. Grandma took a deep breath. I stuck my chin out, crossed my arms, and stubbornly waited for an explanation.

"Addie, you know your Pop and I love you. Someday you'll understand, but I can't explain it to you right now."

"You know I have heard of things like this," I said. "People get older and demented, and then they get all paranoid about the government, Revelations, World War III, you name it. The next thing you know, they've got a fallout shelter full of food and weapons in their basement. You'd rather keep me in the dark than keep me alive," I accused her callously, and she and Pop both winced under the allegation, as I scowled my most disgusted look at her.

Grandma's eyes snapped at me, but she calmly bit her tongue and motioned with her hands for Pop to do the same.

"Addie, I just can't tell you about it yet. It ain't fitting."

"What do you mean 'it ain't fitting'?! What ain't fitting is you keeping secrets from me. What ain't fitting is you hiding stuff with secret passage ways in my house and not telling me why. What ain't fitting is how when there are things I don't understand about you two, you're always telling me how you just can't tell me right now. I'm here to tell you one thing—you may not give me answers, but I'm about to find some on my own, and I'll do it with or without your help. You two may have a death wish, but I don't."

I had never talked to my grandparents like this before. Grandma has always made the rules, and even if I don't do exactly what she wants me to do, I have never called her out like this. So the minute I get done saying my piece and huffing and puffing, I start to feel rotten. It's not that I think I'm wrong. It's just that I've got mounds of respect for both of them, and I don't feel good about how I've just hurt their feelings. I suck in a long breath and try my best to hold it before I say something else for me to feel guilty about.

To my surprise Grandma doesn't snap my head off or barbecue me for dinner. She just looks at me with this long, deep look and sighs. She holds up her hands admitting defeat before looking at my Pop as if to say, "What should we do?," which is something I have never seen her do. In my observation, as tough as Pop might be, Grandma has always worn the pants as the family decision maker. Pop looked at me steadily for what seemed like a long time.

"Sugar, there are just things we don't want to put on you. There are burdens we don't want you to have to carry. Your Grandma and I are just trying to protect you—to help you to have a normal life, don't you see?"

"Well, that's just laughable seeing as how I've spent my whole life bending over backwards to take care of you two. Because even though you've lied to me for years, I've never tried to harbor any anger toward you, because I have always believed you were only trying to protect me. But it's high time you two reevaluated the risky situations I've found myself in lately. I'm in harm's way whether you tell me what's been going on or not. Being out of the loop makes me question my sanity and puts me in a very isolated situation. I'm wandering around blind and in the dark every flipping day."

"It's ludicrous for you to think that I have any expectation of ever having a normal life." I continued on. "I have predictive dreams I can't control. My only sibling was autistic and died from a hit-and-run driver we never found. My parents divorced and left me to move out of state, and the first date I've had in years resulted in a death threat. My Grandma is some crime fighting renegade, who thinks she has psychic understandings of complete strangers, and I've spend my life as a twenty year old college student taking care of people in their seventies.

"We live in the scariest area of town for reasons you have never explained to me, and the two of you have been keeping secrets from me my entire life. Now you've got some bizarre trap door with chains under my house, and you're still holding onto the insane idea that my life could be normal. I will have you know that my life will never be normal, so you telling me why on earth you're hiding stuff from me yet again is not going to change that. I gave up on having a normal life a long time ago. I wish you would, too!"

I stormed out of the kitchen, went to my room, and slammed the door like a spoiled, bratty kid. I burst into tears and cursed myself for not just taking a deep breath and biting my tongue like usual. I was mad, and I was hurt, and I had allowed that to build up like Mt. Vesuvius and erupt with twenty years worth of lava in Grandma's kitchen today.

I turned on my radio where a local band was belting out the Blues, which completely fit the funk I was in. I called Keisha for moral support, and she was kind enough to pick up. Per my promise to be completely honest with her, I recapped the entire bizarre scenario for her down to the last detail.

"Good grief, I can see why you were upset, and I don't blame you." She let out a low whistle. "They're so cryptic all the time, and yet you're the one taking care of them. If anyone needs to know what they are up to, it's you!"

"I know, but I lost my cool and said a lot of things that I shouldn't have."

"Addie, you're wonderful with them, but you're not perfect. Everybody has a right to get frustrated from time to time—even you."

Keisha reassured me through a yawn, which made me feel guilty for having woken her up at this late hour.

She lightened the mood by making up a lot of ridiculous reasons why my grandparents had a secret passageway and a safe hidden under our house, and she reflected on my grandparents' wild antics throughout the years.

"The next thing you know your Grandma will convert your house into one of those dome homes with solar panels, because she'll think the neighborhood thugs are stealing electricity from her, and she sure as heck won't let them get one over on her!" she joked.

I wiped tears from my eyes and chuckled. "You're so right! She'll probably install her own personal watch tower where she can post herself up there like a sniper to take out people who get on her property. 'Trespassing is cause for shooting in Tennessee!' she'll say before she asks them if they have any final words."

We laughed so hard we cried.

"Ad, I don't know what to tell you about all of this, but it'll be okay. They'll come around, and if they don't, you can always live with me. It's closer to campus, and I think you'd like living on your own. I mean, you've never gotten to ..." Keisha responded on a more serious note.

"I know, I know. Sometimes I think about it. But as much as they drive me crazy, I know they still need me—whether they are too proud to admit it or not."

"Everything's going to be all right."

"I hope so. I just have to get some answers for myself. They're obviously not planning on telling me what's going on, and I don't want to die from ignorance."

"Yeah, that's something else I wanted to talk to you about, but it's kind of a big subject, and I know it's really late."

"Like you can't be friends with me anymore, because it will ruin your father's public relations with the city council and because you think I'm psychotic?"

"No, of course not." Keisha laughed a little too nervously. "It's just that I stumbled upon something in class today that could give you at least one answer and maybe lead you to a few more."

"An answer to what?"

"An answer to why you have predictive dreams. Especially because it's an answer that I don't think your grandparents would ever give you."

Chapter 6

Anytime your best friend offers to answer a question you've been asking your entire life, you take it no matter what time it is. So, when Keisha told me she had learned why I had predictive dreams and that the reason was juicy enough that my grandparents would take it to their graves, of course I had to know why.

"Have you ever heard of a caul?" she asked me.

"A who?"

"Okay, I guess that's a no. Um, have you ever heard of being born with a veil over your eyes?"

"How does that even happen, and what the heck does that even mean?"

"It's when a baby is born with an extra layer of skin covering its face and head and sometimes even his entire body like a cocoon at the time of his birth. It's an extremely rare situation."

"All right ... but what does that have to do with me?" I said feeling confused.

"According to hoodoo legend, people who were born with a veil over their eyes are thought to be able to see the future. Addie, if you were born with a veil over your eyes, it would explain all of your predictive dreams. Back in medieval times a caul indicated that the baby was meant for greatness, and it was a sign of good luck. It is also supposed to help one fight against evil forces like witches and sorcerers."

"Now you're just messing with me, Keisha."

I disputed her claims even though my mind instantly

wandered to all of the hoodoo that had been surrounding my family. I couldn't help but wonder if this meant that I could help protect my family from evil threats.

"No, I'm afraid I'm definitely not messing with you. We talked about it in Southern History class today," Keisha said seriously. "People born with a veil over their eyes have a knack for getting into disastrous situations, but surviving them completely unscathed. It is considered a great gift of protection from God. Oh, and those born with veils over their eyes can also never be drowned."

"So, no suicide by drowning for me then, huh?" I tried to tease even though my head was spinning.

"You could attempt it, but according to the legend, you would not be successful."

"Are you telling me I was born with a caul and that despite my humble and stressful circumstances I should be thankful that God's favor has shone down on me in some currently undiscovered way?"

"Maybe. Back in the day people kept knowledge that babies had been born with a veil over their eyes a secret, because it was the kind of thing that scared other people and got the veiled people burned at the stake or hung in the town square."

I shivered thinking about this as she continued, "Births of babies with cauls often run in families as well. Families who have these tend to be really good at keeping secrets, which could explain some of your grandparents' privacy concerning family matters."

It all made sense, but I had no idea how to confirm any of this, and I told Keisha as much.

"Well, there's one more thing with this ..." she started until her voice trailed a bit.

"What is it?"

I pushed her.

"Cauls were considered gifts and great luck throughout history. So, when people were aware of what they meant, their family members kept them and stored them in little jars. They let people going off to war borrow them for protection or sailors at sea keep them on their ships to prevent them from drowning."

"So, knowing my superstitious grandparents, if I were born with a veil, they would probably have held on to it and made sure nothing happened to it."

"That's exactly what I think."

"The only problem is, they'll never tell me."

"Who says they have to? They're not the only people who can keep secrets. I say two can play this game. They might hide it, but that doesn't mean you can't dig it up," she challenged me.

"Keisha Kane, that's pretty rebellious coming from you."

She laughed and said, "Whenever you decide you're ready to start digging, call me up, and I'll bring my shovel."

We hung up the phone, and despite my anger at my grandparents and the fact that my head was spinning from a hoodoo hailstorm I could not escape, I allowed myself to fall asleep. For the first time in a long time I didn't dream anything all night.

I woke up the next morning with my mind racing. I

wondered how many church break-in's there had been that my grandparents had told me nothing about. I rushed to class to find out that I had gotten an "A" on my mock therapy session in psychology class.

I started to feel slightly hopeful that maybe there was something to this theory that I had been born with a veil over my eyes and that this somehow would make me lucky. Then I got a call from Grandma, who said that my Aunt Geena was coming over this afternoon, and she gave me a lecture on the importance of being nice to her.

There was nothing like a phone call warning me about a visit from Geena to ruin my newfound optimism. If there was a contest for my least favorite person in the entire universe, my Aunt Geena would win first place. It was bad enough that she had neglected Grandma and Pop her entire life. The only thing good Amber had gotten from her was her looks—all the way down to the red hair and freckles. Their hair is as orange as sweet potatoes. Amber is just as sweet as the spuds, but Geena is as sour as folks can come.

She looked like an Irish potato farmer, who had just learned she had lost her entire crop and was hell bent on making somebody pay for it. She depended on gambling the way most people depended on oxygen. To make matters worse, I had always suspected that my grandparents funded her expensive habit. Of all our bones of contention, their enabling of her was the worst one. To make the situation even more unpleasant, she and I had never been good at hiding our antagonism for each other. She was selfish, and I hated her for it.

My green eyes are the only physical attribute I acquired from my family, and of course I got those from Geena. Considering how much I despised her, this was just my luck. Green eyes, DNA, and a relationship with Grandma and Pop were the only commonalities I share with her, and none of those are by choice.

Pop likes to tell me how Geena has always had a heart for helping people, but I certainly don't see it. She held down jobs in various casinos for over two decades until she got fired one too many times for playing the slots on the clock and even counting cards a time or two.

She has always been an odd duck. Even though I've never known her to have a steady boyfriend, she has never lacked for male companionship, although none of her guys had been the marrying kind. She thought ice cream was its own food group, especially if it was butter pecan.

In spite of her easy access to delicious local foods, canned soup was what she craved most of the time, especially when she was pumped up to play poker. Strangest of all, she believed that even just one cigarette would kill you, so she tried to talk anybody she met out of using nicotine, regardless of whether or not her audience dipped or smoked.

I hung up the phone in a very foul mood. I had always believed she had taken advantage of Grandma and Pop, and if she was coming over today, I was certain there was something she wanted. At Grandma's request and against my desire to go underground until tomorrow, I went home to their house driving as slowly as humanly possible.

I pulled into the driveway and headed toward the

back door. I was happy to note Geena's speedster wasn't there yet, so I was hoping that would buy me a little time before I bit my tongue until it bled all night. I was surprised to see Pop out in his garden with his shovel digging ferociously.

Like most areas of their property, it was just one more place I wasn't allowed to go. Unfortunately for them though, as of yesterday, I wasn't playing by their rules anymore. I headed straight for him past Grandma's assortment of bottle trees as quietly as I could, curious to see what I would find. Hoodoo herbs, tomatoes, and green beans hid him from my view, but I could see the top of his "World's Greatest Grandpa" hat sticking up above the bushy leaves. However, the old man's hearing was even better than mine, and he popped his head up and spotted me dead on.

"Addie, get back in the house! You know you ain't supposed to be out here!"

But I was done listening to him.

I kept strolling in between corn and okra towards the back of the garden where he was running towards me to head me off. Before I knew what hit me, he grabbed my arm and started dragging me back to the house.

"Ow!" I whined. Pop had never grabbed me before. "That hurts!"

"Well, then you should have listened to me when I told you to get back. You know not to come out here."

"Maybe I'm tired of all the places I ain't supposed to go."

"People with nose trouble tend to be upset when they

gets their noses in messes they can't get out of," he lectured me. "Besides, Geena will be here any minute. Go on, and help your Grandma in the kitchen."

"Addie!" Grandma called for me. She made no bones about pointing inside to show me where I was welcome and where I was not. I went in as Pop finally released my arm and headed back toward his garden.

"I didn't realize you subscribed to the mentality that children should be seen and not heard." \Grandma was mixing up cornbread and cooking butter beans and ham, chicken and dumplings, fried green tomatoes, and baking a pecan pie.

"We don't treat folks like children when they act like adults," she said pointedly while waving a wooden spoon dripping of cornbread batter in my face.

Just then Aunt Geena walked in like she owned the place; Grandma greeted her with a kiss, and she and I exchanged a scowl. She was dressed presentably, but her eyes were red and hazy, so I knew she had been in the smoke-filled casinos like usual.

"This place smells like cigarette smoke," she complained with her nose wrinkled up. "You know, that stuff will kill you. You really need to quit," she lectured Grandma, and I snorted without intending to at the pure hypocrisy.

"You got something to say?" she growled at me.

"Oh, I just thought it was sort of funny how concerned you are about your Mom's smoking but not all the secondhand smoke you inhale playing slots."

"I fail to see how that's any of your business," she

111

snapped.

"I suppose it's not," I responded both as sweetly and sarcastically as I could manage.

"You two hush!" Grandma wagged her tongue at us. "We are going to have a nice, peaceful dinner tonight whether you two like it or not."

I had not known that to happen even once in my twenty years, but the butcher knife she was waving around from cutting up her chicken was enough for me to keep my mouth shut. Pop walked in the back door just as the front door bell rang. I scrambled to answer it since it was a welcome reprieve from any time with Aunt Geena.

Nosy Rosy, our neighborhood gossip and Grandma's friend, stood on the porch peeking in our windows. She looked a bit startled to see me greet her so soon but didn't have the decency to blush.

"Well hello there, darling! I just made some divinity and knew how much your Grandma liked it, so I wanted to bring it by. Is she home?"

Translation being: I noticed Geena's speedster in the driveway, and I wanted to get the latest scoop on your family gossip.

"Sure, Mrs. Rosy. Come on in," I said politely.

"June!" Rosy called to my grandmother, who had always just been Grandma to me, so hearing her call her by her first name always threw me off for a second.

Grandma smiled and walked towards her as she reached in her pocket, pulled out her blue starred ring, and slipped it on her finger. She gave Rosy a big hug, and as she did her face caught my attention, because she looked

112

frozen in time for several seconds.

Oddly enough, I noticed Geena watching her as well as she cleared his throat and picked up a piece of cornbread. Rosy was oblivious to any change in pace as she chattered on about how last night her neighbor on the other side of her had come home drunk with a woman half his age. She looked aghast that the old man would behave that way after being recently widowed.

For someone who kept up with all of the latest scandals, Nosy Rosy was easily scandalized. Grandma's face paled and looked ghost white when she pulled away from Rosy, but she busied herself pouring sweet tea and serving dinner to everybody.

I wondered how many times that scenario had played out with different people over the years and how in the world I had always missed it before. I suppose people only see things when they are ready to.

Rosy jabbered, "My neighbor kept telling me he was going to meet with some man. I told him he didn't need to go do business dealings with nobody he hadn't checked references on first."

"What do you mean your neighbor was going to see some man?" I asked.

Rosy got flustered and clarified, "No, that's not quite right. I meant to say he told me he was going to see *the* man, as if there was only one. Now isn't that silly? We live in Memphis for crying out loud where half of the population is male. How ridiculous is it that he would act like there was only one? My goodness, he must have already been drunk! Bless his poor heart. I need to put that

113

man on my prayer list."

She tisked in a tone that sounded much more interested in his plight than worried about it.

Then just like that, Grandma dropped a plate, and it shattered all over the kitchen floor. I could have sworn I heard her mutter, "What is the Man doing in our neighborhood? He ain't got no cause for doing business around these parts."

I immediately flashed back to the conversation I had overheard my grandparents having about going to a crossroads to see the Man. I wondered if this could be the same person while I helped her sweep up the broken dish.

After fishing around to see if I was dating anybody and hinting around with Geena that it would be nice if she and Amber came to see her sometime, Nosy Rosy eventually left. Geena and I seemed equally amused by her indiscreet attempts at meddling, and it occurred to me that it was probably the first time we had ever been on the same page about anything before.

After Rosy was gone and dinner was consumed, Geena got around to what she had probably been after in coming over here in the first place. She asked Pop for five hundred dollars.

"What makes you think it's okay to keep taking money from them?" I hit the room and hollered at her. "You have got to quit leeching off of them!"

"Child, this ain't none of your business," Grandma said, cutting me off.

"You need somebody looking after your business," I objected. "She certainly ain't. You two are not an ATM machine for her!"

Geena stood up and swayed back and forth a little before conceding, "You're right—they're not," as he walked out the door.

"Do you see what you did?" Pop hissed at me as she chased after her.

"What do you mean 'what I did?!' I just took care of a problem for you. You're welcome!" I hollered after him. Grandma stared coldly at me, and it was frigid enough for me to shudder from the chill.

"Addie, you got to stop being so hard on her. It ain't all her fault." she said coolly.

"Grandma, she's a grown woman. She's responsible for her choices. It's not right the way she takes advantage of y'all, but it also ain't right that you two let her do it."

"You think you know her, but you don't. One of these days when your Pop and I are dead and gone, you two are going to have to look out for each other. You'd better start acting like you're on the same team before it's too late."

"What is that supposed to mean?" I asked. "She has never looked out for me. The only person she cares about is herself, and every time I'm around her she makes that even more abundantly clear. I'm on Team Grandma and Pop; she's on Team Geena. The fact that she doesn't do right by y'all means that she and I will never be okay. I know you wish that were different, but Grandma, it's not ever going to change."

Grandma started wringing her hands and pulled out a cigarette to smoke before saying, "You don't have the right to judge her until you've walked a mile in her shoes.

Someday Addie, you're going to be in her shoes, and having somebody in your life who knows what they feel like would be mighty helpful. Don't be so hard on her—someday you'll regret it."

I fell silent; I was too tired to argue with her anymore. The last thing I wanted to do was upset her when I was only trying to protect her.

"Here," she said, handing me a card.

"What is this?"

"It's just a little something from Pop and me. We know you're disappointed that we can't give you the answers you want right now. We can see how you've been feeling more stressed than blessed lately. We thought you could use that to have a fun afternoon with Keisha and Amber."

I read their sweet card and was pleased to find gift cards to the zoo and to my favorite coffee house. My grandparents didn't apologize, but whenever they had done something they felt badly about, they usually gave me a present. They were too proud to admit any wrong doing on their part, but they loved me too much to want me to stay mad at them for any length of time.

"Thank you."

"You know we always do anything we can for you, child," she said, and I did not miss the message underneath her response. They wouldn't do just anything for me, but they would do whatever they thought was good for me. There was and always would be a difference. Pop walked back in humming. I figured he had just convinced Geena to take a wad of cash before she left, but I didn't ask, and he didn't say.

I helped Grandma with the dishes quickly as I had another date planned with Will tonight, and I didn't want to be late. Considering his recent scare with Pop, I offered to meet him at a local pub. After insisting several times that he did not mind picking me up, he had finally conceded to meet me there. My plans to see Will again reminded me that I had stashed the hoodoo sack from the Destination in Pop's liquor cabinet, because any time I thought about it, it just made me want to drink.

I was too scared to look at it again but too afraid I would need it for future reference to throw it away. So, there it sat like a visitor passing through town in between its new friends, Jack Daniel's and George Dickel.

My grandparents didn't tease me too much about going out with Will, and traffic was better than usual getting downtown tonight. I met him at the pub where a bunch of drunk locals were embarrassing themselves singing karaoke. We had front row seats to the entertainment and were highly amused by the show.

He went to get a second round of drinks for us when I noticed the television in the bar was tuned to a local news channel, and a reporter was covering a story on neighborhood crime. He discussed the recent break-in's at our church and showed video footage from the security cameras of the intruder's. I was immediately gripped to the screen as I realized for the first time exactly how much my grandparents had been keeping from me.

"Hey, what are you watching?"

Will quizzed me as he slid into the seat beside me and

handed me a soda.

"The news is covering the break-in's at my grandparents' church," I explained.

"Y'all go to that church? I didn't know that. Yeah, it's been all over the news for weeks now."

"I have got to start watching the news! What's going on?"

"You don't know?" he inquired incredulously.

"I thought I did, but obviously there's been more to it than I've been informed about."

He proceeded to catch me up. He explained how the church had experienced countless break-in's and had tripled their security but how none of their actions had deterred the intruders. The reporter showed footage of several people dressed in black from head to toe sliding into the church on a rope through the bell tower.

"What sort of ninjas are these people?" I asked, shaking my head as a rhetorical question to myself, which Will took it upon himself to answer.

"I don't think they're ninjas," he observed. "They are pretty bizarre and persistent about whatever they are trying to accomplish over there though."

"How do you figure?" I asked as I watched them interview Gerald Smith, a security guard, who worked with Pop over at the church.

"They break in leaving almost no damage, ransack the place, check out whoever is working security, and leave weird stuff behind."

"What kind of weird stuff?"

"Some kind of bags with bits of strange things in

them. Like I said, it's bizarre. Oh, and the crazy thing is that they have never stolen a thing. So whenever they finally do get caught, it's not like the church can even press charges on them for thievery or any major destruction of property."

"Shhh! I want to hear what Gerald's saying."

The reporter had just asked Gerald if he had experienced any direct encounters with the masked intruders, and he explained that he had one time. Gerald said the black ninjas asked him for only one thing—they wanted him to take them to see Louie Jackson.

My heart stopped and fell through the floor. I don't know what else was covered in that interview. All I knew was that hoodooed henchmen had been breaking into Pop's workplace for weeks now looking for him, and as usual I was the last to know. All I wanted to do was get home and make sure that my grandparents were okay.

I told Will I had to leave, and he looked disappointed but didn't argue too much about it. He walked me to my car and surprised me by kissing me just before I sat down. His lips were warm and soft, and even though my feelings for him were ambivalent at times, I thought I could get used to kissing him. He looked like he enjoyed it too and reluctantly waved goodbye to me as I drove off toward my house.

It was late when I got in. My worries for Grandma and Pop consumed me. I tiptoed into their room to make sure they were safe and sleeping soundly.

I was pleased to see Grandma's feet sticking out under her quilt with her ragged, old bunny slippers looking as tired as I felt. Pop was snoring loudly enough to shake the rafters, but at least that meant he was getting some rest and not being threatened by masked men. So, all of that made me feel a lot better for tonight at least.

I decided to get some shut eye myself, so after I got ready for bed, I laid down in my room. My thoughts turned to Amber, and I had a horrible dream about her. In my dream I didn't know where she was, and all I wanted to do was go look for her. Unfortunately, no one would let me help find her, and they treated me like I had a lot of nerve to even ask. I was terrified and cried out for her, but all that answered my pleas were walls and silence.

I went on to dream about Gavin, which I felt strangely guilty about after my kiss with Will tonight. In my dream we were loading boxes into his car. He was stealthy about keeping what we were doing discreet, so this made me curious about what was inside those bins.

Gavin had a song about being too hot to be real blaring when I hopped into his black ride.

"Hope you don't mind," he said casually in a tone that indicated he didn't care whether I did or not. "It's kind of my theme song."

"I can't believe you listen to pop!"

"What should I be listening to?"

"Oh, I don't know... Devil music maybe?"

Gavin exhaled and shook his head at me with an air of superiority as he maturely ignored my suggestion that his personal music style had to be devil rock.

"Addie, who doesn't like this musician? He's a local, whose main musical influence growing up was the blues."

"He's just not really my style—that's all."

"And you call yourself a Memphian. Tisk tisk, Addie...tisk tisk."

We drove out almost all the way to Oakland, Tennessee with Gavin's rock music blaring the whole way. He cut off down an isolated two lane road and continued all the way until the road ran out with nothing around us but grassy fields. He parked the car and got out as I trailed along behind him. He unloaded the car and stacked the boxes up together in a pile before asking if I had any final words to commemorate them.

I looked at him aghast as he smirked at my shock before he snapped his fingers in front of my face and sparks flew up. He took the flame from his fingers and lit the boxes on fire before blowing on them to fan them into a bonfire within seconds.

"What the heck are you doing? And how are you doing that?"

"I'm helping you out. You don't need all this evidence lying around. It'll be better for you when it's gone."

"How could you possibly make fire from snapping your fingers like that? That's crazy!"

He looked at me wryly as the flames reached toward heaven and said, "John told you I was a devil."

"So, that means you can make fire," I said more to convince myself than him.

"You know I can. You just saw me do it," he answered as he eyed me steadily waiting for a reaction. He seemed impressed that I had stayed so calm during so many potentially scary revelations about him.

"The more you prove you are worthy to obtain knowledge, the more you will have the privilege to learn."

"I mainly just want to know one thing."

"So, go ahead and ask," he dared me.

"Exactly how scared of you should I be?"

He gave me a devilish grin. "You, my dear, have no reason to be afraid. Some other people would have great reason to be fearful of me. I, however, happen to be quite petrified of you."

"Why would you be afraid of me?"

He hesitated before answering, "Because I'm not supposed to get involved. I'm not supposed to help you bury the evidence," he motioned at the bonfire before us. "Because if and when they find out what I'm doing, my lot will be far worse than it already is."

"I appreciate you helping me, but why are you doing this if it will only make things worse for you?"

"Because I can't stay away from you. Because you didn't ask for any of this. And because at the end of the day it's the right thing to do, even if it breaks all of the rules."

I contemplated all of this while I watched the flames lick up the rest of the box pile. I had seen more than my fair share of hot guys in my life but none who could start fires with their hands. I was dying to know the answer to one more question even though I was terrified to find out. But like my Grandma always said, my curiosity usually won out over my God given sense.

So, I asked him, "Gavin...what are you?"

He met my gaze as the smoke curled up around his face, and he answered, "I'm the Man."

Chapter 7

Not only was Gavin a devil. He was the Man.

I sat up in bed in a full on panic attack. I slipped out of my room and ran to the bathroom where I splashed water on my face.

Gavin was a legend whispered behind closed doors and feared by all, yet I could not reconcile the gentleness he had always shown me with his evil reputation. My chest hurt, and I sucked in air like I was barely keeping my head above water. I wondered if Keisha could find out anything in her Southern History class about him today for me.

I forced myself to get ready for class quickly and darted out the door as fast as possible to avoid unwanted questions from Grandma and Pop. I tried unsuccessfully to sidestep Grandma, who was trying to entice me to stay long enough to eat biscuits and gravy. She eyed me suspiciously when I declined her delicious offer and left. There was no doubt she was tempting me to try to pick my brain for information about Will and to find out what else I knew that Pop and she were trying to keep hidden. There was absolutely no way I was going to give her the satisfaction of sticking around.

I made it to campus relatively quickly and was surprised to see how crowded Shelby College was today as I had forgotten that Amber's high school was taking a tour of the college. I quickly remembered as soon as I saw all of the students wearing matching T-shirts following the campus's student council guide around. I brightened at the possibility of seeing my favorite cousin as I looked for her in the crowd. I spotted her glowing red hair in the back of the tour group. Her smattering of freckles was so cute on her, and it was strange to me how she always attempted to cover them up.

To my shock, I looked down to see that her hand entwined with a male classmate; I had no idea she was dating anyone, and it was completely unlike her to leave me in the dark about something that significant. They were clearly in their own little world and were quite oblivious to anyone approaching them, including me.

I headed towards them intending to introduce myself. I wanted to check this guy out and determine whether or not he was good boyfriend material for her. They turned their heads as they heard me walk up behind them, and the glow on Amber's face at seeing me there was a complete contrast to my reaction when I saw whose hand she was holding. For out of everyone in the entire Tri-State area that she could be dating, she was holding the hand of a Skullbangerz gang member.

I flashed back to the day when the Skullbangerz had chased me down, and the gang leader had threatened to cut me into little pieces and mail bits of me to Grandma for Christmas. The pipsqueak who had been with him and had clearly enjoyed tormenting me was staring right back at me.

"What the heck are you doing holding hands with him?" I cried at her. "Have you lost your ever loving mind? You don't get to touch her!"

I pointed at him as I grabbed her other hand and pulled her away and back towards me.

"What is wrong with you? Since when is that any way to greet my new boyfriend? Gosh, you're so rude! What is your problem?"

My mouth dropped open like a catfish. I had never seen Amber snap at anyone, and as crazy as she had always been about me, I couldn't wrap my brain around the way she was speaking to me now. To make matters worse, her new "boyfriend" grinned slyly back at me as he was clearly enjoying the way the tables had turned.

Amber took my silence as an invitation to continue ranting, so she did, "I've always been nice to the people you've introduced to me. I don't think it's asking too much to expect the same from you!"

I found my voice again. "Amber, you don't understand. This guy …"

"Chris." She cut me off. "His name is Chris."

"Okay, whatever. Chris here is a member of the Skullbangerz, and they chased me down a few weeks ago and threatened to kill me. I would be dead right now if Grandma hadn't pulled a gun on them."

Amber looked at him quizzically and asked, "Chris, is that true?"

"Why in the world do you need to ask him whether it's true or not? I just told you it happened—that should be more than enough answer for you to know it's true. You know there's no reason on God's green earth why I would ever lead you astray."

"Of course that's not true," Chris answered Amber while casting a calculating eye towards me. "That's ridiculous. I love you. I would never try to hurt anyone

125

you cared about. She's clearly mistaken me for someone else. It was an honest mistake – it could happen to anybody."

"You see, Addie?" Amber grinned a breathtaking smile at us. "There's just been a mistake. Chris wouldn't do anything like that. It's all just been a big misunderstanding."

"The heck it has!" I roared back at her. I noticed for the first time that we were attracting too much attention from the back of the tour group, so I lowered my voice. "Amber, you don't even know this guy. Where is your head? You know I would never lie to you. You've got to believe me—he's dangerous."

"This is not up for discussion," she said as she stared back at me coldly. I had never known she was capable of being anything but warmth. "I love him, and he loves me, and we're going to be together, and there's nothing you can do about it. Don't be saying all these lies about him. You need to apologize for making false accusations, even if it was an 'honest mistake.'"

Chris put his arm around her waist and looked pointedly at me as he kissed her on the cheek in a clearly antagonistic dig at me. I visualized putting my hands around his tattooed throat and choking the life out of him, but I was interrupted before I could get the satisfaction.

"Is there a problem here?" a security guard inquired. I must have been so caught up in the heat of the moment that I had missed the fact that we had created a big enough scene for campus police to get called.

"Oh no, officer," Amber turned on the Jackson charm.

"Thank you so much for the concern. My boyfriend and I were just enjoying the tour. Lovely campus you have here! And my cousin, Addie, over here was just going—weren't you, Addie?"

I was smart enough to know when I was out of tricks, and my bag was plumb empty. But I didn't want Chris to think this was over, so I said pointedly, "Thank you for checking on us, officer. There aren't any problems here that we need you to fix. I can take care of everything myself later."

Chris scowled at me, and the security guard scratched his head and responded cautiously, "Well, as long as there ain't no trouble, I guess I'll be on my way."

Amber took Chris's hand, turned her back on me, and ran off to catch up with the tour group. Somewhere in my heart a piece of my soul died.

I was late for class, but I still had to make one phone call on the way. I called Keisha, who was also running late for her Southern History class. I asked her to find out whatever she could about the Man today. With a little explanation about him from me, she promised she would do her best.

I got through today's classes on autopilot and then drove back home as quickly as I could. I had to tell Grandma about what I had observed with Amber so we could figure out how to help her.

Amber's behavior had been so bizarre and out of character that I would never have believed she could have acted that way except that I had seen it myself. I was relieved to pull into my driveway at home and walk through my front door.

"Grandma! Pop! I'm home!" I called out as I slung down my backpack, kicked off my shoes, and collapsed onto the sofa in the living room. Grandma poked her head in and wiped off her dripping brow. She was making fudge and snicker doodles and had chocolate clumped onto the tip of her nose.

"How was class, child?" she inquired.

"Horrible!"

"Oh, don't be so dramatic! Going to college is a privilege you ought to be thankful for."

Even as she lectured me, she checked the time on her old pocket watch.

"Grandma, I'm not complaining about school. I ran into Amber, and her new boyfriend is one of the guys who tried to attack me a few weeks ago."

She snapped her head to look at me and examined my face clearly hoping I was joking with her. Her face fell when she could see my heavy shoulders and somber expression.

"Addie, you got to tell her to stay away from him. He ain't no good."

"Grandma, I did! She wouldn't listen to me. She accused me of lying. That boy fed her a bunch of fried baloney, and she ate up every bite. I don't know what's wrong with her," I reported feeling perplexed by Amber's behavior.

Grandma turned white and started spinning her blue starred ring around before hunting up her nicotine fix. Her hands shook as she tried to light up, so I helped her by holding up her match.

"I knew that bunch was mixed up in hoodoo. They must have cast a love spell on her."

"They did what?" I asked incredulously as my voice went up an octave.

"They bewitched her. She can't be thinking right. She's under the influence of witchcraft. We'll have to break the spell to get her back."

Grandma was talking to herself more than me.

I studied her and felt surprised that she was sharing any of this information. I decided to take advantage of her brief moment of honesty and see what else I could find out.

"I have always loved your pocket watch, Grandma. Where did you get it?"

"Oh, that old clock has been passed down in our family from generation to generation," she said as she dismissed my comment with a wave.

I persisted, because usually when Grandma was evasive, that meant things were more interesting than what they appeared to be on the surface.

"So, where did it originate from?"

"I'm not sure exactly, child."

She turned back to her baking goods with her mind obviously on her other grandchild. "It got passed on to me, and someday I'll pass it on to you," she continued. "Want a snicker doodle?"

She stuck a cookie in my face in a less than subtle attempt to change the conversation.

"Thanks." I took a bite and continued, "Well, it looks

so unusual. I've just never seen another watch like it."

"No, and you won't neither. And don't you be forgetting that I've got jewelry that I'm passing on to you, too. My blue starred ring is a family heirloom, and you've got to make sure you get that. I don't want nobody else having it now, you hear?"

"What's wrong, Grandma? Are you thinking of kicking the bucket sometime soon? I'm going to the hardware store later; I could always get you a bucket."

Grandma ignored my joke. She had her blue starred ring on now, and she was twirling it around her finger and staring off in a trance-like state.

"Nobody escapes the will of God. When He don't want me here no more, He's going to pluck me right up into the sky. Nothing comes between God's people and His providence." She checked her pocket watch and said, "Time is running out. I need you to respect my wishes, Addie. I don't want nobody else having my ring."

She turned to me looking as serious as a heart attack.

"Now you promise me! You give me your word that you'll do as I say! The last thing I want is the wrong people getting anything of mine. So, you make sure they don't!"

"Grandma, I know you're just wanting to make sure I get the things you're setting aside for me when you're not here some day, but all this talk about death is just morbid. You've got more vitality and adventurousness than anybody else I know, so we don't need to talk about this right now."

"Addie, you got to promise me." Grandma pressed the subject intently.

"Grandma, all I really want is you, and I'll take you any day of the week and five times on Sunday over any of your belongings. So, could we please talk about something else now? All this talk about dying is creeping me out!"

So, she eyeballed me long and hard and relented, "Okay...I'm going to let it go for today. But don't you forget you promised. I'll feel like I can't ever go on to Glory if you don't take care of things after I go. I know I depend on you way too much already, but this is real important. If you don't ever do nothing else for me, you've got to do this."

"Grandma, you're just inventing things to stress about. You need to get the doctor to give you some drugs or something. Instead of worrying about taking care of yourself or trying to move into a safe neighborhood like a sane person, you're spending all of your energy trying to make sure nobody else besides me inherits your ring and your pocket watch when you keel over. I swear, Grandma, you beat all I've ever seen."

"What did I tell you about all that swearing?!" she raised her voice at me. "God don't like for His children to swear. You go on into the bathroom, and wash your mouth out with soap!"

"Grandma, if I had a dollar for every time we had a conversation about what you want me to do when you die, I could retire at a very young age."

"Addie, we have these conversations so much, because they're just that important," she stated clearly. "You go on and leave me be for a bit. I've got to consult with Pop about what to do with your cousin. I've heard about how to cast a love spell, but I don't know how to undo one."

"You know, I saw what's really going on with the church break-in's on the news. You should have told me that the masked intruders have been looking for Pop."

She stared back at me steadily before warning me, "I told you that you don't want to know how deep the rabbit hole goes. If you get so curious that you fall in, there won't be no way that anybody can pull you back out."

Then with that warning, she wandered past her assortment of bottle trees outside to see Pop, who was piddling around in his garden. I figured they would be gathering up an assortment of hoodoo herbs to try to rectify the wrong against Amber. There was no telling how long they'd be out there, and I was worried and restless.

A phone call from Will was a welcome reprieve, so I invited him over to have some of my Grandma's snicker doodles and fudge and to watch TV. He showed up looking as fine as ever; time with him would be a peaceful escape from all of the other drama in my life. We sat down on the living room couch, and he flipped channels until he stopped on the chick flick channel.

"I figured maybe we could find a romance on here," he said, trying way too hard to sound casual.

"What makes you think I like romances?" I asked him warily.

"All girls like romances," he announced as sincerely as if he had just said that women couldn't be doctors or men couldn't be nurses.

I snatched the remote back from him and said, "I

don't like romances. I don't."

I emphatically pointed at my chest.

"What? How come?"

He looked shocked.

I had never liked romances, because I didn't believe they were anything that would ever actually happen for me. I knew other people had stories about getting chased in an airport by a handsome guy with flowers or riding off into the sunset with Prince Charming on a white horse. However, I would never have the luxury of being in love, because that would involve making decisions based solely on what I wanted to do.

Growing up I had to make decisions based on what was best for my autistic sister, Amy, especially since my parents were too neglectful to pay much attention to us. Then after she died and I moved in with Grandma and Pop, I had always made decisions based on whatever was in their best interest.

Romance would only ever be enjoyable for me if it didn't come with the guilt of neglecting my loved ones who needed me.

"I just don't like romances. That's all."

Will grinned and snatched the remote from me clearly oblivious to the fact that he had sent my defenses up and walled him out.

"Geez, how old is this TV?" he whined.

"It's one of a kind—a living legend." I bristled defensively. "Vintage is in nowadays. Don't hate."

"Yeah, well, I hate the fact that the picture is all staticky and that the screen cuts off the edges on all of the shows."

I folded my arms across my chest and muttered, "You can still see most of it."

"Addie, how do you live like this? I mean seriously!"

"What is the big deal? It's just a stupid TV!" I snapped back at him.

"No, I mean how do you handle all of this with your grandparents? They have no cable, no Internet, they eat dinner at 4:30PM, and I bet they've never even heard of social media."

"I don't get on social media either, and I'm surviving," I sniffed stubbornly.

"See! That's what I'm talking about. Being with them puts you so out of touch with the rest of the world. Plus, y'all are real violent."

"Violent? What are you talking about?!"

"Um, your Pop threatened me with his hunting arsenal before our first date, you tried to run over some guy with my car, and you're getting aggressive at the mere suggestion that your family is violent. Sheesh, Addie, don't you want more out of life than this?"

He waved his hand around in judgment of my house.

Will looked at me like I was an alien he was prodding for signs of intelligence, and it offended me. He had no right to criticize us for why we were how we were. I knew Grandma and Pop were old school.

I realized being on a geriatric schedule put me in a different mindset than the rest of my college friends. I didn't, nor had I ever, cared about the latest anything, but I cared about them more than anything in the world.

I may have never been in love with a guy, but I had always been in love with them. So, the fact that he didn't understand that and had the nerve to question this had just placed him on my last nerve.

"Will, I'm tired. I need to wash my hair. It's not you—it's me," I announced coolly. "I have things to do, and you need to go do whatever you want to do with someone else besides me."

It was the rudest I had ever been to a guest in my home.

"You know what? That crazy lady was right about you. She said she needed to meet with you about some hoodoo or voodoo or some other wacky weirdness. I told her she was looking for the wrong person, because surely you couldn't be mixed up with some wonky woman wearing animal bones."

"What are you talking about?" I whispered as my blood turned cold.

"Some African American lady with natural hair, whose eyes looked ... off ... something ain't right about her, and apparently something ain't right with you either, so maybe you should look her up. I mean, whatever—I'm done trying to hook up with you. You're obviously a head case, and I could get any girl I wanted. I don't have time for your baggage. I'm out."

Then with that admission, Will walked out, and I burst into tears. Not only had my only almost boyfriend in years just called me psychotic, but a dangerous woman was hunting me down.

And people wonder why I don't date.

Chapter 8

My grandparents were working hard to get Amber's love spell removed, and the spell I had been under for Will was officially gone. Nobody talked to me badly about my grandparents and survived; they might be nuts, but they were all I had. Anybody who wanted me to turn on them was someone I needed to turn away from. I went outside and walked around our big yard by Grandma's bottle trees in the muggy heat.

I had seen other Southerners have one bottle tree, but I had never seen anyone besides Grandma have a yard full of them. I had noticed the number of bottles seemed to have doubled since the Skullbangerz attacked me, and I wondered what that was all about. A black snake slithered by me and curled up around one of the bottle trees. In spite of the heat I suddenly felt a chill.

I needed to get my head cleared, so I called Keisha and asked her to wander around the zoo with me. I informed my grandparents that I was heading out to use the gift card they had given me.

Then I jumped in my beater and drove to meet Keisha at the zoo. She had always been the most stable person in my life, and a hug from her was like warm sunshine. After we caught up with each other, we wandered around to look at the miniature elephants, the giraffes, and the polar bears. Being somewhere I associated with pleasant memories of elementary school field trips was comforting for a change.

She told me she had asked about the Man in her Southern History class. Her professor told her that even though he is known as a devil or a trickster, he is neither good nor bad. People who have something they really want can go down to a crossroads for nine nights in a row to try to impress him so that he will make a trade with them. During that time he will intimidate them to see if they are worthy of what they want, and if they are, he will strike a deal with them.

"What do you mean people meet him at a crossroads?"

"It's where two roads intersect or where two different railroad tracks cross at a junction," she replied as if this was the most obvious thing in the world. I had to hand it to Keisha—she was good at handling the unusual and never acted like I was crazy for being curious about it.

"Is he malicious?" I asked feeling fearful of the answer.

"No, he doesn't use black magic. Bokors use dark witchcraft, but the Man is a business man, so he's supposed to be neutral."

"What kind of trades does he make?" I questioned her feeling fascinated by this new perspective.

"He makes bargains for special skills or knowledge."

"So, he doesn't try to kill people or sell their souls?" I asked.

"No ... of course not, Addie, why are you so interested in this?"

I hesitated but then decided to keep my promise to remain honest before I replied, "You know how I have those dreams about the guy I've never met?"

"The good looking man you've got the hots for?"

"Gavin. His name is Gavin."

"Okay, go on," she prodded me while hiding a grin.

"Well, I've been dreaming about things in the future, and he's there, and we're...together, for lack of a better word," I confessed feeling somewhat embarrassed.

"Whoa, you talk about him like he's real. Do you think he actually exists?"

"Yes, I really do," I admitted at the risk of sounding crazy. "I just don't know him yet. But the problem is that the last time I dreamed about him he told me he was the Man."

"Oh no, Addie! I'm so sorry. I know you have to be disappointed. It's too bad y'all could never be together."

I bristled defensively and snapped a little more harshly than I intended to at her. I had never taken kindly to anyone telling me what I could or couldn't do.

"I didn't say we could never be together. I just said he told me he was the Man, and I wasn't sure what that meant."

For the first time in my life Keisha looked at me like I was insane.

"I don't know if you just heard right me or not, but he's a devil from hoodoo legend," she argued. "Even if he exists, it's unnatural. You can't be with him. The very idea is ridiculous."

"You don't know him." My face hardened, and my stubborn streak flared up as I countered her logical concern with an emotional one. "You can't talk about him like that. He's good to me. He's not what you think. Don't be so judgmental."

"You're calling me judgmental for being worried about you wanting to pony up with some possibly imaginary guy you've never met after I just told you he's the trickster?"

She snorted and stared at me in disbelief.

"Keisha, there's good in him. I've seen it."

"So said every other woman who's been swindled by a sociopath or stuffed into the back of a trunk!"

"Listen, just forget it. I obviously can't talk to you about this. You don't understand, and I shouldn't expect you to. I don't even know him, so it's stupid to even discuss this anymore."

I forced myself to end the conversation with her since I felt like I had been punched in the stomach.

"Addie, I'm sorry. Like I said, I don't know if it's true or not, but I just felt like it was only fair for me to tell you," Keisha apologized clearly feeling a sense of false guilt for being the messenger of bad news.

"Thank you for letting me know, but I can't do this right now—I've got to go home."

I decided to leave the zoo; I felt like a cloud raining darkness everywhere I went this week. We parted ways without the friendly banter we had enjoyed at the start of our visit today.

I drove home feeling despondent. It started to rain, which just suited my mood. I got back to the house and out of the car to find Grandma yelling at a black rooster. To say my grandparents were off the chain would be like saying the sun was a bit warm.

I walked up on her slowly to try to understand what

she was saying. To my surprise the rooster wasn't trying to run off, and he wasn't attempting to flog her either. It almost seemed like he was waiting patiently—if a rooster could wait patiently for someone.

"You've been showing up here masquerading yourself as every black animal in the book. I done told you I'd let you know when I needed your help. I know you're worried, but you're getting on my last nerve. I got this under control, and when I don't, I'll let you know. Now scram! No roosters allowed in this neighborhood. Can't nobody do nothing about the crime, but the animal control would pick you up faster than you could fry an egg on the Tennessee pavement in July. Get! Shoo!"

She squawked and flapped around looking more like a bird than the rooster did. The rooster turned and cocked his head to the side, eying me for several seconds before flapping off. Grandma realized for the first time that she had an audience and looked flustered for an entirely different reason now.

"I didn't expect you home so early," she said in between wheezing breaths.

"I didn't expect you to be having conversations with chickens while I was gone. You should have introduced me seeing as how that would have been the polite thing to do."

"That bird brain better get far away from here if he knows what's good for him."

"Would you care to elaborate on the one sided conversation you just had with that cock?"

She narrowed her eyes. "That there was a private conversation. If you needed to have been included, you would have been."

I shook my head in disgust and strode into the house and slammed the door behind me.

Pop was in the kitchen surrounded by bottles and jars of herbs, plants, and strange smelling substances. He grinned at me oblivious to the fact that I was having the world's worst day.

"I think your Grandma and I figured out how to reverse that love spell on Amber."

"As much as it stinks in here, I don't think you could get her close to any of this," I said as I wrinkled my nose.

"No, sugar. We put the remedy into this bracelet. All she has to do is put it on her wrist, and it will break the hold Chris has over her."

"That's great! Grandma can take it over to her right now," I said hopefully.

"Whoa, Nelly! You've got to think this through. This crooked Chris guy is going to be suspicious of anything that comes from our family. You confronted him in front of Amber, and your Grandma pulled a gun on his friends. He ain't inclined to forget any of that, so we need to get somebody involved that he wouldn't be distrustful of to help pull this off."

"Somebody like who?" I asked.

"I ain't quite figured that out yet. I got to consult with your Grandma to chew on it some more."

Grandma walked in, and they got caught up discussing their plan. As usual, their adventurous idea didn't include me. I was angry and exhausted, so I decided to go to my room to lay down for a bit. I must have been plumb worn out, because when I went down, I went down for the count, and I slept all night long. It was a shame that I went to bed, because there was a whole lot of action that went down while I was sleeping.

I dreamed another scary dream about Amber, and in my nightmare she was in trouble, and I was powerless to help her. While I was facing down fears in my sleep, Grandma was about to address hers head on in real life. She and Pop were taking advantage of the time I was out of their hair, so naturally they were up to no good.

"It's about time I go see him. I hate to admit it, but I need some help," Grandma confessed to Pop as she watched and waited for the sun to go down.

As soon as the last sliver of sunlight slipped out of the sky, the two of them began pulling bottles off of the trees.

"It's been too long since I took these dark spirits down to the Crossroads. It's high time I released them. Some of them is too dark for even the sunlight to burn up."

"It's time for them to pass on to the supernatural world now," Pop agreed as he plugged the bottles and lined them up in boxes on the bed of his truck. "That don't mean I like you going down there by yourself though."

"Fiddlesticks!" Grandma fussed. "I ain't no more scared of him than the man in the moon. He's all smoke and mirrors anyways."

"I ain't worried about the Man," said Pop. "I'm worried about the company he does dealings with."

"They know better than to mess with me. Besides, he'll be there waiting for me at midnight, and as soon as we get the trade worked out, I'll be home."

"If it weren't for the girl sleeping in there, I'd come with you."

"I know. You always go when you can. But I'd rather you look after her. I don't need no looking after."

Grandma finished stacking the rest of the plugged bottles in the truck bed.

"I just about got a pot de tete ready," Pop said.

"We just got to decide who would have the best chance of getting through to Amber with the bracelet. The pot de tete would keep him from falling under the spell of any black magic, but he's got to get close enough to Amber to put the bracelet on her for our plan to work."

"You just let me worry about all that." Pop patted her hand and comforted her. "You best be on your way. If Addie wakes up in the middle of the night, I won't have a good excuse for where you are."

She held out her hand for the keys to his old truck, and after a brief hesitation, he handed them to her. She kissed him on the cheek, climbed into the driver's seat like she was sixty years younger, and pulled out. Nosy Rosy was peeking through her lace curtains from her bay window as Grandma started to drive away.

Grandma hollered a greeting to her to let her know she had just been busted for spying. Rosy ignored her greeting and hastily yanked the curtain shut as if that would conceal her snooping.

She drove down to the railroad over by I-55 and South 3rd Street where two railroad tracks intersected. It was pitch black at the Crossroads, but the bright moon and stars lit her way to meet Gavin. She reached for a crate of bottled spirits when he gently took it from her to help. They nodded in acknowledgement of each other and worked together solemnly to release the dark spirits into the world of the dead.

After they were done, and the spirits hissed and whistled their way into the darkness, he said, "I was hoping you would come see me tonight."

"I told you I would come when I was ready to."

"I can't stop thinking about her," he admitted after a brief hesitation.

"She's hard to forget, but I sure wish you'd try."

"I don't want to forget." Gavin shook his head stubbornly and argued. "I want to fill my head full of memories of her."

Grandma looked at him sadly and acknowledged, "You know I've always had a great deal of respect for you..."

"And I you," he interjected.

"But your role puts you in the path of so many shady, greedy people who would be much too dangerous for her, and I can't take that kind of chance on her life no matter what the feelings might be."

"I would die before I let anything happen to her," he swore.

"And then what would that accomplish?" Grandma said. "You would both be dead, and the cause would be for naught. The whole world would unravel by a single thread, and it would all be because I was foolish enough to bless this union. God's face would never smile on that."

"I know her situation is precarious, but I'll do

whatever is within my power to help her."

"Until when?" Grandma looked aghast. "Until it comes out that you broke the cardinal rule and got involved? Then you would have your own wars to wage and would be of no help to her."

"June, I love her," Gavin confessed helplessly with his palms spread. The wind whistled and the trees waved while Grandma chewed on that revelation for a spell.

"You and everybody else." Grandma admitted slowly, "I know she fancies you. She's been sharing dreams with you for years."

"She's fantastic," he breathed.

"She's also young and unprepared," she countered.

"Because you won't prepare her."

"Don't you understand that I'm trying to protect her?!" Grandma cried in exasperation.

"You are crippling her!" Gavin retorted. "She is extremely capable and talented. I have seen it for myself. She deserves so much more credit than you are giving her. How do you think she will feel if you die? After you leave her alone to fend for herself with the realization that you never gave her the knowledge she needed to be ready? Can't you see what that will do to her?! It will destroy her!"

"I just need more time," Grandma muttered as she nervously patted down her pockets hunting for her cigarettes.

"You've been using that tired excuse for years. She's gotten so strong. You still think of her as a child, but she's an old soul, and she's ready to know. She has more than earned the right."

"What makes you say she's an old soul?" she asked curiously.

"She is her Grandma's child."

His answer pleased her, and after a brief hesitation, she conceded, "You're a good man, Gavin."

"I try to be," he said humbly.

"You are."

"Well, don't spread that around. I need my menacing reputation—it's good for business." he stated simply.

"And it keeps the wrong kind of business away."

"Exactly!" he agreed.

"You know you've got a bunch of impostors running around town I would hate for you to get picked up, just because the cops think you are involved."

"From the intruders at your church? Yeah, I saw that on the news," he shrugged clearly unconcerned.

"So, what are your thoughts?" she asked curiously.

"I dress much better than they do," he reflected.

"You know that ain't what I meant," Grandma fussed as she rolled her eyes.

"I got an alibi for every night they been causing trouble. "Besides, any talk is good for my line of work—even if I can't accept the credit for any of it."

"You know you ain't nothing like your father," she pointed out cautiously.

"I don't want to talk about him," he snipped defensively.

"You need to talk about him. Talking's good for the soul. You ain't never been responsible for the choices he makes," she countered.

"That's easy for you to say. He ain't your father," he grumbled.

"You ain't the only one who's got a parent they ain't especially proud of."

Gavin waited patiently with interest for her to go on.

"My father was an abusive slave owner." she whispered with shame.

"But you're..." his voice trailed off as his incredulous shock was evident on his face.

"An advocate for equal opportunities? Yes, I realize the irony."

"How did you go from having a slave owner father to speaking out for civil rights back in the 50's?" he inquired with amazement.

"It helps me remember I ain't him."

Gavin waited carefully before cautiously confronting Grandma, "You say I'm not my father, but my relationship to him is enough to hold you back from blessing my relationship with Addie."

"She don't even know you're real yet. She thinks you're a fantasy ... and you better wash that grin off your face at the very idea—this is still my granddaughter we're talking about."

"The logical side of her isn't convinced I exist yet, but her heart has always known. Someday she'll meet me and know it's all real."

"That don't mean any of it's happened yet," she argued.

"And it won't happen if she doesn't choose it."

"She don't realize she can pick a different future than the dreams. She thinks she's powerless to them."

"That's why she needs you to show her how! You were both born with a veil over your eyes. You could help her use that gift, because you understand it better than anybody."

"It ain't time yet," Grandma said. "I keep telling you that, and you just won't listen."

You should make a trade with me," he proposed. "Bless my life, and bless my relationship with her."

"Why does a blessing from an old woman mean so much to you?"

"Everybody wants to be redeemed."

"Gavin, you're the one who decides who you want to be and how good you are. Your life choices are much more powerful than my blessing. You ain't your father, but you know he ain't right. He's dangerous. I can't support you being with her, because it connects her to him. It's nothing personal, but you and I both know that Bokors don't abide by the same rules as the rest of us."

"You say I shouldn't blame myself for having an evil Dad, but then you punish me for it."

"It ain't fair. I never said it was." she admitted.

"Please give me your blessing. Bless me to keep me as a child of the light. Bless my life as long as I love her.'"

"You're smooth to tug at my heart strings with that line. You know I love Dr. King, but do you really think a blessing from me is enough to keep you from going dark like your Daddy?"

"You forget that I have seen what you can do. You

can't downplay your abilities with me."

"The girl don't know he's a traiteur."

"She hasn't ever seen him heal?" he asked in surprise.

"He healed her knee a few weeks back, but he ain't never healed anything significant enough in front of her to draw attention to his gifts."

"What about all his herbs and powders?"

"She just thinks he's obsessive about his garden. She don't know all that is part of his role as a healer."

"It's odd she hasn't noticed him reading cards or casting spells though."

"He ain't never thrown no bones or laid no tricks in front of the girl. He does all that when she's asleep or away from the house."

"We can make a business deal. It will be an official trade," Gavin proposed as if he were about to make a toast.

"I figured this was coming. Everybody else has to come see you for nine straight days at midnight just for a shot at getting your attention. But you been visiting me as every black animal you could come up with for weeks just itching for a visit with the fabulous June Jackson. It ain't your fault; it's on account of my natural aura—all the men folk want to pencil in time with me,"

Grandma teased him.

"Your granddaughter gets it honestly," he teased her back.

"Let me hear your proposal."

"You bless and protect my life that it will be filled with far more light than darkness. You bless my relationship with Addie in whatever capacity that may be.

You bless me for loving her, and you bless me tenfold if I can ever get her to love me back."

"And in return?" she pressed him.

"I will use all resources at my disposal to aid her as long as she shall live. There is nothing I have that I will withhold from her. I will swear to protect her for the entirety of my days. I will stop anyone who tries to get in her way."

Grandma resisted the temptation to tell him not to say the word "swear."

"You knew that deal would be too tempting for me to pass up," she confessed. "Don't forget that I have seen what you can do. I love my girl too much not to want to afford her with every resource and chance in the world. And she will be the keeper of the cause. She's the only hope I've got."

"Does that mean we have a deal?"

"Yes...it does. But you know what I need first."

"Of course," he acknowledged before he held out his hands. Grandma studied him hard, and she slipped on her blue-starred ring. She slid her hands into his and went away mentally to a far away place for several seconds while Gavin waited patiently. She drew a sharp intake of breath and pulled away from him in shock.

"It's all true," she conceded.

"You know I respect you too much to lie to you."

"I must admit I'm confused," Grandma said in surprise. "You're so worried about going dark, but you've got so much love for her. You and I both know light and dark can't co-exist."

"What are you implying?" he asked cautiously.

"I'm not just implying. I'm telling you that it don't make much sense for you to be worried about being evil when evilness don't know nothing about love. Your heart is swollen up with affection. I ain't saying it's impossible you'd go dark. But it would go against what I see, so staying light is a lot more plausible for you than you turning into your Daddy."

Gavin took her hand and kissed it in gratitude and relief, and all he could whisper was, "Thank you," to her; she patted his hand understanding this was better news than he had ever hoped for.

Grandma promised to perform his blessing this week. She wiped a tear from her eye before telling him that she had to go as there was one more stop she had to make tonight. Gavin walked her back to her truck, opened the door for her, and stood there until she drove back out into the night. For the first time in a long time he felt hopeful again.

Grandma drove as quickly as possible out to John Hamilton's house. She was not concerned about the late hour; she knew John well enough to know he never slept anyway. He was on guard at hearing her on the back porch of his cottage, but he relaxed and smiled immediately after catching a glimpse of her face.

"Did you bring me some of your delicious, fried apple pies?" John asked Grandma as he walked her inside and deadbolted his front door.

"Not this time, I'm afraid. We've got some business to discuss."

John had been preparing for this mission his whole life. Like me, this was a calling he had been born into, but unlike me, he had always informed about it. It mattered little to him whether he would have chosen this for himself.

Just like his father and grandfather before him, he would fulfill his role, which had been set before him long before his existence had ever been written into history. He believed in the fulfillment of the ring and in the idealism June Jackson clung to. His family had a deep enough history with mine to realize that her vision was something to believe in our broken, crime-ridden world. He had seen too many people look for short term fixes to the brokenness of poverty and injustice, and he was interested in a solid, long term solution.

So, if she had asked him to run across the Interstate during rush hour traffic, despite his natural fears, he would have been committed enough to do it regardless of the risk. John was bold, brave, and impulsive, and Grandma truly admired all of this about him. I was my Grandma's child just as he was his father's.

"What's wrong?"

"There ain't nothing wrong with me, but something's wrong with the cops."

"More wrong than usual?"

"I understand the question. I don't like them none neither. But yes, it's almost like they're half blind lately."

She furrowed her brow, but John didn't seem convinced.

"I fail to see how this is different from any other day,"

he stated wryly.

"I'm telling you—something is off with them." Grandma shook her head firmly and argued. "They aren't investigating the church break-in's nearly enough. The media is still covering the situation, but the cops are just going through the motions with it. We had somebody try to break into our garage, and I called the cops just to see what they would do. They were much more interested in our family than even pretending to chase him down. I even called them to tell them about Addie getting hunted down by that gang. Would you believe they wouldn't even bother to come out to the house to write up a police report? Nothing we have called about has been solved."

"What are you trying to say?" he asked.

"I think somebody has hoodooed them to stay away."

"You mean somebody laid some tricks to keep them from unraveling what's going on?"

"Maybe. Or maybe somebody's got their ear and is pulling them away from us, and they're too spell bound to resist eating up all the lies."

"It's also possible there's some money getting passed under the table. Money talks."

"It does, and I'm sure the Skullbangerz have plenty of it to spare with all of their drug deals around here."

A thoughtful silence passed between the two of them.

"There's only one person I can think of who would lay tricks for a big enough price without any regards for the consequences."

Grandma nodded her head grimly, "She came to my mind too, and you and I both know that Hoodoo Helen is just about the last person I want to go see."

"That woman's sketchier than a sketch artist," John said in disgust as he shook his head.

"On that, my good man, we can agree."

"Mrs. June, why are you so set on pegging the cops on this bad bunch now? I've been after you for years to take care of all this."

"I suspect it was time I finally listened to you. You were right. I just need to make sure everything's taken care of and safer for the girl, that's all," Grandma fibbed.

John eyed her suspiciously. He didn't believe her story for a Memphis minute, but he was smart enough not to call her out on it. In turn, she was smart enough not to tell him how she knew that he knew she was lying.

"Do you still want me to take care of everything like we've always talked about?" he asked.

"You had better, because you one of the only ones left I can trust. You make sure you do just like we talked about. You got to protect her. She's going to need you something fierce."

Like me, Grandma had the gift of divination to see what was coming before it arrived. Unlike me, she had been trained on how to use her gift and trained on how to hide the future from others. For the truth was, Grandma knew the end was near for Pop and her. To protect my life, she had used her gifts to hide my future from me.

So, I had experienced no bad dreams to warn me about what was coming. She made sure I didn't hear the tornado siren about the storm ahead, and that's why I was the last to know I would be the last one left standing.

Chapter 9

Grandma had met with Gavin the trickster and John the guardian, and now Keisha was meeting with Mr. Kane the interrogator, but unfortunately for him, Keisha was distracted today. Her father was trying to talk to her about deciding on a major, the importance of selecting one that would support her lifestyle, and all of the other first world issues he was great at reminding her to worry about. The problem was that Keisha was tuning him out, and it was becoming an ongoing irritation for him.

"Keisha, are you even listening to me?"

Mr. Kane's booming voice snapped her out of her daydream.

"Oh, sorry, Dad. I was just...thinking about something else. What were you saying?"

"I'm trying to talk to you about your future. You have big decisions to make. I don't think you're taking your responsibilities seriously."

It was a speech Keisha had heard her entire life. It never mattered how many "A's" she got, how few speeding tickets she received, how composed she was at his political events, or how graciously she treated his high profile visitors. It was never good enough for her father.

"I know it's important, Dad. I told you I've got everything under control. You don't have to worry. Seriously."

She told him for the five millionth time, but he was already distracted with another project. His cell phone, which never quit buzzing, was ringing again, and he lost focus from barking at her long enough to answer it.

"Hello? Yes, it's me. So, what did you find out? Were they meeting like we thought?"

After a thoughtful pause he swore a stream of profanities, which made Keisha wince and almost tune him out until he hollered, "Any time there's corruption in the ranks it is my business! You tell Chief Stamper I want a thorough investigation to get to the bottom of this now!"

Then he hung up.

"What was all of that about, Dad?" Keisha inquired as he wiped his wet brow. The combination of the hot weather, stressful job, and high blood pressure kept him sweating most of the time.

"I think there's some funny business going on with the local law enforcement. I keep pressuring them for answers and for a financial report, and they keep dragging their feet. These folks are about to give me a stroke!"

"I think all that salt you keep putting on everything will give you a stroke faster than those folks will!"

"I got to get back to the office," he said as he kissed her on the forehead. "I'm late. I'll see you tonight. Don't forget we've got that charity event to attend, okay?"

"How could I forget?" she asked.

After he left, Keisha drifted back into her own thoughts. I would have felt guilty to have known they were consumed with worry over me. I saw my grandparents as mostly invincible, because they had survived more strokes, heart attacks, and assaults than anybody I had ever heard of. However, my faith in them blinded me to their increasing frailty, which unlike me, Keisha was not oblivious to.

She was starting to get angry at them for keeping me in the dark. She was worried about how I would make it after they were gone when so much of my identity was tied up in them. My stories about getting stalked, jumped by the Skullbangerz, and followed around by the conjure doctor had only served to heighten her anxiety.

Keisha didn't eat much normally, but she had eaten even less since I had begun confiding in her. My burden was lighter, but her shoulders were heavier, and she felt isolated in her promise to hide secrets for me. Had I known, I would have broken the promise I had made to stay open with her. However, she kept her worries hidden to protect me. She finally understood why I had panic attacks all of the time as she put her hands in her pockets to keep them from shaking.

On the other side of town I was crying on my front porch. It was the anniversary of Amy's death, and my stress combined with her absence made today particularly hard. Pop's rocking chair provided a comforting sway and familiar squeaking, and I rolled back and forth in the rickety, old chair trying to clear my head.

Through blurry eyes I looked up to see a black Labrador Retriever trotting down the street. I didn't recognize him, but he didn't appear to be lost. I cocked my head to the side watching him as he walked through my front yard, up the porch steps, and laid down at my feet as he whined like he knew me.

I loved animals, but in spite of my incessant begging over the years, Grandma and Pop had never agreed to a house pet. So, I reached down carefully and stroked this dog as he closed his eyes contentedly. I seemed to be charming a lot of animals lately, and I chuckled wryly to myself about how I attracted more mutts than men.

I petted the lab, and he laid there for a very long time warming my feet until I stopped crying. Then he sat up, licked my cheek, and lumbered off. I watched him in amazement as the unexpected comfort from a canine trotted out of my sight again.

I forced myself to pull it together before going to class. I survived geology as best as I could, considering the only rock I was really interested in was the musical kind. Naturally I was smart enough not to mention this to my overzealous professor, who spent so long discussing sedimentary rock that I wanted to chunk pebbles at his head.

On my way home from class I stopped by my favorite coffee shop to pick up a drink. The hazelnut, vanilla, and dark roast coffee swirling together in my mug were divine. A local musician was singing songs from her latest album, and a crowd had gathered in appreciation of her chops. However, the high from the caffeine and the music was quickly undone when I caught a glimpse of the news in the cafe.

The reporter was covering a story on television. Apparently the church break-in's had spiraled out of control more than I had ever imagined. He was showing footage of Grandma's church, and there was a close up of a man bound and duct taped in a chair with blood running down his arms.

I drew a sharp breath and barely held on to my caffeine as I wondered whether the blood was from him or from some twisted hoodoo ceremony. As the camera zoomed in, I could see that the security guard was Gerald Smith, Pop's friend and co-worker. There across Gerald's chest was a clearly written message, which dangled by a rope around his neck. The ominous threat had been delivered in blood, which was dripping down his torso and onto his legs.

"Give us Louie Jackson, and this all goes away," the note read.

In my mind at that moment there was no more coffee house. There was only Grandma and Pop. I sped out of there like the devil himself was after me, because after today, he just might be.

On the other side of town, Amber was at Audubon Park with her own set of problems. She was completely enamored with Chris for she thought he hung the moon. She was so high off of the love spell that she saw what was going on around her but processed it differently than she normally would have done.

When Chris grilled her about her family and she didn't have all the answers, he gave her a black eye. Because she thought he was flawless, she turned around and blamed herself for upsetting him. She groveled, apologized for not having the information he needed, and pampered him even more than she had already been doing. She saw him hand money to some cops under the table at a bar one night, but she assumed the transaction was simply innocuous. Considering her spellbound circumstances, poor Amber had no other way of seeing things.

I arrived home to find Geena, Grandma, and Pop sitting solemnly at the kitchen table.

"What's up, shorty?" Geena remarked snidely as a less than subtle attempt to insult my lack of height.

"Hey, don't hate. Good things come in small packages. You ain't got nothing on me. Besides, all of y'all look like you're headed to a funeral." I slung my heavy backpack onto the linoleum floor. "If we don't come up with a good plan to establish some safety precautions soon, we might be headed to yours though."

"You think you know everything, but you have no idea. It's easy to think you know what to do when you ain't got all the facts," Geena whined and scowled at me behind red, hazy eyes. I couldn't help but wonder how quickly she had blown through the five hundred dollars.

Grandma lit up her cancer stick, and Geena waved the smoke away disdainfully as I rolled my eyes at her.

"That stuff will kill you faster than the mess you've gotten yourself mixed up in," Geena muttered under her breath.

"So, do you have anything intelligent to say, or are you just going to be childish and cryptic?" I retorted.

"I was just telling your Grandma and Pop that Rosy has finally installed a security system in her house. I've been trying to convince your grandparents to get one for years."

"I don't need no newfangled nothing."

"Grandma, you might have a death wish, but I don't," I argued back with arms folded. "And I don't think Pop needs to be going to work at the church anymore until all of the threats are behind us."

"Ain't no sense in worrying about that, sweetheart. Church put me on temporary leave on account of it," Pop grumbled as if his being on leave was a mere suggestion that he would be renegotiating with them.

"Good! You don't need to be over there. And I agree with Geena—we are long overdue for a security system."

It was only reluctantly that I agreed with Geena, which he grinned smugly about.

"Ain't no need for no dad-blamed machine when I got these babies to protect us," Pop indicated flexing his muscles before giving them a big kiss of pride. Geena snorted, and I glared at both of them.

"Would you just get the security system already?" I turned to Grandma in a final, desperate grasp at a sane solution as I pleaded with her. "Puh-lease?! It's bad enough I've got to live over here. Could you at least buy me some form of insurance to stay alive?!" Grandma's face softened, and I knew I had spread the manipulation too thick for her to resist.

"Okay, child," she sighed and nodded. "There ain't no reason to have it. As long as...never mind. If it makes you feel better, we'll get it." I smiled; this was the first good thing to happen today.

"My work here is done," Geena announced before she stood up and pushed her chair back just as my cell phone started ringing.

I answered the phone on speaker when I saw it was Amber, but it was immediately obvious we had been pocket dialed. She was bawling, and a male voice was cursing her and calling her everything but a child of God. She was begging him to believe her that she didn't know anything when we heard a loud smack, and my phone went dead right along with my heart.

Geena had always been scary and intimidating, but now her face looked like the pits of hell. We mobilized into action. Grandma handed me the car keys, and Pop handed Geena the hoodooed bracelet and a pot de tete. Geena and I headed out together without so much as a word.

"I assume you know where she is?" Geena growled once we were in my car.

"Last I heard she was headed to Audubon Park."

"Let's fly!" she banged on the inside door like it was a chariot carrying her across the sky. I sped faster than I ever had, and there was no bickering between the two of us now. At one point I heard her mutter, "Can't let nothing happen to that girl. She's the only good thing I've ever done."

We drove by the mall and hightailed it to the park. I circled around looking for Amber when we spied her slumped over on a bench crying as Chris towered over her with his menacing, clenched fists. We parked, and Geena scrambled out of the car even faster than I did.

When I spotted her black eye, my first reaction was to lunge to blacken both of his. I headed straight for him with every intention in the world of pounding his face into the pavement, but Amber stepped in between us begging me to stop. Geena studied her and caught sight of her daughter's battered face.

Any doubts I ever had regarding Geena's commitment to her family flew out the window as a dangerously dark cloud consumed her. She handed me the charmed bracelet and pointed me towards Amber before she ran to Chris, pinned him to the ground, and started pounding him with all her might. Amber screamed and ran towards Chris, but I grabbed her arm, pulled her back, and slid the bracelet onto her arm.

The moment the bracelet slipped onto her, her entire demeanor changed as if someone had fired up an inferno inside of her soul. Rage filled her, and she turned on Chris and kicked his family jewels repeatedly. He howled in pain as I heard police sirens wailing in the distance.

It suddenly occurred to me that Chris was probably underage, and while Geena was my least favorite person in the world, I certainly didn't want her to get locked up for defending her only daughter. I grabbed her shirt and yanked at her hollering for her to get off Chris, but she was only seeing red and not reason. It wasn't until I told her we had to get Amber out of there to keep her safe that she finally backed off Chris. Geena shook her shoulders to shrug off her overwhelming anger long enough for Chris to scramble off.

The only advantages we had with Chris were that maybe he was old enough to be an adult as well as the likelihood that he wouldn't own up to anything since it would incriminate him as well. He would also probably be more worried about the consequences he would receive from the Skullbangerz for failing his mission.

Amber cried and hugged Geena and me. I was so thankful to have her back. She had always been so upbeat and happy, but her experiences under the spell and at the hands of Chris's abuse had taken a toll on her. Her brightness had been dulled, and I hoped that given time to heal she would soon shine once again.

We drove quickly toward Grandma's house dodging the police in the distance. Geena fiddled with my radio before deciding on a rock station that was playing a love song for a bad boy. She turned it up and remarked, "I figured this melody would have a special place in your heart."

I turned my head back away from the steering wheel and snapped, "What is that supposed to mean?"

"Oh, I don't know," she smirked. "You tell me."

Then just like that, whatever camaraderie we had shared in Amber's escape mission dissolved. I flipped my hair at her and sped silently the rest of the way home. Working together with her to save my cousin was one thing; confiding in her about anything private was completely different.

We pulled into the driveway to see a flower delivery guy pulling out. Curiosity led me up the driveway and into the house where a bouquet of pink roses surrounded with baby's breath set in a blue vase on the kitchen counter.

"Looks like you got yourself an admirer!" Grandma cocked her eye at me as she blew a cloud of smoke my direction.

"Who's it from?" Amber asked as she stepped into the house.

"For land sakes alive! Louie, get in here, and do something for this child!" Grandma hollered at Pop upon seeing Amber's face. She winced and tried to hide her bruises with her hair as if that would make any difference.

Pop fussed over her muttering prayers and Bible verses under his breath while cooking up another one of his strange smelling concoctions. Grandma fixed her up some chicken soup and soda and insisted she rest on the couch while Pop hastily prepared the hoodooed help for her.

I lifted up the card under the flowers to find a message to me from Will which read: "Thinking of you, Addie. Sorry I was a jerk. I miss you. I hope you'll give me another chance. Love, Will."

I rolled my eyes but couldn't help but be impressed by the bouquet.

"The whole house smells like a funeral parlor," Pop teased.

"Like anything could smell worse than what you're cooking," I said.

"Don't you be forgetting where I left that pepper spray for you to use," he muttered. "You never know when you'll need it to chase them boys off."

I ignored Pop while Geena sat with Amber until she drifted off to sleep. I wondered for the first time whether Pop's herbs had a sedative effect on his patients, as I thought about how quickly I had slipped off with the motion potion he had pasted upon my knee.

"I've got to do something to keep all this juju away from these children," Pop murmured as he gently stroked

Amber's hair out of her face. While Amber slept, Geena paced the house roaming as she often did. I didn't much care where she was. I was just glad she wasn't pestering me.

"Pop and I got a surprise for you, but we ain't telling you nothing about it until tomorrow," Grandma announced mysteriously.

"I don't know that I like getting surprises from you." I narrowed my eyes suspiciously. "They would probably involve casting snakes or getting chased by critters." She waved her hand dismissing my worries. Her electric blue rollers bounced around on top of her hair, and the ears on her bunny slippers flopped in motion with her hand.

"This one you'll like. You'll see. Just wait until tomorrow morning. Now get on into your room, and get you some rest."

"You are still letting Rosy's referral come over and install your security system tomorrow, right?" I pressed her to insure she hadn't changed her mind.

"Yes, Bill Thompson will be here tomorrow. Now don't you worry your pretty, little head about nothing else. You go on into your room, and have yourself some shut eye."

Strangely enough, I did feel tired suddenly. If I hadn't known better, I would have thought Grandma had some secret powers of persuasion. I went into my room, got dressed for bed, and fell asleep to a night filled with nightmares.

Gavin took center stage in my hellacious dreams as a forest fire, and I was trapped in his destructive path. I knew he would burn and consume me with an almost certain death. However, his warmth was so enticing that I could not summon the strength to resist his temptation.

I felt like I had nobody and nothing left to lose, and this had made me reckless and desperate for any high I could get. So, without any more regard for the risk of the heat, I jumped into his flame even though I knew I would soon be turned to ash.

I woke up with a start at how hot I felt. My room was sweltering, so I threw off the covers and turned on my ceiling fan. My face was flushed, and I went into the kitchen to get a glass of ice water. The lightening sky indicated it was early morning, and Grandma was eating a stack of pancakes.

"You know all that sugar isn't good for your diabetes," I reprimanded her behind a yawn.

"Breakfast food is its own food group, and you got to eat all the foods in the pyramid to stay in balance, child."

She gave herself another shot of insulin to counteract all the maple syrup.

I poured myself a cup of black coffee and was startled to hear a fluttering sound nearby.

"What's that?"

"That's coffee, child. Seems to me like you need a cup. You must not be awake yet." She was teasing me, but her eyes told me she was keeping secrets from me again.

"No, no..." my voice trailed off as the fluttering quieted and then started back up again. "That! What's all that noise?" I persisted as I began wandering through the house to investigate.

"That ain't nothing to worry about. Just some silly, old birds," she minimized, but I heard the fear in her voice.

I walked up on the window ledge to find that outside everywhere I looked was filled with black birds, and they were all staring at our house. I dropped my cup, and my coffee filled up every crack in the floor like black oil. Grandma fussed and wiped it up with a dish towel. However, I didn't even notice the caffeinated crevices, because I was too horrified by the flock that had surrounded our house. Every tree, bush, and blade of grass was full of the creatures, and I screamed in shock.

"Shhh! Ain't no sense in making all that racket. They are just migrating this time of year. They'll go on like they always do."

"They do not do this every year, and it's obvious they aren't focused on migrating anywhere. They're staring straight at our house! What is wrong with those bird brains? That is so creepy!"

"Oh, they ain't nothing but some of God's creatures," she said lightly in an effort to be reassuring, but her tone was shaky and tense. "Don't worry your pretty, little head about that. You've got a big day today, so don't let no strange sights destroy it."

I had almost forgotten she said there was a surprise in store for me, but I didn't think I would be interested in anything that involved leaving the house anymore. Suddenly, Keisha's car turned down our street. She slowed down to barely a crawl as the birds took their sweet time getting out of her way.

With great deliberation, she obtained enough room to

roll into our driveway, and her face was aghast at the flock. She walked gingerly up the house shuddering, and she seemed incredibly relieved to get into the house.

"What's going on out there?" she asked intensely with her thumb jabbed towards the birds.

"Bird migration," Grandma said. "Coffee?"

She perked up in a less than subtle attempt to change the conversation.

"I think I need something stronger than that to steady my nerves after driving through those birds."

Without another word, Grandma poured her a coffee and added some whiskey to it. She handed the cup to Keisha, who nodded in appreciation and took several quick swigs.

"Addie, I got you packed and ready to go. Keisha is taking you out for some fun," Grandma announced like the plans were already settled. I began to object when Grandma held up her hand to cut me off. "Don't get smart with me, Missy! I expect you to cooperate."

"We're going on a weekend get away!" Keisha blurted out.

"I can't leave town! I need to be here at night."

"Who said we were leaving town?"

"We knew you'd say you couldn't leave town, so you're staying downtown!" Grandma smirked as if she had outsmarted me this time.

"We're going to stay at the Mississippi Magnolia Hotel for the weekend!" Keisha squealed. "And your Grandma already packed your bags, so you don't have to prepare a thing."

"Why are we staying at a hotel when we live in town?"

"Addie, have you ever stayed at the Mississippi Magnolia before?" Keisha asked the question she already knew the answer to as she twisted her hair and cocked her head to the side.

"No, of course not." I admitted begrudgingly.

"Well, then there's a first time for everything." Keisha smiled coyly. "We're going to be there for three whole days."

"I think all of this is sweet and all, but I don't need to stay overnight." I objected thinking especially about the weird animal behavior right outside of our house. "I haven't stayed away from my grandparents since I moved in 12 years ago."

"That's exactly why you need to get out of here." Grandma squawked and pushed me towards the door. "Maybe your Pop and I want to party for a change, and you just might be cramping our style. Did that ever occur to you?"

"Grandma, don't change the subject," I protested as I pulled away. "I don't feel comfortable leaving you two alone at night, especially considering there is someone out to get you. Amber's still laid up recovering from her injuries in the next room, and your yard looks like a scene from a horror movie. There's no reason for y'all to spend money for me to stay at a hotel when I can just stay at home."

"Addie, you never let your hair down, and you're going to have a good time this weekend even if it kills you."

"Um, it just might," I argued stubbornly.

"Addie, Amber is doing a lot better already. She and Geena can check on us while you're gone, so there's nothing to worry about."

"I don't feel comfortable entrusting the trouble making two of you into the hands of my sixteen year old cousin and her irresponsible mother!"

"Now Addie, we don't need nobody coming by to check on us," Pop raised his voice. "We will do just fine on our own."

"Amber will be going back to her Daddy's in just a little while. She promised to keep her phone on her all weekend just in case we need anything, and we'll call you if any problems come up."

"Your house could burn down, and a nuclear bomb could go off, and you would never call me, because you'd say you 'had things under control,'" I argued. "Your promise to call does not put my mind at ease."

"Addie, we will be just fine," Grandma pleaded as she put her hands on my shoulders and looked me squarely in the face. "We love you, and we want you to have a good time, so please just go enjoy yourself for once in your life. I hate to say this, but you're the oldest twenty year old I've ever met."

"Thanks for the insult. For the record, I don't like leaving y'all in Geena's and Amber's hands, but since none of you are giving me any choice in the matter, I guess I'll just go."

I made a futile, final stand crossing my arms just as

Grandma spontaneously hugged me hard with Pop quickly following suit. Then Grandma wiped a tear away when she thought I wasn't looking, and the unexpected emotion and affection from them puzzled me.

Fifteen minutes later, against my better judgment, Keisha and I had escaped from the flock and were heading downtown. My distraction about all the birds slowly melted away at the temptation of experiencing a weekend of freedom. Before I knew it, we had arrived at the historic local site and were walking into the Mississippi Magnolia.

"There sure are a lot of tourists taking pictures today," I commented.

"We've got dinner reservations at Chez Centre," Keisha announced with pleasure after we had checked in.

I frowned despite my intrigue.

"Can we afford to eat there?"

"Addie, just enjoy yourself, and try not to worry about everything for once."

After we unpacked in our luxurious room and freshened up, we walked around downtown browsing the shops before we checked in with Chez Centre for our reservations. The hostess seated us at a beautiful table covered with a crisp, white linen tablecloth. I was relieved to note there were no gang members or hoodoo conjurers in sight.

"What are you going to order?" Keisha asked at the restaurant as we examined the menu.

"I'm going to go out on a limb and order the crab claw soup."

After we had placed our orders and the food came

out, I had to admit, "This is the best soup I've ever eaten."

"What's up with our waiter?" Keisha giggled.

"What do you mean?"

"Every time I crumple my napkin and set it down, he comes by the table to reshape it to look like a pyramid."

"You're kidding!" I choked on my soup.

"No, I'm serious!" she whispered adamantly. "Watch!"

She wrinkled her napkin and tossed it onto the table. Before we could even count to ten, our attractive waiter had glided over to our table and begun sculpting the loose linen into a triangular triumph.

Keisha fidgeted with that cloth all evening just to watch the cute waiter mold it back for us. After we finished dinner and dodged advances from several of the men at the restaurant, we went to a local club to have some fun.

"Wow, they're packed," Keisha observed when we arrived. "Oh, look! A blues band is playing—they're really good!"

We sang and danced all night. Keisha and I had so much fun that weekend, it should have been illegal. She was relieved to be away from the political responsibilities of her father, and I was relieved to be away from the chronic needs of my grandparents. I should have been more worried about Grandma and Pop, but it was such a relief not to feel responsible for anyone for a change.

Not surprisingly, they didn't call my phone a single time even though I kept it on me all weekend. I couldn't remember the last time I felt so carefree, and it left me believing that my future might actually be bright.

When the weekend was finally over, it was hard to pull ourselves out of our big, fluffy bed to leave. We checked out of the hotel, and one look at the bill reminded me why we didn't do things like this more often.

I yawned as she drove us back to my house and wondered how worthless I would be if I followed my lazy weekend up with a nap in my room. I was relieved to find all the black birds gone when we arrived. I waved goodbye to Keisha and strode up the driveway. I shuttered as I stepped around piles of feathers, which were scattered across the ground before I entered the house as she drove off.

"Grandma! Pop! I'm home!"

I dropped my bag onto the floor. However, the moment I stepped into the kitchen, I knew something was wrong.

There was no smell of coffee or breakfast, and the house was incredibly dark. The drawers and cabinets throughout the house were wide open with their contents strewn all over the floor. The cars were in the driveway, so I knew my grandparents hadn't gone anywhere. I wandered through the house to see that the TV was off when Grandma and Pop normally kept it on all day until they went to bed at night.

"Grandma! Pop!" I called again more anxiously as I wandered back to their bedroom. Nothing in my life could have prepared me for what I found there.

I saw Grandma and Pop lying in their bed totally still. I was wondering why they hadn't popped up by now to ask me how the trip was and to fuss about their having slept in so late. Yet the room was completely silent, and the only noise I could hear was the ticking of their grandfather clock.

"Hello, sleepyheads! Rise and shine!" I teased as I approached them. Yet as I stepped closer and the sunlight hit their faces, I knew what was wrong. I couldn't hear them breathing. I ran over and touched them to shake them, but their hands were ice cold, and their lips were blue.

I violently retracted my hands upon feeling their chilly skin, and I was nauseated to see how stiff they appeared to be. I knew without accepting it that they were dead, and I was starting to realize that they had died before today. I felt like the room was spinning, and my chest was caving in. I started screaming like a mad woman, but there was no one who could help me.

I had to call for assistance. I had to do something. Maybe I could do artificial respiration. Maybe I could perform CPR. But when I reached over to them again to try to bring them back, it hit me again how far gone they were. I started to heave and vomit. I had just walked into my worst nightmare – only this time there would be no waking up.

Chapter 10

All my life I had struggled with dreams so real I thought I would never escape them. The difference today was that this nightmare was no dream.

"What am I supposed to do?! Call 911?! Call a neighbor?! Call the hospital?!" I screamed a torrent of rhetorical questions that no one would ever answer.

Then suddenly in the midst of my insanity, I remembered Grandma talking to me. I could recall her telling me, "If anything ever happens to your Pop and me, call so-and-so, before you do anything else…" as her voice played back over and over in my mind.

My head was swimming. I couldn't think.

"What did you tell me to do?! Who did you tell me to call?! Why won't you answer me?!" I yelled at Grandma as my voice went into high pitched hysterics while Grandma lay there ignoring my desperate cries.

"Think, Addie, Think!" I began pacing and muttering to myself. "Wait … John …. John somebody …. she told me to get her safe deposit box ... I'm supposed to call him before I call anybody else . John … John Hamilton! Yes! John Hamilton!"

My mind flashed back to the visual of him as the attractive African American man from my dreams. I spun around away from Grandma and Pop and willed myself to walk into the kitchen to retrieve Grandma's address book. She was one of the only people I knew who still used one of those things, and she kept up with everybody and his brother in it.

My brain was racing like a hamster on a wheel. I knew the rational thing to do was to call 911. However as my heart swelled with despair, I remembered promising Grandma that I would do as she had asked, even though at the time I had never thought it would be necessary.

I found John's phone number in her book. I was relieved to see it started with a "901" area code, so at least he would likely be close by. My hands shook violently as I dialed him up while I sobbed uncontrollably.

The man's voice I recognized from my dreams answered the phone. With devastation I suddenly realized why my predictive dreams of him had never included my grandparents. They were never going to live long enough to introduce me to him.

"John?" I whispered tentatively.

"Addie?...Addie Jackson?" his deep voice whispered cautiously back.

"Yes, it's me," my voice cracked on the line. I heard him gasp a deep breath into the phone almost as if he knew my world had stopped.

"My Grandma told me that if anything ever happened to Pop or her that I had to call you," I stubbornly fought back tears, as I forced myself to speak. "I don't know what she would expect you to do seeing as they're dead now, but I promised to do as she asked..." I rambled as my voice trailed off into hopelessness.

He interrupted me quickly and authoritatively in his low, gravely tone, "I understand. I am well aware of what you need. I'm going to take care of everything. Don't worry about a thing."

I wanted to tell him that he didn't know the half of everything I had to worry about, but then he asked me, "Are you okay?"

It was an incredibly stupid question from a man, who seemed anything but foolish. My chin quivered as flashbacks of what laid in their bedroom ran through my head.

"No, I am not," I said as my dizziness, nausea, and chest pain immediately resurfaced.

"Addie, I'll be right there. I'll be driving a black pick-up truck. Don't let anyone else in, and don't tell anyone else about what's happened. I'm five minutes away," he stated.

I hung up the phone and threw up again.

I curled up in Grandma's chair at the kitchen table shaking and crying. I was too terrified to evaluate anything else at the house. My scary sanctuary had become my living nightmare. Before long, a big, black truck pulled up in the driveway, and I noticed Nosy Rosy's curtains flutter. A serious, lanky African American man strode quickly to the front door and knocked loudly.

"Who is it?" I inquired in paranoia even though rationally I knew who he was. I laid my head against the door wishing this would all just go away.

"It's John Hamilton," he replied in that same deep voice. I took a big breath and opened the door. Waves of compassion and sadness filled his face as he said, "Addie, I'm so very sorry. What happened?"

I began to squall, and in between gulps and gasps, I told him what I had found when I came home, and he listened patiently with tears in his eyes.

"Addie, I realize you don't know me, but I've known your grandparents my entire life, and they knew my father and his father before him. I know how proud they were of you and how much you meant to them. So, I realize how devastating all of this must be for you."

"I just don't understand. They were fine," I stammered in between jagged breaths. "They were walking around doing great just two days ago. This doesn't make any sense. I never should have left them alone. This is all my fault. The one time I let them talk me into leaving them, look what happens!"

"Addie, I know you're very upset, but I need you to do something for me. It's not going to make a lot of sense right now, but I need for you to trust me. I know you're very straightforward normally, but I have to protect you, and in order to do that, you're going to have to lie."

He spoke in such a way as if he knew I was not going to like what he had to say.

"What're you talking about?" I asked, a puzzled look on my face.

"Addie, I don't know what has happened to your grandparents, but I'm going to figure that out. In the meantime, you can't tell anyone about calling me or me having been here," he said with a softer tone. "I also need you to take me to the trapdoor where the safe is. We have to protect what's in there."

"What do you mean I have to deceive everybody?" I narrowed my eyes in suspicion. "Who do I have to lie to, and about what specifically? I've been lied to my entire life, and I've hated every minute of it. The last thing in the world I want to do is repeat that pattern of trickery, and how in the world do you know about that trapdoor?"

"Addie, we don't have much time." His face strained as he was clearly losing patience with me. "I don't know how long we have before they find out what's happened. I need you to let me go into the trapdoor and take the safe. I also have to take your Grandma's ring and her pocket watch. You can't tell anyone I was here—not your family, not the police—nobody. You also can't tell anyone about the trapdoor, the safe, the pocket watch, or the ring."

"What are you talking about 'they'll find out what's happened?' Who is 'they' anyway? And fat chance of me being able to tell anybody anything useful about all of that stuff, because neither Grandma nor Pop ever explained or prepared me for any of this."

"Your grandparents were only trying to shelter you, Addie. They didn't know what would happen when this day came, and in addition to guarding you, they were protecting a higher calling."

"What on earth are you talking about? Who are you anyway? What gives you the right to talk to me about my grandparents and what they wanted? I don't even know anything about you, so why should I trust you?" I grilled him as the paranoia I had lived with my entire life reached dizzying heights.

"Addie, we are simply out of time, and it's very important for you to trust me," John implored desperately. "Your Grandma leaned on me to look out for you, so you are going to have to lean on me a bit, too. I'm going to take some things out of your house. As I've already told you, you have to pretend that my coming over and having this conversation never happened. Trust no one right now, and don't let anyone you haven't met before inside. I don't care who knocks on your door, don't let them in! After I leave, I promise I will never be far away. I am giving you this locket—put it on right away. It has a tracking device in it for me to be able to keep up with you. If you are ever in trouble, all you have to do is push this button on the back, and I'll come to your aid immediately."

I was surprised to see that the locket was one that Pop had given me for Christmas one year when I was a kid. I felt guilty that I had never worn it much, but apparently it, like so many other areas of my life, had been part of a bigger plan I had not be informed about.

"Once I leave, you'll want to call 911," John continued with his instructions after I slipped the locket on. "Tell the police exactly what happened when you arrived. Call your family, but spare no time. Tell your family and friends that you're upset and don't feel like talking—tell them whatever you have to to get off the phone quickly. As soon as you've done all of that, everyone's gone, and you're certain that nobody's loitering around, call me. Then I will come, pick you up straight away, and answer all of your questions. But Addie ... it is absolutely imperative that you do exactly as I say."

I sized him up as best I could; I sensed no deceit or malice in him. I didn't like taking orders from anyone, especially people I didn't know, but in a way, taking orders from him was indirectly taking orders from Grandma. And since she was lying lifeless in the other room, I felt I at least owed her the respect of honoring her wishes, even if they seemed completely insane to me.

"Okay, Mister, you've got yourself a deal. But you had better answer every question I've got. I don't like having some kind of crazy tracking device around my neck, and the minute you start getting creepy on me, I'm going straight to the cops, you got that?"

John fought back a smile and nodded as he said, "Little lady, you have got yourself a deal."

I followed him to the living room where he pushed the couch back to reveal the trap door. To my surprise, he pulled out a key and opened the lock.

"How come you get a key? I don't even have access to that!"

He ignored me and took the ladder deep down into the ground. I heard the chain of the safe clinking around, and he rustled with more keys and used an alternate one to remove the safe from the chain. He climbed back up out of the ground and locked the trap door back. He surveyed the area quickly and rearranged the furniture to push the couch over the trap door to conceal it again. He covered the safe up inside his coat and then slipped the watch into his pocket.

"Watch until I get inside my vehicle," he instructed me. "As soon as I drive off, call the police. Once everything here is done, I recommend that you stay with me for a while until we can find a safer location for you."

"Now listen here, Mr. Hamilton, this is my home, always has been .... And I understand that somehow you think it's your responsibility to look out for me and all, but I can take care of myself."

"Addie, I know you're a very strong person, but this is something much bigger than you. You need to stay somewhere more secure than here, and I'd rather it be with me than anywhere else."

"You're telling me that I should leave my home to go stay with some strange man I've never met on the day I find both of my grandparents dead? Mister, I'm not the kind of girl who has sleepovers with guys—especially not on a day like this."

"Addie, you may not like or understand all of this, but I'm going to look out for you whether you like it or not, so you might as well just get used to the idea," John asserted firmly. I got the impression he didn't handle the word "no" very well from anybody.

"Why do you feel so much responsibility to me—to someone you've never met before?" I asked since curiosity had gotten the best of me, as it always seemed to do.

"Because, Addie, my job is to keep you safe. My whole life has been preparing me for this. I am your keeper, your guardian, and your protector."

With that omission, he slipped out the front door as mysteriously as he had slipped in.

"Lock all the doors and windows! Do it now! And don't forget to do exactly as I say!" he ordered before he rushed hurriedly into his truck and wheeled out of the driveway.

As soon as I saw his vehicle disappear down the street, I noticed the security system my grandparents had paid to be installed. There was a red, blinking light stating that it needed to be activated before use. My grandparents had been right—the blame thing was a big waste of time and money. If ever there was a weekend when they would have needed it to work, this would have been it.

I picked up the phone and called 911, and before long the police arrived and asked me all kinds of questions. My house was swarming with emergency medical staff, cops, detectives, and fire fighters, even though I tried to tell them that nothing was burning. They asked me to tell the story of what had happened here again ... and again ... and again.

Finally I couldn't take it anymore; I got in touch with Keisha, who came right over. She took Grandma's address book and went into the living room with the cordless phone to call family and friends. She honored my request in reiterating to loved ones repeatedly that I did not want company or food and that we would let them know when the funeral arrangements had been made, but Amber understandably insisted on coming over anyway.

She burst into tears as soon as she saw me. She had experienced enough grief this week with being battered and abused by Chris. She loved Grandma and Pop tremendously, and the last thing she needed was this. She rambled on about how badly her dad and she felt, since when they had left Grandma and Pop everything had been fine with them.

My grandparents and Geena had allegedly had some sort of argument that day, and she felt really guilty about it, especially now that they were gone. She told me they never called her for assistance after she left, so she had no idea there was anything wrong with them.

I wasn't paying much attention to what she was saying, because it was all I could do to keep it together. A big part of me was angry at myself for leaving them, angry with them for encouraging me to go, angry with Amber for not paying more attention, and angry at Geena for upsetting them the last day of their lives. I was trying to maintain my composure with Amber, but I was too full of grief and rage to be sincerely understanding.

Thankfully, one by one the crowd finally dispersed. After the last of them left, I had a hard time convincing Keisha and Amber to leave me alone for a while. Only by crying and arguing about how all I wanted to do was go to bed and cry did they eventually go despite their better judgment.

As soon as they were gone, I called John Hamilton, who drove right up, so he must have been in my neighborhood already. He cautiously opened his car door, looked from side to side before getting out, and strode quickly to the front door to meet me. I felt fairly certain Nosy Rosy was watching yet again. If that woman had any say, we would be front page news in the local newspaper by morning.

"Addie, we have a problem," he announced after he stepped inside and locked the door behind him.

"Listen, man, I've got a lot of problems, so I'm not sure which one you're referring to at the moment."

"Something extremely important was missing from the safe, and I need to get to it ASAP." He scowled as he paced the house intently searching. "I'm hoping you know where it is."

"What is it?"

"The ring is missing!" he exclaimed in obvious distress. "It's supposed to be in there, but it's gone. Do you know why that might be?"

I had so many questions, but I figured I had better answer his first.

"Which ring do you mean? The blue one with the star in it? No, I'm not sure where it is. Grandma would wear it when we would go out, but she always hid it when she came in. Why? What's wrong?"

John ran his hands around the back of his neck and stretched his head back as if getting more oxygen would help him to think better.

"Addie, we have to find out what happened after you left. Something went seriously wrong while you were away."

I refrained from being a smart Alec with my new personal bodyguard and had the self discipline at least to put myself in check.

"What do you need me to do?"

"Amber and Geena were here Friday, right? Your grandparents mentioned it to me. I need you to call them to find out everything you can about what happened while you were gone."

"I seriously doubt either of them would have been nearly as observant with Grandma and Pop as I would have been."

"Please just call them now," John insisted and handed

me his cell. "Use my phone; it's safer than using your land line."

So, I called Amber's cell phone, and she picked up on the first ring.

"Oh, Addie!" Amber wailed, "I'm sooo sorry!" as she continued the apology I had interrupted during her visit not long ago. I had neither the time nor the emotional strength for all of that at the moment.

"Listen, Amber, I need you to stop crying and listen to me," I rudely interjected. "It's important. I need to know everything that happened Friday after I left ... please ..." as if adding a "please" onto the end of my discourteous tone would somehow make my coldness justifiable.

"Okay," she sniffed on the line and exhaled slowly as if trying to calm herself down. "Mom and I got there, like, around noon; Grandma was cooking, and Pop was watching the news. Mom came in with me and started eating whatever Grandma was fixing. I wasn't hungry, so I went into the living room to watch the news and talk to Pop. Then after a little while, I heard Mom and Grandma start to yell at each other. I couldn't hear what they were saying, because the TV was super loud, and I don't think Pop wanted to get into the middle of it with them, because he just turned the TV up instead of going in there to see what was wrong."

She continued to ramble, "I went into the guest room since I hate watching the news, because I mean, it's all like sooo depressing, you know? But I didn't want to listen to them argue either, so after a little while, Mom came to get me and said it was time to go, because sse had things to

187

do. She looked real mad and drove super fast the whole way home. I thought it was strange that we left so early, since I thought we would be visiting a lot longer, but she just said I needed to go back to my Dad's, so she dropped me off at home."

"Addie, you know how the house looked … ransacked?" she spoke carefully, as if choosing to use that word, only because she couldn't think of a better one. "Well, I swear, it looked totally normal when Mom and I left. And I didn't hear from Grandma or Pop or see them anymore, because the last time I heard from them was when Keisha called to tell us that they were … dead." as she swallowed the fatal word and fought back tears.

My brain was in overdrive processing all of the details and trying to fit them in with the information I already had. As distrustful as I had always been of Geena, this news of the argument between my grandparents and her was particularly upsetting. I reluctantly pulled myself out of my distracted thoughts to try to focus on what Amber was saying.

"Amber, where's your Mom now?" I asked mildly as I willed myself to withhold my suspicion that Geena had been responsible for their demise from her only daughter.

"Um, I don't know. I guess he's at home with a date. I know Keisha told him about Grandma and Pop, and she called me to talk about how bad he felt, but I haven't talked to him since."

Geena changed boyfriends the way most people changed out their socks. As unappealing as she was to me, it was bizarre to me that so many men threw themselves at her. Naturally Geena would turn her parents' untimely deaths into her own personal pity party. I knew I had to get in touch with her, because something told me that talking to her would answer a lot of my questions.

"Amber, I need your mom's phone number."

"Yeah, her phone number changes every other week, doesn't it?" she made a halfhearted attempt at a joke.

"Yeah, I gave up on keeping up with her digits a long time ago."

"Addie ..." Amber paused after giving me Geena's latest cell number. "If you're going to call her, I'd do it soon. You know, so she can talk to you before she goes out to gamble."

My heart hurt for her as I thought for the first time in a long time about how Geena's gambling must have affected her throughout the years.

"You got it, Amber. I'll call right away."

I hung up the phone and turned to John in disgust.

"Geena makes me sick."

"What do you mean?" he asked.

"She's a complete vulture—a bad person," I ranted. "Everywhere she goes, trouble follows. And she doesn't accept responsibility for any of it. I can't stand her."

"Huh," was all that John said as he thoughtfully considered my words. Unlike Pop, he didn't make excuses for her. Unlike Grandma, he didn't guilt trip me into being nice to her. Unlike Amber, he didn't seem embarrassed by her. And unlike me, he didn't seem enraged by her.

I couldn't tell if he agreed with me or not, but his facial expression led me to believe he knew a lot more about Geena than I ever had, but now was not the time for him to fill me in on any of Geena's layers. Right now he mostly just seemed interested in how Geena appeared to come off to me.

"Well, Addie, she's not all bad … nobody is, you know."

"I think she's manipulative, and I can't stand for people to take advantage of other people—especially senior citizens."

I refused to concede his point.

John didn't respond, and I tried to shake my agitation off, because I knew that precious time was slipping away from us. I called Geena's newest phone number and reached her voice mail; I left a message urging her to call me back ASAP and left my cell phone number. I hung up my cell and sat there stewing while my mind raced.

"We've got to talk to her, but I don't feel like we can tell Geena why we need information from her," I told John.

"You don't trust her, do you?"

"Not in a million years!"

"We're going to her house." John grabbed his keys. "Come on."

"Somehow I figure you already know how to get there, huh?" I asked assuming I already knew the answer.

"I know exactly where she lives, and I think finding her will be the missing piece of this puzzle," John responded confidently. "Let's go."

That afternoon after considering John's suggestion I stay elsewhere tonight for safety reasons, I had reluctantly packed an overnight bag for myself. I was undecided about whether or not I would seriously consider staying at his house as he had proposed. John noticed the luggage sitting by the front door and did a good job of not reacting to it.

"I'm not agreeing to staying at your house," I said as I pointed my finger at his face. "I'm just taking some supplies to keep my options open. So, don't you go getting any wild ideas or anything."

"Did I say anything?" His mouth twitched into a half smile, and his shoulders relaxed a bit. "I don't believe I said anything." he remarked clearly amused. After he saw that I was securely buckled into his vehicle, he sped off.

"Do you always drive this fast, or is it just when you're responsible for keeping people safe that you drive like a mad man?"

His eyes tightened, and he slowed down a little but still maintained a pace that was too quick for my taste. In lightning speed we arrived at Geena's place.

"So, how exactly are you going to fit into this whole scenario?" I asked John a little too bluntly.

"It is a strange situation for you to show up at your aunt's house on the day your grandparents died with an African American man she knows you've never met prior to today, isn't it?" John said directly. He clearly caught on quickly.

"Yes ... and in your truck, no less." I pointed out while he let the car idle, as the air from the A/C blew coldly against my cheek.

"Addie, I'm going in with you, because I'm afraid of what might happen if I don't. I'm going to tell Geena that

I'm the executor of your grandparents' estate, because it's true, and it's all she really needs to know. You ask her about what happened Friday, and if you don't get all the answers you need, I'll be here to assist with that."

Judging from John's size and physique, I had a pretty good idea by now about what kind of "assistance" John could provide, but I was hoping it wouldn't come to that. I was developing the idea pretty quickly that John was going to do what John was going to do regardless of what I had to say about it, so I begrudgingly acquiesced with a simple, "Okay, fine."

We walked over the steps and onto the porch before proceeding to knock on the wooden door hidden behind the squeaky, screened entrance. There was no sound from inside, but I saw that Geena's green car was in the driveway, so I knew she was home.

I knocked even harder and listened for any noises from inside. I heard the sound of creaking floors. A few loud noises and swear words later, Geena answered the door.

Geena was always quite a sight to behold. Her wild, crazy red hair looked madder than usual today, and her freckles practically glimmered in the sunlight. She normally opened doors like she was ready to start swinging at somebody. Today she was wearing little more than a T-shirt.

"Man, you have got to put some clothes on!" I exclaimed as John and I tried to look at everything there but Geena.

"Well, hello there, Addie. What're you doing up here?

And with the likes of him no less?" She folded her arms and leaned against the doorway. "I was expecting a little male company, if you know what I mean. You two are kind of throwing off my evening plans."

I had no interest in hearing about my aunt's love life.

"Geena, I came by to ask a few questions about Grandma and Pop. This is John Hamilton; he's the executor of their estate."

I introduced my new bodyguard as I tried hard to only focus on Geena's face.

She stuck her chin out and glared at me in disbelief.

"I know who he is. You act like I just got married into your family yesterday. Ain't no reason for him to be managing their affairs though. I'm perfectly capable of taking care of everything. I don't need no help from him or nobody else."

If John had had feathers, I could literally have seen them ruffle up.

"Listen, Geena, Mr. Hamilton was hired by Grandma and Pop to support their wishes in the event of their deaths. I need to ask you a few questions about how things were when you were with them on Friday."

"Look here, Addie, I ain't got nothing against you, but I ain't about to sit here and have this conversation with this here black guy standing on my property like he belongs here!"

While it wasn't off base for Geena to refer to John as black, it was off base for her to do so with a dismissive, contemptuous tone which clearly indicated her comment was intended to be a put down. She had really done it now, because the quickest way to see the smart mouth side of me was to say something racist in my presence.

"I'm not going to stand here and have you disrespect John like that. Grandma and Pop would be ashamed of you! Listen to yourself. He hasn't done nothing to you. There ain't no need in talking about him like he ain't even here." I scolded her as if I were lecturing a child.

"Addie, I don't know what's going on with you, but I don't like it, and you is my niece, and I ain't about to sit here and stand for it!" She bellowed back at me. Considering Geena's history and the horrible example he had set throughout the years, the idea that his opinion would ever carry any weight with me was preposterous.

"What I do and don't do is none of your business," I coldly responded as Geena scowled and gave John a look that could kill. "So, why don't we talk about the important stuff – like how things were with Grandma and Pop the Friday before they died?"

"Fine. I went over there to check on them with Amber just like she promised you we would. Unfortunately, once we got over there, your Grandma was being her normal, ornery, unreasonable self. We had a tiff, and Amber and I left. They didn't call me to let me know they needed nothing, and next thing I know they're both dead. Now if you'll excuse me for saying so, I've done lost both my parents in one weekend—I sure don't need to be getting any grief from the likes of you!"

"Geena, I'm devastated about losing them, too, but I've got to try to put the pieces together to figure out what happened."

"I didn't have nothing to do with whatever happened to them, if that's what you're implying, and I hope that ain't what you're implying, because I don't like it if you are." Her eyes became dark and defensive, and I tried to hide my frustration.

"Nobody is implying anything. It's just that I'm hoping maybe you can shed some light on things. When I got home the house was ransacked, but Amber said it wasn't like that when the two of you left. I keep thinking ... did somebody break in after Amber and you left? Then Amber told me that Grandma and you argued about something. What did y'all get into it about?"

I pushed her to keep talking.

"What we were fighting about ain't none of your business," she growled. "I'm a grown woman, and I don't need to explain myself to a teenager."

"Everything with them is my business; I've been taking care of them my entire life." I glared at her. "And since you seem to have forgotten—I'm twenty years old now, so I'm grown, too!" I was tired of spinning my wheels with him when all I wanted was to crawl into my bed, pull the covers over my head, and wake up from this awful nightmare. So, I decided to lay all the cards out on the table.

"Geena, I think something bad happened between Grandma and you on Friday—something real bad. I want to know what y'all were fighting about, and I want to know if anything was missing from the house when Amber and you left. I need you to tell me why the house was all messed up," I persisted almost implying an accusation towards her.

"I didn't break into their house, and I didn't tear it up!" she bellowed. "I didn't do nothing to them, and what I talked to them about ain't your concern! And I sure don't appreciate you calling me a thief!"

It stupidly occurred to me for the first time that confronting my angry aunt, who was paranoid in general, was probably not the brightest idea I ever had, but I stayed on the path, especially after John gently put his hand on my shoulder to show his strength and support.

So, I spelled my question out as plainly as I could. "Geena, did you take anything from their house?"

"I only took what'd be mine someday anyway." She stubbornly lifted her chin. "I didn't take nothing valuable. I don't know what's got into them lately. They know how I get down in a hard way sometimes, and they ain't never denied me before. But Friday Mama wouldn't help me with nothing."

"So, you asked Grandma for money, but she refused to give it to you, so you two had a disagreement about that?"

"Yeah, and Dad told me 'no,' too, because she threatened to make him sleep on the porch if he didn't back her up. She always been crazy, and your Pop knew she would've actually put him out in the heat, and that humidity ain't no joke!"

I fought back a smile at her description of my Grandma; I had to at least give my aunt credit for understanding how her mom operated.

"So, after you asked for money, and they both

refused, what happened next?"

"Aww....it ain't nothing, really." She tucked her head down in obvious guilt. "I didn't have money to pay the water bill, and I needed some cash. I was pretty furious with them for not helping me out, so I took some of your Grandma's jewelry to pawn it off so I could pay my bill...Now, look here...I see the look in your eye, Addie, and don't you even think about laying a hand on me! What was I supposed to do? I got to have water—I'd die from dehydration without it!"

"So, you stole from your own parents, when they've given you everything." My voice trailed off, and I willed myself to stop talking, because what I needed from her was more important right now than my desire to kill her.

"Geena, where is Grandma's jewelry?" I switched gears as a light bulb came on in my head. "I'll give you money for the water bill, and you give me her things, and nobody has to know anything about you stealing from them."

"What do you care about that antique jewelry for anyhow?" She narrowed her eyes suspiciously. "Why'd you drive all the way over here to come get it from me? What's it to you?"

"Addie's Grandma willed that jewelry to her, so legally, it belongs to her," John interjected smoothly. "We are simply here to retrieve what is rightfully hers."

If Geena hadn't been so distraught, I felt certain she would have been asking about what had been left to her in the will to see what she was going to get out of this, but fortunately for me, her thought processes were not up to par today. She sized me up with curiosity and John with disgust, as she contemplated my offer.

"All right, fine...but the water bill's three hundred bucks. You got that kind of money? You give me the cash, and I'll give you the jewels. Besides I don't feel like going down to that pawn shop no how. I owe that man money, and he'll be giving me heck about it."

John immediately reached into his wallet and pulled out three hundred dollar bills that he handed to Geena. Just to be difficult, Geena counted them out loud, slowly and deliberately, to antagonize John. I thought provoking John was a lot like poking a hibernating grizzly bear with a stick, but I didn't say anything, because if John got into a fight with Geena at this point, that was perfectly fine by me.

When Geena finally got through counting the money, she reluctantly let me pass and allowed John inside, too, even though she was visually boring holes into the back of his head. She had the jewelry in a black garbage bag, and she reminded me of a white trash Santa with the way she slung the bag over her shoulder. She carried it over to me and heaved it carelessly onto the floor.

"There," she announced, as if everything were settled.

John slowly reached for the bag and started going through it.

"What's the matter with him? Didn't he just hear me say it's all there?"

"Yes, Geena, he heard you." I answered calmly. "Just give us a few seconds, and we'll be out of your hair."

John relaxed his shoulders and expressed a sigh of

relief after finding something in the bag that I couldn't see from where I stood.

"Okay, Addie ... we can go now."

"The two of you are about the strangest visitors I ever had, and I've had some strange people up in here." she mused.

"Now that's one observation I truly don't doubt, Geena."

Geena paused. "I don't know if this means anything to y'all or not, and I didn't even think about it when the cops was talking to me, but....your Grandma was saying that the security man was going to be coming by after Amber and me left...he was coming to install that new system we'd talked about. It was the same guy that nosy, old Rosy had used. I forgot about it until the two of you started grilling me! Like I said, I don't know if that means nothing to you or not, but I just thought I'd tell you."

I had almost forgotten about the security installer, as my mind flashed back to the security system at the house, which had never been activated. I didn't have a clue what to make of all this, but I was almost drained, and maintaining a civil conversation with Geena was sopping up my last drop of energy.

"Thanks, Geena. We'll let you know the funeral arrangements as soon as we have them," I said, and then we left without any more ado.

There were a lot of things I should have asked about during the drive back to Memphis, and I knew John would have answered any inquiry I would have made. But I was too worn out to talk anymore, and no matter what secrets and skeletons John revealed to me today, none of it would bring Grandma and Pop back, and they were all I wanted anyway.

So ten minutes into our drive home, I started to sob. My cell phone had been ringing all afternoon from everybody in Memphis. I had hit decline so much that I finally just turned it off. John reached into the back of his cab and found a quilt that he tucked around me. I noticed after curling up with it that it was one Grandma had made. He didn't speak, and I didn't either, but when I looked over at him, I saw the tears running down his tough face. Sometimes there just aren't enough words.

John drove me to his house, got me situated in his guest room, and gave me a sleeping pill to help me rest. I was too depressed to care what happened, and all I wanted to do was escape, so I took it without a second thought. That night I had no dreams or nightmares. All I saw was darkness, and an empty future waiting for me.

The next morning I forgot for a split second what I had lost yesterday, but then the walls came crashing back down on me again. I cried for a long time before forcing myself to pull it together and get dressed just like Grandma would have wanted me to. John and I had much to do today, but I certainly wasn't looking forward to any of it.

There were so many events in Memphis I would have loved to help plan. Picking the musical selections for the local symphony would have been inspiring, and deciding which caterers were chosen for the annual barbeque festival would have been divine. However, selecting flowers and writing obituaries for my grandparents' funeral was the one event I would have given my last breath to have never had to face.

Today John Hamilton and I sat down with the funeral home to discuss arrangements for the service, which would be held tomorrow. John was kind enough to plainly spell out and interpret funeral jargon into simplified terms for me to follow.

"Addie, fortunately, your Grandma and Pop prepaid for their funeral expenses, and they prepared instructions about how they wanted their services handled down to the last detail," John said. "I can handle the legalities and carry out the plans so you don't have to."

For the first time since I had met John I studied him hard; I realized what a blessing for me it was that my grandparents had the foresight to hire him to take care of things after their passing. I was probably staring at him too long, because he finally looked over at me and frowned.

"Is everything all right? You okay?" he asked with concern.

I knew I wasn't okay, and I knew that I would never be okay again, but I was composed enough to nod politely before looking away.

John told me that in my grandparents' will they had left everything to me. Part of me was surprised about this since they had two living children.

"Addie, you always took care of them, so they wanted to make sure that when the time came, they would take care of you," John explained. "I'll just have to wait until we get the death certificate to make everything legal."

"I don't think my Dad will be upset about the will, but I know that Geena will be spitting nails."

Right then I was too numb to care much how anybody felt about anything. I was appreciative Grandma and Pop had made provisions for me, because I didn't see how I would be handling anything well ever again. Even though their house was scary, it was at least nice to know I had a place to stay and John to look after me for a while.

"They were always going to make sure you were taken care of, Addie...even after they were gone," John said as if he had read my thoughts.

The hours, minutes, and seconds leading up to the funeral were a blur, and before I knew it, the service was here. All during the funeral I was like a deer in headlights, so Keisha never left my side.

"I have never seen this many people show up for a funeral before. I thought that normally this kind of crowd only turned out if a young person died, but obviously, my grandparents had more connections than I had realized."

I was glad to see that they had been important to a lot of other people besides me.

"It's so crowded here that the parking has spilled over onto the street and all the way down to the elementary school," Keisha said with a bittersweet expression on her face. "Your Grandma loved the color pink, didn't she? She would have loved all the pink petunias."

They would have matched her bunny slippers, I thought.

Everyone was dressed in their Sunday best. A lot of the cops from the force, who had come by our house to help with the burglar and then later when Grandma and Pop had died, were present; it was strange to see them in their church attire, rather than in their uniforms. The minister delivered a beautiful sermon, so I'm told, but I didn't hear any of it. I was just sitting there in a daze staring at their coffins and waiting to wake up from all of this.

Keisha nudged me to try to get my attention.

"Addie, are you okay?"

I shook my head and wondered how many times people were going to keep asking me that dumb question.

"I've just had so many dreams in the past that felt real that I keep telling myself that this is just another bad dream."

"You just tell yourself whatever you have to to get through today," Keisha spoke with encouragement that I couldn't feel.

"Well, so far, this lie is working as well as any, I suppose."

After the funeral, my house was flooded with people carrying casserole dishes, banana puddings, salads, divinity, and other varieties of food in large quantity— none of which I thought I would ever feel like eating. My parents had both flown into town, and they were each sobbing and trying to coax me to come to live with this one or the other. I knew they were just worried about me, but all I really wanted was for everyone to just leave me alone to die.

People would walk by and hug my neck or kiss my cheek and cry.

"I'm so sorry," friends would say, and I would think, *Why? It wasn't your fault.*

"They're in a better place," visitors would tell me, and I would mentally reflect, *Sure they are, but call me selfish, because I want them here with me.*

Acquaintances remarked, "At least they're not suffering anymore," and I was confused. *I knew they had their share of health problems, but I didn't think they were suffering enough that they had to die.*

However, I didn't say any of the negative things I was thinking, because for all of my sassiness, my grandparents had raised me right. I knew that sometimes when there's nothing helpful to say, people say all the wrong things, because they are trying to right something which can never be righted.

So, Keisha and I had practiced two lines for me to repeat all day. "Thank you for coming" and "I appreciate your concern" were what I repeated whenever people made those wrong comments.

I felt like a robot with a frozen, Southern smile, who was only programmed with two responses, so I reiterated my script all day long. I liked keeping it simple and appreciated not having to concentrate on much of anything right now, because I sensed that after everyone left, the walls would fall down around me. John wasn't there, because he said it wasn't about him, and he thought that the less attention on him the better. But I knew he was only the press of a button away, and I was surprised by how much the remembrance of that comforted me.

The brief comfort was fleeting though, because it

wasn't long before the bottom fell out of the sky, and depression rained down on me like the flood of Noah.

Chapter 11

I'm at the bottom of a well, and in my well, there's no light anywhere in sight. I slipped part way into it when Amy died, but I fell all the way to the bottom on the day my Grandma and Pop died.

I can't believe the earth hasn't stopped turning, because my world certainly has.

I don't answer the phone or the door, and they both ring all the time. There are flowers and food and a lot of other supplies I haven't identified yet piling up on the front porch, and I just let it all accumulate.

The last time Keisha came by my place she yelled at me through the peep hole, threatening to get the fire department to break the door down if I didn't answer it, and I just couldn't care less if she did.

I don't feel anything; I'm totally and completely numb. It's like the snow that fell this past winter wrapped my heart in ice so I'm preserved but not actually alive anymore.

I don't know what day of the week it is. I don't know if I'm scheduled for any responsibilities today, and I don't know when I'm supposed to go back to class.

I just stay in bed with the television buzzing in the background, and the days, minutes, and hours are all running together. I've discovered my Pop's liquor stash, and I've developed a serious interest in it.

I can't remember the last time I ate. I'm not sure how long people can go without eating before they expire, but if I go that long, so be it. It's not that I want to give up the ghost; it's just that everybody I've lived for is dead now, and my heart has died right along with them.

Chapter 12

I have abandoned my friends and family in favor of my new best friend, Mrs. Vodka. In my fog I'm vaguely aware that I'm entering a new phase in life, and it's one I want to hide from forever.

The phone rings for the millionth time, and I pick it up planning to hang up on whoever is on the other line when I hear Keisha's voice calling for me in the background.

"Hello," I answer begrudgingly.

"Oh, Addie, thank God you're all right. I've been worried sick about you."

Silence from me.

"Addie, I never hear from you anymore," she pleaded clearly concerned about me.

"Keisha, I just can't do this today."

"Now Addie Marie Jackson, why would you even talk like that?" she asked, raising her voice an octave.

"Everyone I've ever cared about has died eventually, so there's no point in staying attached to you. One of us will be dead before long anyway."

"Addie, I've known you your entire life, and I'm still here. I am not going anywhere."

For now, I thought.

"And why is it that you haven't been to church lately?" asked Keisha. "You must need it now more than ever. The choir sang the most beautiful version of 'Amazing Grace' Sunday—you would have loved it."

"I'm in a spiritual wasteland," I slurred.

"What's that supposed to mean?" Keisha adjusted the receiver of her phone to hear me better.

"Keisha, that's just the season I'm in, and I don't feel like there's any 'Amazing Grace' for me."

"How can you say that?" she asked in exasperation.

"I feel like God has forsaken and abandoned me."

"Addie, God's presence is not limited by our lack of faith in Him anymore than you can make gravity go away by not believing in it."

"Look, I know He's still there; I'm just so sad and overwhelmed that I can't feel Him right now."

"God is always bigger than our feelings."

"You're right. Just give me some time, okay?"

"Okay. Just don't forget that I'm still here. I never see you anymore."

"I don't want to see anybody, Keisha."

"Fine then. Just stay away from me. All of us are getting pretty used to it by now," she said softly revealing the sour grapes I had not realized were there. This was a surprise punch I had not seen coming.

"I'm sorry I can't be what you want me to be," I said sadly.

"I just want you to be you," she said longingly and with sincere vulnerability.

"Yeah, well, I died the day they did, in case you haven't noticed."

I hung up the phone. I knew I would feel terrible about the way I had spoken to her later, but right now I was too inebriated to care.

Then I heard knocking at the front door. I know I

smell of whiskey and wine, and my depression is reflected in the dark circles under my eyes, but I don't care enough to conceal them. I realize I've probably lost twenty pounds in the past ten days, but my alcohol induced state has decreased my inhibitions, so I crack open my door with little shame.

John Hamilton is standing there holding breakfast to try to entice me to eat. In growing awareness of my personal presentation, I let him in as I trip over the bottles on the floor. He goes into the bathroom and starts running a bath for me, and he sets out my soap, shampoo, and conditioner. Then he enters my room to pick out some clothes and puts them on the bathroom counter as well.

"Are you ready to get up now?" he asks gently, and I know it's a loaded question.

"As ready as I'll ever be," I reply soberly after staring at him long and hard.

"Then go get cleaned up, and come in here and eat your breakfast," he says. "When you're finished, we'll start again."

So, I put one foot in front of the other. I scrub myself raw as if the scalding water will burn away my pain, but all it leaves me with is a painful, red complexion. I take my time freeing myself of my funk, and John gives me space to breathe and time to spare.

I finally finish freshening up, and I eat the omelet he brought. It's good enough to make me feel as though I might be among the land of the living again someday. When I have a full belly for the first time in what feels like forever, I begin afresh. He took a good, long while pouring the rest of Pop's liquor stash down the sink, and I'm too ashamed to object. He feels badly for me; he thinks I look lost, so he decides to lead me until I have the strength to lead myself again.

"Let's go somewhere for a while," he suggested. "There are things you have a right to know, and it's time for you to learn about them if you so choose."

He handed me my jacket, and I followed him docilely out to his truck. In spite of my independent streak, it was just easier to follow his lead rather than make my own decisions right now.

I vaguely noticed us taking a detour down a side country road followed by countless twists and turns. We drove past numerous giant oak trees before we wound up in the town square of Collierville. John pulled over and parked beside the town's post office and shut off the truck.

"What are we doing here?" I asked feeling confused.

"Well, that's up to you really. Let's start from the beginning," he suggested eagerly. "Do you want to hear everything from me, or would you rather hear it from your Grandma?"

I was offended by the question, since he knew I couldn't talk to her.

"What the heck is that supposed to mean?"

"I'm simply asking if you would rather hear your family's secrets from your Grandma or from me," he repeated patiently.

"Well, I would've loved to have heard them from her, but somehow that wasn't high on her priority list, because as you can see, she's dead now, and I'll never get the chance to hear anything from her ever again."

"I wouldn't be so sure about that," he remarked mildly. He peered from one of my eyes to the other several times as if checking to make sure I meant what I had said."Okay, it's your choice to make, so I'll respect your decision." He reached into his pocket and fiddled with something for a minute before pulling out a key and displaying it for me like it was the most important thing he had ever held.

"What's that for?"

"You're going to be getting some mail. You don't need to tell anybody else about this. It's the only post office key to your box. I suggest you keep everything associated with this under your hat for your own good."

"Why do I need a post office box to pick up my mail when I already have a mail box?"

"Because I'm sure every greedy thug in your neighborhood has gone through your mail more times than you would care to count. So, that's why she got you a box."

"She?" I questioned him.

"Your Grandma," he stated as if it were obvious.

"Okay, so she gave me nothing helpful to equip me to survive without her, but she paid for me to have a mailbox so gang bangers don't steal my grocery coupons. Super."

"No, Addie. She got you a mailbox to receive mail from her."

"That's the worst gift in the world. I lived with her— she could have just written me a card and handed it to me whenever she wanted to while she was alive, but she never

212

did. Besides, it would have been easier to just walk across the house and tell me whatever she wanted me to know. Now that she's gone, I'll never get mail from her," I vented as I futilely kicked the floor board of his truck.

"Addie, I am trying to tell you that you're about to start getting letters from her," he said seriously. "You probably already have one now."

"How is that possible?" I retorted and whipped my head up at him. "She's dead. I saw her. The dead don't do mail."

"She wrote you a lot of letters while she was still alive. She wanted to help guide you with them someday when she wasn't here anymore. That's why she left you the key in her safe deposit box," he explained as if it were normal for this sort of thing to happen.

I was a flood of emotions. *Dang her for knowing I wouldn't be able to resist the intrigue of getting mail from her! She hadn't called me a curious cat for no reason,* I thought.

"If you choose to read her letters, your life will never be the same. The world will look differently, and you may never feel safe again."

"How would that be any different that it already is?"

"You don't have to read them, as the things you learn in there may upset you. You may become burdened from carrying secrets you won't be able to share with others. The road of knowledge about your family confidences could be quite lonely for you, just as it was for your grandparents. But if you decide to educate yourself, you will understand a great deal about your family and the power that has surrounded them for almost seventy years. Therefore in many ways, you will have insight that most could only dream of. So, Addie… what are you going to do?"

Curiosity won out over caution, so I took a deep breath and held my hand out for the key as visions of the dead cat Grandma had warned me about flashed through my psyche.

There were worse things besides being dead, after all.

John slowly leaned forward to hand it to me.

"Okay, but this changes everything…" he warned as he laid the cold key in the palm of my hand.

I turned the key around and around; it looked ancient and was engraved with my initials, "AMJ." The metal was carved and sculpted in the most interesting, beautiful pattern I had ever seen.

I had begged my grandparents for answers my whole life, but I had never wanted them like this. I headed into the post office thrilled about receiving mail from Grandma but terrified about what it might say.

Upon entering, I discovered that my post office number was "777"—three numbers representing the Trinity and seven days for God's creation. The more I learned about my grandparents, the more confirmation I received that they did nothing without purpose or plan. I found my metal box and slid the key into the key hole, which squeaked as it opened. There was one long, sealed, security envelope laying there waiting for me.

It was addressed to my full name in Grandma's handwriting, but there was no return address. The post marked date was the day my grandparents had died, which sent a chill down my spine. John advised me to read it in his car away from the watchful eyes of others, and he sat guard on the hood of his truck to remain vigilant and to give me some privacy. After a brief hesitation, I ripped it open to find the following message penned in her scrawling handwriting:

Dear Addie,

If you're reading this letter, that means your Pop and I have gone on to Glory. There's a lot in this world I ain't sorry to say "Bye" to, but you, my child, were the hardest for me to leave. I've watched you grow up your entire life, and not a day has gone by that I have not been proud of you. I have always believed that there ain't nothing in this world you can't do if you put your mind to it. I would still be there with you if there had been any other way.

I suspect John Hamilton has caught up with you by now. You need to listen to him – he knows what to do. He's bold and brave, and he will help you any way that he can. He's going to look out for you now that I'm not there no more. He's a good man that you can trust, and there ain't a lot of them left.

I know there's a whole bunch of questions you been wanting answered for a long time. Your Pop and I never knew when the right time was to tell you everything, and we always wanted you to be unburdened for as long as you could. We kept hoping we could fix everything so you never had to know any of this, and my biggest regret is that we failed the great cause. We're passing the torch on to you, my child. You're our only hope. You've probably already suspected that there's a lot about my life that we kept secret from you. It wasn't always that way. Sometimes you don't pick your life—sometimes it picks you.

When I was growing up, I'm ashamed to tell you that my father was a slave owner. It don't matter what

215

them history books tell you—slavery existed in the South for decades after it was banned. My father was a mean, heartless man, and he was cruel to my mother, so you can only imagine how he treated his slaves. My mother was a closet sympathizer to them, and I watched her sneak off many times in the middle of the night to give them food and water while my father was sleeping. She inspired me to reach out to them, but of course I had to keep this hidden from my father, or he would have beaten all of them.

There were two slaves named Moses and Zephorrah, who took a particular interest in me. They were a married couple, who lived in the slave quarters on our property. Despite their horrible circumstances, they were kinder to me and modeled a healthier relationship for me than my own parents did. I know my mother saw me slip away and visit them often, but she never told my father, and I never told her I knew she snuck food to the slaves. I have always believed that she stayed with my father, because she thought he would kill her if she tried to leave, and the truth is, she was probably right. If she had died, she would have left the slaves and me unprotected, and she just couldn't do that to any of us. Times were different then—she didn't have no education or no means. She had made her bed, and she had to lay in it – bloody nose and all. She's why I always wanted you to get your education so you don't ever get dependent on nobody who ain't good for you.

It wasn't long before the yellow fever epidemic blew through. Moses and Zephorrah became deathly ill, but the traveling doctor was so busy taking care of the white families that very few slaves received medical attention. It wasn't right, but that's how it was. I was under strict orders from Mama to stay away from them due to their high level of contagion, but I was too worried to turn my back on them.

At some point in the illness it became very clear that Moses and Zephorrah were not going to recover from their sickness, so they tried to prepare me for this. I was devastated at the thought of losing my friends, who had become my only confidants in my short, lonely life. Before they died, they confided in me about their involvement with hoodoo, which was a form of witchcraft some slaves were using to try to protect themselves from their abusive masters. They told me that the two of them had been chosen by their families with the purpose of freeing their family from slavery. They said they had been working on accomplishing this their whole lives, but they were going to have to die bitterly unsuccessful. Their forefathers had been slaves, who traced their ancestry all the way back to Egypt. These predecessors had stolen a ring from their pharaoh, because it was believed to have special powers. After acquiring the ring, their ancestors fled for their lives and escaped only to be captured into slavery by new masters. Their family worked over the years to protect the ring at all costs, and many slaves sacrificed themselves to hide the ring and the powers that it held.

The ring was significant, because when placed on someone's finger, it enhanced that person's natural ability. For example, if someone was a fast runner, when worn, the wearer would have incredible speed. The hoodoo on the ring was so strong that whenever the ring was worn, you could view other people's most significant event just by having any kind of physical contact with them. The effects were subtle enough that others would not normally notice that anything was amiss.

There is so much more that I need to tell you, my child, but Rosy is coming up the porch to give me the latest scoop, so I will tell you more in my next letter. I must implore you to guard my ring and my pocket watch with your life. So much blood has been shed to protect them; those who want them would think nothing of sacrificing yours to have them. And Addie, you must burn all of the letters I send you straight away. They must never get into the wrong hands. I love you, my child, and I promise to write you again very soon.

Love,

Grandma

Tears filled my eyes as sadness filled my heart. John had stopped watching for warning signs and had started watching me curiously instead. He walked over and climbed in the truck and sat beside me for support. I hugged her letter across my heart and knew I could never burn it. It was a connection to her, and destroying it would destroy part of my soul.

"I need somewhere safe to hide this," I told John between tears.

"Okay, then that's what we'll do," he said.

"I'm not ready to talk about it yet," I continued.

"No one said you had to."

"I do need two things though," I said, feeling more determined than ever.

"Sure, what would they be?" he asked.

"I need Grandma's ring and her watch," I said in a tone that scared even me. "I'm going to have to guard them, and I can't let anybody else have them without prying them off my corpse."

"They would have to pry them off both our corpses to get them." he confirmed.

Just then my cell phone started pinging like crazy.

"I must have been without a signal for a while," I remarked. I entered my password to check my messages as John started his truck and headed west toward Memphis. I bypassed a couple of voice mails from Geena that I had no interest in when my phone rang. I picked up to hear Amber on the other end of the line.

"Addie? Is that you? Thank God! I've been, like, calling you for forever! Where have you been?"

"I went to go see your mama. I'm with John, remember? Is everything all right? What's going on?" I asked trying to determine why I heard so much fear in her voice.

"Oh, Addie! I got ran off the road today! My dad's so mad. He thinks it was my fault. His car's all banged up, and I'm probably going to be grounded for the rest of my life. He's never going to let me drive again!" she whined as she began to squall.

"It's okay, it's okay, just calm down. Are you hurt?"

"Yeah, I mean I got banged up, but it's not bad enough to go to the emergency room." She sniffled. "But I swear, Addie, that car ran me off the road. You've got to believe me—Dad doesn't. He just thinks I was fiddling with the radio station or yapping on my phone, and you know that, like, usually would totally be something I would do. But honestly, I swear somebody was trying to push me into that ditch. They even threw some sort of weird powder at me as they were driving off. I tried to tell the cops, but my dad kept cutting me off, and he wouldn't let me talk!"

I shuddered fearing the worst.

"Amber, I want you to tell me exactly what happened."

"Okay, I was driving on I-240," she explained. "And before you say anything, I know I shouldn't have been trying to drive on the Interstate. But I had ordered a pizza, and then after I'd ordered it, they go and tell me they don't deliver. I mean, what kind of a pizza place doesn't deliver, right? So, I ask for the manager, and I get this chick on the phone just smacking her gum and..." she rambled.

"No, Amber, what happened with the guys trying to run you off into the ditch."

I attempted to get her back on track.

"Oh yeah, that. I was coming back from picking up the pizza, and this black car started tailgating me. It was the weirdest thing I'd ever seen. I looked up in my rear view mirror to see who it was, but there were two guys in the car wearing ski masks! Ski masks, Addie! I mean, how freaky is that? Memphis is hot as blazes, so who does that? That's so bizarre. Anyway, they kept riding my bumper and swerving around me. I think they were just, like, really trying to scare me. So, I tried to get out of their way, but they were getting more and more aggressive. I called the cops, and they told me to come into the station around the corner, but on my way there, the sedan totally steered me into the ditch. Dad thinks I'm just trying to get out of trouble for driving his vehicle on the interstate. He thinks this will teach me a lesson or something stupid like that. But Addie, I promise—that was exactly what happened!"

He implored me to believe her, which I had no trouble doing. My mind was racing. I didn't know what to say to Amber. I didn't want to upset her anymore than she already was, but I didn't want her to be naive about the kind of people who were out to get our family either.

"Amber, where are you right now?" I asked her.

"I'm at home," she howled. "The way this day has gone, my dad isn't going to let me leave the house ever again."

I wanted to tell her that that was probably the best

thing for her, but I bit my tongue.

"Amber, I really want to help you with this, but I need to call you back in a little while. Can you hang tight for me just a bit?"

"Yes, I can 'hang tight,'" she sighed dramatically. "But I can't guarantee that masked men won't come after me while you're taking your sweet time."

"I promise I'll call you back as soon as I can."

Then I ignored her melodrama and hung up the phone.

"What's going on? What's up? You okay? What's wrong?" John wheezed as one long sentence.

"I'm okay, but Amber's not. Men wearing ski masks, who were driving a black sedan ran her off the road. She's all right, but her mom's vehicle is messed up. She tried to tell her dad and the cops what happened, but they didn't believe her."

"Well, that's really serious." He let out a low whistle and looked very concerned. "They are trying to provoke you to get your attention."

"What are you talking about?" I questioned him.

"I think they're trying to lash out at you to obtain the ring by attacking your closest family member," he surmised.

"How is she my closest family member?" I whispered feeling very disturbed by his perspective. "Wouldn't my dad rank higher on the list than Amber?"

"Not necessarily." He shook his head. "Of your remaining living relatives, you are closer to Amber than anybody else. My guess is that they're more interested in drawing you out into the open than worrying about your blood line."

"But how do they even know about Amber? I thought I was the only one who was going to be burdened by all this. She's got nothing to do with any of this, and there's no reason for her to be involved."

"Well, you didn't deserve any of this either, but that doesn't mean it's not affecting you," John softly replied.

"I know, but I so desperately wanted to protect her from all this. What do we do about it?" I pleaded.

"Well, I guess I could just run double shifts to watch out for her, too." He frowned. "It would be dangerous to tell her about hoodoo, because it's safer for her if she's ignorant about it."

"John, you can't rescue my entire family forever."

I looked at John sadly.

"I can sure as heck try," he narrowed his eyes in determination as he sped back to Memphis.

I laid back in my seat and distracted myself by flashing back to a conversation I had had with Grandma prior to her death. I had just refilled my grandparents' pill boxes when I wandered into her bedroom and found her sitting on the edge of her bed crying and wiping her eyes. Naturally this worried me, so I slipped in to sit on the bed beside her.

"Grandma, are you okay?" I patted her knee.

"Oh, I'm fine," she blushed clearly embarrassed to have been caught crying. My Aunt Geena had just called and left a message apologizing about how she would have to miss dinner with her on account of having "the flu." The last time I checked the flu was not spread from excessive casino sprees, but I didn't ask Grandma if Geena was why she was crying.

"Lord, I wish that girl would quit those slots," Grandma said, tearing up, which confirmed my fears. "If I hadn't burdened her with so much, I bet she never would have started gambling."

I exhaled thinking about how ridiculous it was for her to feel guilty about Geena's choices. I really wanted to help pick her up out of her funk.

"I was just thinking about things from a long time ago," she reflected.

"What kind of things?"

She accepted the tissue that I handed her and dabbed her eyes.

"I was thinking about how old Amy would be if she were still alive. I always felt bad about what happened to her. I should have been able to stop her dying – it was all my fault."

"Grandma, that's completely ridiculous! I said in puzzlement. "Amy got hit by a car—there wasn't anything you could have done about that."

I immediately felt a pang of guilt for telling Grandma she should not feel responsible when I had been blaming myself for the same thing every since Amy's death.

"Well ... I'm used to being able to protect my family," she sniffled through tears. "But I was having an off day that day. I was in the hospital when she got hit, and..." her voice trailed off devoid of explanation that would have filled in the gaps for me.

"I didn't have everything I needed when I went in, and then I found out what had happened to her when I got out...Addie, I just never forgave myself. I swanie I didn't."

"Grandma, I am so dumbfounded by what you're saying! It's distressing to me to see you so upset. You can't protect everybody all the time, and nobody blamed you for Amy dying. For Heaven's sake, she got killed by a hit-and-run driver while you were in the hospital! There was no way you could have saved her - you're not making any sense!" I said as I wondered what exactly she wasn't telling me about all of this.

"I know, I know ... you're right ..." She immediately started regaining her composure. "I just wanted you to know that I didn't know ... I mean, I wasn't aware. I mean ... I never wanted anything to happen to either of you, and I'd do anything I could to change what happened, but I can't now."

"Grandma, to be perfectly honest, it really hurts me to hear that you've been blaming yourself about something that's clearly not your fault – it makes me feel sad."

"I'm sorry for being a silly, old woman," Grandma started apologizing and straightening up. "Are you sure you're okay? I mean, we can keep talking about this. I don't want you to be upset!"

I expressed my concern, but Grandma shook her head, dried her tears, kissed my cheek, and waved me off.

"We ain't got nothing else to talk about. I ain't upset no more." Then just like that she had ended the conversation.

I knew that the more gifts people were given, the

224

more God expected from them in the life He had blessed them with. I wondered how many bad things had happened over the years that Grandma had felt like she should have been able to prevent but had been unable to and felt responsible for. I was curious how much of that stress and obligation had played a role in her fading health, and I suddenly knew that if anything ever happened to Amber, I would be in June Jackson's exact shoes.

I tried to call Amber back several times to check on her even though I had no idea how to help her. She never answered the phone, and I assumed she was already spreading her story to all her friends. I would normally have taken greater steps to reach her, but my head was too full with my own stuff to put as much effort into her as I should have.

If I had only known how much danger she was in, I would have moved heaven and earth to reach her.

Chapter 13

Against his better judgment, John agreed to take me back to my house to stay on the condition that he stayed there with me. John was an insomniac, whose only rest involved brief dozes on my couch.

Despite our platonic relationship, him sleeping at my place only poured gasoline on the neighborhood gossip that Nosy Rosy kept fired up.

To my surprise there was a green glass jug filled with wildflowers on my front porch when we arrived. Will was too upscale to make a delivery like that, and everything about them reminded me of the wildflowers Gavin had picked for me in my dream.

A note was attached which read, "Addie, I am so terribly sorry for your loss. You are always in my thoughts," but there was no signature to indicate who it was from. I couldn't wrap my brain around what I was looking at. John, of course, felt compelled to inspect them to insure they weren't a weapon of some sort, and as soon as he was satisfied, he set them on my kitchen window sill. I didn't know who had sent them, but I was certainly glad for something to brighten up my dark day.

As I walked into the house I noticed to my dismay through the back window that Geena's car was parked in the driveway. I knew it would only be a minutes before she would kill my buzz from the bouquet. I heard noises coming from the back door and immediately tensed up as Geena stumbled through the rear entry way.

"Well, hello there, Addie," she slurred.

"What are you doing? Did you drive over here like that?"

Despite the fact that Geena didn't normally drink, at the moment she was obviously drunk.

In the lamp light her red hair glowed brighter than ever.

"There are worse things than dying," she muttered as she swayed bck and forth, and scowled at John.

For one of the few times in my life she had finally said something I agreed with.

"I got a splitting headache," she whined.

"I'll make you a pot of coffee if you like," I said begrudgingly as I straightened my shoulders.

"I'll take it," she said as her eyes rolled around for a minute; I expected her to pass out, but she surprised me in staying awake.

John eyed Geena like she was a chemistry experiment with explosive tendencies.

"So, how are things at the old homestead anyway?" Geena asked me nonchalantly, but something told me she was more than a little curious.

"Oh, fine, I suppose," I lied in my best casual tone while the coffee brewed. I was far too prideful to tell her that memories of Grandma and Pop haunted me every second of every day in their house.

"Yeah, our family is real good at saying things are 'fine' when they ain't, huh?" she replied sardonically.

I was not about to be reeled in that easily, so I fished up a mug and a stirrer for her caffeine fix.

"So, how much you done figured out yet—that's what

I really want to know."

"I don't know what you're talking about," I responded nervously.

"Girly, I been in this family a lot longer than you. We both know some strange things done gone down around here."

I dodged her conversational hook.

I could feel Geena's frustration steaming off of her as she snapped, "Addie, you ain't the only one who knows."

"Knows what?" I questioned Geena while staring at John in confusion.

"About that ring." she whispered.

My face turned white as a ghost, as Geena passed out on my kitchen table. I could never figure out whether Geena was a friend or foe, but maybe she was a little bit of both.

"Whoa," John let out a whistle and ran his hand across the back of his neck; he started sweating and seemed jumpier than usual.

"If she knows about the ring, why would she have taken it from Grandma and Pop?" I asked John.

"I don't know."

John checked to make sure Geena had a pulse.

"Darn it, John, help me figure this out!" I pleaded with him.

John studied me hard for what seemed like a long time.

"Why are you just sitting there looking at me like that? We have to do something!" I cried.

"Addie, I need you to trust me."

"Trust you with what? Information? My confidence?"

I rattled off rhetorical questions feeling overwhelmed.

He reached over and took my hand and led me over to the couch where he sat down beside me.

"Geena has her own interpretation of things, and I want you to take what she says with a grain of salt."

"What is that supposed to mean?" I asked as I pulled my hand away from him as I was starting to sweat.

"Geena is bitter about a lot of things ... and that bitterness combined with her gambling losses have warped her viewpoint."

"Why do I feel like you're trying to manipulate me right now?"

"I just don't want her to try to turn you against me." John said after a brief hesitation. "Geena can be strategic whens he wants to be. Just remember what you know about me if she ever speaks ill of me. Your grandparents would only put someone, who they knew would take good care of you in charge of looking after you. Addie, I would fight to the death to keep you safe."

"You're being cryptic, and you're not making any sense."

"I'm your biggest ally. Just remember that," John said confidently, as he looked me dead in the eye and spoke as straight as an arrow.

Geena stirred at the table, and we froze to wait and see what she would do. She stretched and tried to stand up unsuccessfully.

"Geena, do you need some help?" I said trying to offer her my assistance.

"I don't need no help from no one—least of all him!"
he snarled as he attempted to point his finger into John's
face but missed by a long shot.

"Let me help get you into the guest bed," I coaxed as
I tried to prevent a showdown between the two of them.

"If you only knew what he was capable of, you'd
never let him in your house again!" Geena hollered.

I winced, and John glowered at her but said nothing.

"I know about that ring, and I know about that
watch," Geena continued slobbering. "I know about the
hoodoo, too. I know what it's like to have people try to kill
you your whole life to get something you didn't want to
have anything to do with. I know how it feels to never be
free and to have your parents trust some man you never
even met more than their own flesh and blood."

My mouth dropped open.

"And you!" she sneered at me. "You with your
college education and your going off to have a bigger and
better life! Did you really think it would be that easy? Did
you really think you could just run away from it all? You
just keep on looking for that great new life, kid, because
I'm here to tell you that you'll never find it. The only
escape I ever found was in the cards you stick your pretty,
little nose up at. Now I know you think you got it all
figured out. But I know things. Lots of things. And don't
you be forgetting it!"

Geena adjusted her shirt in a feeble attempt at
appearing dignified before she announced slyly, "You
know there's more than one, don't you?"

I narrowed my eyes.

"More than one what?"

"Ring," she sneered smugly before she walked crookedly into the guest room and crashed onto the bed.

"Oh no," I whispered.

"What is it? Do you want me to take her back to her house?" John asked anxiously.

"That's going to be me in twenty years," I whispered in a moment of clarity.

"Addie, that will never be you." he disagreed.

"No wonder my grandparents felt so responsible for her! Their secrets burdened her beyond her breaking point. I always thought she was the last person in the world I could trust, yet now...Geena just became my greatest, living resource. How could I have been so wrong about her?"

"Wrong to assume she is an irresponsible gambler? I don't think you were wrong on that account." John argued wryly. "Geena has always resented me. Your grandparents trusted me to take care of things for them. There was a time when your Grandma thought Geena would be the one to carry on their quest. But all the secrets and burdens of the ring pushed her over the edge, and she never recovered from all of the darkness. Geena always thought they should have included her more in the last few years. Despite the way she treats me, she doesn't really mind my race, Addie. She minds my role."

I chewed on this new perspective about Geena.

"I was wrong to judge her," I confessed. "How dare I condemn her? Whoever gave me the authority to decide she was no good? She has born this burden my entire life

231

and never complained about it to me. Shame on me!" I reprimanded myself. "What was she talking about with there being more than one ring? Having one is overwhelming enough—I don't know what to do as it is." I shook my head and said, "What in the world are we supposed to do if we find another one?"

John sat in silence.

"As long as I have to protect the ring, I will never be free. I'm so stupid."

"No, you're not. Why would you say that?"

"I've spent my entire life wishing something interesting and exciting would happen for me, but this isn't what I would have picked for my worst enemy. I just wish I could will it away. Wait … maybe I could."

Suddenly, an idea hit me.

"Could what?" he asked.

"What if I could give the ring away? Maybe if I found someone or some organization that would use it to do good—then I could render up this cross."

"Addie, I don't think that's the best idea," he cautioned me.

"Well, why not?" I whined.

"Because your Grandma tried that one time, and that's when things got even worse for her."

"What are you talking about?"

"She tried to donate it—fulfill the mission that Moses and Zephorrah entrusted to her. She went to P.E.A.C.E. in the hope they would use the ring to free people around the world, who were enslaved in bondage."

"P.E.A.C.E.? The charity that supports minorities and

advocates against slavery around the world? What happened?"

"She used the ring to see that even those who ran P.E.A.C.E. were power hungry and corrupt," he said sadly.

"But I thought they promoted equal rights for minorities and humanitarian aid around the world."

"Yeah, she did, too, but even charities have flaws. Of course there were good people there," he explained, "who were sincerely trying to make a difference. But unfortunately, the people with the power and authority were willing to exploit others for their own gain, so they were not to be trusted."

"So, what did she do?"

"She changed her mind about handing the ring and watch over halfway through her rendezvous with them, but they didn't respond favorably towards her change of heart."

"How so?"

"They threatened to kill her if she didn't give them up, and they never gave up trying to steal them from her."

"Do you think P.E.A.C.E. had anything to do with their deaths?" I asked.

"I don't know—her meeting with them was so long ago that it's probably unlikely."

"But significant enough to look into."

"True, but if we're going to go after an organization as reputable and dangerous as P.E.A.C.E., we had better know what we are doing." he cautioned me.

"How so?" I inquired.

"Their company is powerful, and I don't believe they

would think twice about doing us in if they knew what we had in our possession. And if what Geena claims is true, and there's another ring hidden somewhere ..." John's voice trailed off.

"We'd be dead for sure," I completed his sentence.

"Without a doubt."

We slipped into silence before catching sight of the news playing on the television.

"The media is covering more stories about the Skullbangerz," John remarked. "Looks like the leader, Jaydon Swisher, is at it again. He's been leaving hoodoo symbols sprayed in graffiti all over this side of town for weeks now."

The very mention of Jaydon made me shudder; the visual of him towering over me waiting to punch my face in still haunted my nightmares.

My land line rang, and for whatever reason I decided to pick up. It was Will on the other end asking me if I had gotten his roses and all of his messages. I mentally noted he didn't say he had left the wildflowers, and considering who I was speaking to, I didn't ask him about them either. He apologized profusely for being rude to me the other night, and despite my angst against him, I told him about my grandparents' passing.

To my surprise, he was supportive and sympathetic, and something in the tone of his voice reminded me of when they were still here. So, when he asked me to go to downtown for the annual Southern Music Festival to get extra credit for his Music History class tonight, I agreed to go. I should have been more worried about Amber, but I had no idea how to help myself much less her. So, I pushed my concerns into the back of my brain to deal with later.

All the way across town Keisha was sweating bullets. She was worried sick about me and didn't know how I was doing. Her father's stress level had reached epic proportions with all the corruption and crime in the city, and she hadn't had a full meal in days—not that anyone had been paying attention to her enough to notice.

I was drowning in my own problems, and while she felt sympathy for my situation, she also felt neglected by me. If there had been any time in her life when she could have used a friend, it was now. She thought we had been making progress since I had been more open with her lately, but every since Grandma and Pop passed, she felt like we were back to square one.

She was hearing rumors I had been spending all of my time with the executor of my grandparents' estate. She didn't understand why I was not seeking her out instead, especially considering the depth of our relationship. She was afraid I was keeping secrets from her again, and despite her best efforts to suppress it, anger was starting to creep in.

I was itching to check the mail again. John wanted to go with me, but I told him I wanted him to keep an eye on Geena, but really I just wanted to be alone. So against his wishes, I grabbed my keys and left him scowling on the front porch as I drove toward Collierville. My head was so fuzzy that I got lost and ended up on the wrong side of town.

I stopped at a gas station to try to get my bearings when a car full of guys yelled some racial slurs at me. I didn't know them from Adam, but that didn't mean it didn't hurt my feelings. I knew they weren't really yelling hurtful words at me necessarily; they were yelling them at unkind people who looked like me.

My experiences in being on the receiving end of this had made me defensive of the victims of it. Knowing Grandma's history now made me yearn to talk to her again, but I would have to settle for her mail instead.

I got back on track but felt nervous on the drive to Collierville. A couple of cars had followed me too close for comfort, and I had had too many bad encounters lately not to treat every suspicious person as a threat.

Upon arriving at the post office, I was thrilled to find another letter in my mailbox. I hastily carried it to my car to absorb every word with my doors firmly locked.

It wasn't long before I was falling down into the rabbit hole my grandparents had warned me about.

Dear Addie,

I'm sitting here watching you sleep. I remember when I used to sleep as soundly as you, but it's been years. I know when all of this comes out in the wash, you won't sleep good no more, and I can't tell you how sorry I am about that, child.

In my last letter I was telling you about my ring. It's a beautiful ring to carry so many burdens, ain't it? When you wear it, and you touch someone else, you'll slip into their most significant memory to date for as long as that event occurred. The only way to get out is to take the ring off. For the person whose memory you're sampling, it only

236

looks like you've stared off into space for five seconds. The funny thing about significant events is they're always subjective, because what is significant to one person might be barely memorable to somebody else. As people progress through life, their significant events change as they experience new, important chapters in their lives.

Having this level of insight without someone's permission, knowledge, or awareness is part of what makes it so valuable—and so dangerous. To make matters worse, Moses and Zephorrah made the ring even more impressive by adding their own powerful batch of potion to it. They had been experimenting with hoodoo to try to travel back in time to before their ancestors were enslaved. They were trying to prevent them from ever having been captured. They were working to change the history of their people.

The two of them had acquired an antique pocket watch – the one I keep on me all the time. This clock was very important because of its history, but I ain't never been sure as to why. Unfortunately for all of us, Moses and Zephorrah died before being able to explain it to me. What I do know is that Moses and Zephorrah would turn a dial on the clock to a date and time and use it with the ring to travel to a different period in their current location.

They were trying to master controlling where in time the ring took them, but they were never able to make this very reliable. Because they weren't able to work out the kinks with time travel, they never accomplished what they had hoped to achieve with it.

I have to stop writing for now. You're starting to stir. You're a beautiful girl, Addie. Don't let any of this steal your strength. I believe in you, and I wish you the best of luck. You're going to need it.

Love,
Grandma

237

When I finally stopped reading, I stared off into space in complete disbelief. My mind was racing, and while what I had learned would have been hard for most people to believe, in a very twisted way, it made my grandparents' lifestyle seem much more rational to me.

I had not experimented with Grandma's ring or pocket watch, because they didn't feel like they belonged to me. I kept waiting for Grandma and Pop to show back up at their house and act like their deaths had been the world's worst April Fool's joke.

With all the letters I was getting from Grandma, it was easy to convince myself of this lie. You could say I was in denial, but it was a much better place than my reality. I felt unprepared and inept to deal with any of this, so I was choosing not to.

I kept both the ring and the watch in my pocket all the time so I could return them to my grandparents if they ever decided to come back. I could not fathom why they had chosen me for any of this, especially considering everyone else seemed to want a piece of the pie but me.

I was restless and twitchy. I missed my Pop's liquor. I wondered if I could pay somebody to buy me more. Grandma had warned me that someday I would end up in Geena's shoes. I assumed she hadn't meant I would become a gambler, but I certainly understood now why she had picked that bad habit up to begin with.

John would be horrified, but that made it all the more fun. I slid the letter into my front pocket and drove to the nearest gas station. I scoped the parking lot and found my first unsuspecting victim. Being underage meant I would have to pay someone to get my fix since to my dismay John had poured all of it out.

I was able to flirt and sweet talk a cute college student to hook me up, and I gave him enough to treat himself as well. I waited restlessly while he went inside to buy it and was relieved to see him come back out and hand it over to me. I was as happy as a kid on Christmas morning; I couldn't be genuinely happy under the circumstances, of course, but inebriation was better than depression. I popped open the bottle of whiskey and downed several swigs on the way over to Will's place. I was starting to forget why I had been mad at him to begin with.

Chief Stamper called while I was weaving in and out of traffic. It seemed like the Memphis police force rang me up an awful lot since my grandparents' deaths. I should have talked to John more about it, but I didn't feel like discussing much these days. I was tired of all the questions; none of them brought my grandparents back, and none of them had given me any kind of closure.

The official report indicated my grandparents had most likely died of carbon monoxide poisoning, but this made no sense to me. I had refilled the batteries in their detector right before Keisha and I went to the Mississippi Magnolia for the weekend. If the batteries had been low, Grandma would have heard the detector beeping and replaced them or fixed it altogether.

The chief was starting to make me sweat. He was particularly interested in the time line between when I got home and found them both dead to when I called the cops. He kept asking me if there was anything else I wanted to tell him—almost like he was giving me every opportunity to confess something that wasn't there. I finally got snappy and hung up on him—something I would never have done while sober.

By the time I got to Will, I was well liquored up. Considering I had only started drinking when my grandparents died, he had never known me to drink. Whereas Keisha, Amber, or John would have been highly concerned that I was drinking, Will was entertained by it.

He was looking better than usual, and we kissed a lot on the way to the concert. He at least insisted on driving us there, and it was wonderful to have the night off from worry. My buzz was fantastic, and I didn't care about anything this evening. I made a mental note to drink more often, because right now that seemed like just about the best idea I'd ever had.

The traffic trying to park for the concert was un-believable. The crowd was full of tourists—half of whom didn't speak English, and they were all singing their favorite rock 'n' roll songs in funny accents. The crowd used lighters and cell phone flashlights to illuminate the night. However, I was so lit, I was in no position to try to light anything up as we made our way up the hill to the show.

Will and I couldn't take our hands or mouths off each other long enough to light one up. If I had been sober, I would have been a lot more mindful of the crowd around us, but I just wasn't myself tonight. So, you can imagine my surprise when Chief Stamper and a huge collection of police officers parted the crowd and headed straight towards me.

"Sorry for all the PDA, Chief Stamper. Are you going to lock me up for being a bad girl?" I teased and giggled boldly as Will's face turned white.

"No," Chief Stamper said seriously. "But I am going to lock you up for the murders of June and Louie Jackson and the abduction of Amber Jackson. And after getting a whiff of you, it seems I will also be tacking public intoxication onto your extensive list of charges."

Chapter 14

Getting arrested was not part of the plan for my hot date with Will. However, my life never seemed to turn out the way I planned, and tonight was no exception. I noticed for the first time the anger of the concert goers, who were now glaring at Will and me for disrupting their sacred annual event with our blatant disrespect.

The enthusiasm Will had worn while making out with me had been wiped clean off his face. Then I saw John Hamilton pushing through the crowd and running toward me just as fast as he could. The officers saw him coming and barricaded him back, but he began hollering my name at the top of his lungs and trying to force his way through.

I began bawling as they started to read me my rights, handcuffed me, and dragged me away. I caught a glimpse of Chief Stamper ordering his men to arrest John for interfering with official police business.

The tourists started snapping pictures and recording videos of my arrest on their phones. I didn't use social media, but I was willing to bet I would be plastered all over the Internet after today. My arrest had woken me up from my intoxication faster than any cold shower ever could. I was completely and totally humiliated.

An officer roughly shoved me into the backseat of the cop car and slammed the door on me. Just knowing I couldn't get out started to make me claustrophobic, and I felt a panic attack coming on. He ordered the crowd to clear out and then rushed me to the Memphis police station.

I was worried about John and how he was making it, but the officer wouldn't tell me anything. He dragged me into the station and kept a painful hand on me. I recognized him from one of the many house calls his crew had made when my grandparents were alive, but the camaraderie that had been there before was completely gone now. I wanted to know what had happened to Amber, but he refused to tell me, and the not knowing was gnawing at my insides and making me sick.

He shoved me into a chair while a lady with long fingernails clicked away entering all of my information into the computer before fingerprinting me, taking my unattractive picture, and booking me.

After they forced me to strip down to nothing and turn everything in to a container the size of a shoe box, I was searched inhumanely in places I did not know I had. Despite my vocal opposition, they put Grandma's ring and pocket watch in the box, too.

I cursed myself for being so careless with them and forced myself not to cry. The glimpses I caught of the other inmates were terrifying. I felt certain I didn't have enough tattoos or a long enough rap sheet to fit in here.

Before long, I was being interrogated. My focus was going in and out, as this whole nightmare just felt surreal. I had thought things couldn't get worse than my grandparents dying, but clearly I had been wrong.

"Miss Jackson, answer the question!" Chief Stamper barked at me.

"I'm sorry ... what did you say?"

I tried to zone back in.

"I said when did you concoct the plan to kill your grandparents?"

"Sir, I've never killed anybody." I answered truthfully.

"So, you're saying carbon monoxide all by itself, not you, killed them poor souls?" he asked incredulously.

"No, sir, I never said any such thing."

He might have been good with words, but to my advantage, I was, too.

"Girl, you better start talking soon if you know what's good for you!"

The Southern summer heat had seeped into the interrogation room. Chief Stamper wiped beads of sweat off of his forehead, as I tried not to stare at the sweat rings under his armpits.

"I get a phone call. I know my rights."

"You had better call a minister and get right with God." he lectured me.

"We've been over and over this. I didn't kill nobody, and I want my phone call. And I want to know what's going on with my cousin, too. I'm worried about her, and I didn't hurt her neither."

"Well, if you ain't calling the preacher man, you had better get you a real, good lawyer," he scowled at me.

"You don't get to tell me what I need. Your men were real rough with me when they cuffed and dragged me in here. If my Grandma were still alive, she'd have already put you on the prayer list at your church for the way your men have treated me."

Chief Stamper adjusted his belt buckle and stuck his finger in my face.

"Addie Jackson, you better 'fess up! I been knowing your people a long time, and nobody wants to put no woman on trial for murder—especially no pretty, little college girl like yourself."

"This conversation is over. I'm done talking to you. You'd better give me my phone call fast."

I stood my ground.

The chief glared at me as we had an old fashioned, Western stare down. He whirled on his heel as swiftly as the heavyset, aging police chief could and slammed the door behind him leaving me alone with my thoughts. I was like a duck in a pond. I appeared calm and cool on the surface, but underneath I was paddling like mad.

I bored holes through the wall where the gray paint was peeling off. After what seemed like forever, an officer finally swung open the squeaky door and motioned for me to follow him.

"I'll show you to your cell," he muttered gruffly in a clear indication I would not be getting my phone call yet. I was worried as I wondered what had happened to John, because John hated cops the way cats hated dogs.

He led me to a solitary cell, and I suddenly understood why I had been given an orange jumpsuit where some of the other inmates had been wearing green stripes. Orange jumpsuits and solitary confinement were reserved for their most dangerous criminals, so I was about to feel very alone for a very long time.

He roughly escorted me to my cell. All that I had in my room was a cold metal toilet, a hard bed, and a sink and a barred door as the only escape. I had been informed I would only get one hour out of my cell a day, and books and writing utensils were highly prized items inmates fought and stabbed other inmates to obtain. I had no idea what exactly I was supposed to do for the other twenty three hours a day I was cooped up in here for. I felt certain that slipping into madness would be at the top of the list.

I don't know how long I sat on that metal bed, but for the first time in my life I had a whole lot of time to think. It was ironic that I was locked up for several wrong things I didn't actually do. Maybe I was naive, but I wasn't completely worried about staying in here for life. I knew darn well that I didn't do what they were accusing me of, and I figured they couldn't execute me on suspicion alone. However, there was a whole heap of wrong things I had done that no one would ever convict me for.

I had been judgmental towards Geena and treated her rudely for years, and now I finally understood more of why she was how she was. Here I was locked away, and I may never even see her again to tell her I was sorry.

I had not been a good friend to Keisha for weeks. It had been all about me lately, and she had always been a fantastic friend, who deserved so much better than that.

I had also not done nearly enough to insure Amber was okay when she had reached out to me for help. Now that she had been abducted, a big portion of blame for that needed to be heaped onto my head. Because even though I hadn't had anything to do with her being picked up, I had known she was in trouble and hadn't done enough to help prevent her pain.

To top it all off with the stupidest thing I had done, I

had relocated my mind into a fog of disbelief since my grandparents' deaths. As I sat in my cell, I was detoxing from denial and sobering into reality quickly. I had been careless and reckless since Grandma and Pop had passed; they had always cared for me, but in their absence I had stopped caring for myself, and they would have been so disappointed about that.

To make matters worse, I had not protected the ring and watch that Grandma had entrusted to me, and now I had no control over who exploited them while I was locked up. I had been so very stupid, and I was filled with overwhelming regret.

I couldn't get past the feeling that if I had never stayed away for the weekend with Keisha, my grandparents would still be alive. I should have been there to save them. So, while I didn't actually kill them, maybe my negligence had led to their demise. Maybe I did deserve to be locked up after all. My mind flashed back to the last day I saw them alive, and I wondered if they knew that would be our last goodbye.

I knew that Chief Stamper had said carbon monoxide had been the cause of their deaths, but that was before I had gotten picked up for murdering them. So, if the cops' latest theory was that somebody had killed them, and I didn't do it, that raised the question as to who did.

I reminisced about memories of Pop at the young age of seventy, chasing after a thief, who stole his car. I remembered how agilely Grandma could climb up in Pop's big truck and drive it like it was nothing. I thought about how in spite of their health problems they had always lived like they were invincible, and they had done this so well that I had grown to believe they were untouchable, too.

It felt like I had woken up for the first time since they had passed. I no longer believed something as common as carbon monoxide would have ever been strong enough to take them down.

My mind raced, and the hours ran together. I didn't know how long I had been in there, and I was already losing track of time. I finally grew so tired that I dozed for a bit, and for the first time since their deaths, I dreamed of Grandma. It was a flash back to a conversation we had had long ago, and it made me happy and sad at the same time.

I had confided in her throughout the years about my dreams of my mysterious guy, Gavin. I had just woken up from another night of crazy, recurring dreams. I had been crying in my sleep, so Grandma woke up and shook me until I finally came out of it.

"My chest is caving in; I feel like I'm dying," I gasped.

"Addie, just calm down. Breathe in and out of your belly like this," Grandma had firmly advised, as she poked her finger into her belly button trying to give me some sort of twisted relaxation demonstration.

"See, Addie? You're okay; you're not dying." she consoled me.

"I can't catch my breath. I feel like I'm going to pass out."

"Here, child, take this tissue, and hush your crying. Bless your heart."

She patted me sympathetically. I clutched the wall and raggedly gulped in air.

"This is awful; I feel like I'm having a heart attack. Why do they have to feel so real?"

"Get up, and follow me into the kitchen. I'm going to fix you a cup of hot tea, and you're going to drink it!" she reproached me sternly. Grandma padded into the kitchen with her bunny house shoes on her feet and her arms guiding me. After I had consumed my cup of tea and stopped shaking she pestered me into talking about my dream.

"I dreamed I was downtown with Keisha when I got approached by the hot mystery man. It was a complete nightmare. I tried to ignore him, but he was hard to miss."

"Now Addie, why in the world would some hot guy approaching you be considered a nightmare? I have dreams about washing endless loads of your Pop's smelly socks. Them loads is piling higher and higher, and them socks is smelling worse and worse. So, if you want to trade dreams, I'm all yours. I could use a good looking, younger guy in my life; your Pop just gives me one headache after another."

"Well, if I ever meet this guy, you can have him, Grandma," I chuckled.

Grandma poured herself a cup of tea, too, and sat down.

"Child, you are young and naïve," Grandma snorted. "Give me the dirt already!" she demanded as she goggled like a thirteen year old girl.

"Well, the next thing I know, he's right beside me, and

I'm looking up into his gorgeous face. He looks like a Greek god, but he looks like trouble, too. It was so bizarre that I forgot to breathe. I never act like that around guys, but something was pulling me toward him like a magnet."

Grandma started fanning herself and swooned, "Lord, go on. Don't stop now!"

"So, he introduced himself, and said his name was Gavin. So, I told him my name, too. He said he wanted a tour guide to show him around town, so I asked him what he was into, and he said right now he was into me . . ."

"Oohh, now it's getting good again!" Grandma squealed.

"I tried to tell him that I'm not big on going out, so he'd probably do better picking up one of the local party girls." I rolled my eyes at her and continued. "But then he says he had hoped I would show him some of Memphis's famous Southern hospitality and that he's disappointed that I don't have better manners."

"Humph! Now you lost my interest again. My grand-baby's got great manners—who does he think he is anyway?"

"Well, then I scowl right at him, but he's got the most incredible cloudy blue eyes I've ever seen."

"Ooohh, child, I'm all ears again." She widens her eyes at me.

"So, he says it's a shame he can't spend more time with me since this is the most interesting conversation he has had in a very long time."

"Of course it is! Nobody outshines my girl! What'd you say back to him?"

"I told him that if this was the most interesting conversation that he's had here so far then I felt sorry for him, because he was not that interesting."

"Oh no, you didn't! Addie Marie Jackson! No wonder that man thought you were rude! What is the matter with you?"

Suddenly, she whooped me upside the head with her newspaper.

"Ow! Lay off! Look, I am not interested in him or anybody else. Relationships are just one more stressor I don't need in my life, so shooting him down early was the right thing to do."

"Loving somebody else and having him love you back is one of the best things in life," Grandma lectured as she shook her head. "Love is not a stressor; it's one of the most important things to live for!"

"Well, I just don't think I'm cut out for all of that anyhow," I said softly as I tucked my head and leaned back out of her newspaper range.

"Doll, you're underestimating yourself again," she replied gently and looked at me sadly.

"Would you believe I had that stupid dream at least five times last night? If I ever meet a guy named Gavin, I'm going to run like the dickens. Just thinking about him makes me uncomfortable."

"But why, sugar?" Grandma asked in puzzlement.

"Because I just don't trust a lot of people, and I've got this line drawn inside me about how close I'll let people get. I like to keep people at a distance until I'm positive I can trust them, because I don't have the time or the energy to be upset."

I took a deep breath and exhaled as I shivered and shuddered.

"I feel like I've got too much responsibility to have a meltdown, and that dream shook me up so badly, because every time I think about Gavin, I can picture him teasing me and dancing around in front of that line."

Grandma sat there for a while before responding, and I could tell she was thinking hard. She finally just shook her head in disbelief.

"Addie, you're never going to get the right guy if you're guarding yourself like a fortress against every one you meet. Of course I don't want you to be foolish—you have to listen to your heart, your head, and your intuition about people. That's how I made the decision to choose your Pop, and as much as I give him a hard time, I know I made a good choice when I married him. But, Addie, don't be so guarded that you miss out on love, because that's what will happen if you're more worried about guarding your heart than being open to giving it to someone who would take good care of it. And I got to tell you—I like this Gavin guy. He's got spunk and something else I can't quite put my finger on, so, when you meet him, I don't want you to run."

Grandma had jumped over the line that kept people from getting to my insides. She was looking back at me from the other side of that line, and I was still kicking. I was completely exposed and vulnerable with her, and apparently, I had been this way all along, and I just thought I had hidden it better. I was stunned, and my eyes started welling up with tears. Grandma gazed at me compassionately with her sad eyes, as she spun her blue starred ring around her finger like she often did when she was concentrating on something.

"Addie, you're so used to toting your load by yourself that you're not comfortable letting anybody else tote it with you," she spoke kindly. "You know, you don't have to be in control all the time—nobody is. And trying to stay in control all the time keeps you from missing out on the surprises life can bring you."

"You knew I had been messed up, and I just thought I was hiding it better."

"It didn't matter though, hon," she spoke with a trembling voice as she teared up, too. "It didn't change a thing for you with me. I'm so proud of you that I can't even see straight."

"I know you're right, and I know what you mean, but I just don't like it." I exhaled and dabbed my eyes. "Relationships are messy enough, and romantic relationships are ten times more complicated. And since relationships involve people I don't have any control over, that scares me. I like to be in control, and I try to stay calm and collected, so I didn't like the way that dream made me feel one bit."

"You're going to be okay, kiddo." Grandma patted my hand. "I promise."

"Maybe I'll be a nun; they have a lot of restraint. And no one expects them to be anything but disciplined and serene. They serve God and the church, and their lives are intentionally simple and drama free."

Grandma's mouth dropped open, and the corners of her mouth twitched.

"A nun...that's your big plan?" she inquired dubiously.

"Yep, I think I could be a nun."

"But, Addie...we're Methodist."

"Yeah, I guess that might be a problem."

"A habit would swallow up your small stature, and it sure wouldn't do your figure any justice."

"Yeah, you're probably right." I conceded.

"And don't you think that taking orders from a priest all the time would most likely get old? I mean, if you want to live your life with no voice and just take orders from a man every day and have nothing to your name, you could just live with your Pop for a few years. I'll go on a cruise to Mexico, and you can serve God here while I serve myself some fruity drinks with umbrellas in them. Yep, I can see it now. Me on a big, fancy yacht. Waves splashing over my toes. Great view of the beach. Cabana boy feeding me grapes. Yep, it could really be a good life—for me at least."

"Well, Grandma, you just keep on enjoying your fantasy. All I know is that I'm going to stay extra busy all week to shake that dream. I will stay happily single for the rest of my days."

"We'll see, child." Grandma raised her eyebrow doubtfully at me. "We'll see."

I didn't know why Grandma had encouraged me to trust Gavin, but considering her trust issues with people in general, I couldn't forget her advice. I didn't know how I was supposed to ever meet him or even if he actually existed, but my life was getting stranger by the day, so I had just about concluded that anything was possible by this point.

I woke up distressed to find that I was still in my jail cell and was sad to have returned from my dream to my miserable reality. I kind of wished I had become a nun, because maybe then I could cry, "Sanctuary!" and barricade myself in a Catholic cathedral as a safe haven from prison. Orange was really not my color, and jail cells were not made for those of us with claustrophobia.

So, to say I was furious about my plight would have been the understatement of the year. I was curled up in a ball on the bench in my cell with my back facing the hallway. I felt like a fish out of water there with all the female inmates wearing tattoos and frowns the way most people I knew wore blush. I didn't know how I would last a night there much less the rest of my days.

I started wondering if the warden would give me a bed sheet and how hard it would be to hang myself with it if he did. I didn't really mind the thought of dying anymore—anywhere that Grandma and Pop were would be heaven to me.

I sat there reevaluating my life when some prison worker slid a tray of slop into my cell, but I didn't touch any of it. At some point hunger would make me consume it, but I wasn't that desperate yet. I wondered what my family and friends were doing and whether they had heard what had happened to me. I hoped someone out there would bail me out, but I didn't know who would have the means to or who would care enough to go to all the trouble.

Suddenly I heard some wardens talking and walking down the hallway. The smell of warm apple pie wafted down the walkway, and after the offer of slop for dinner, the whiff of baked goods was amazing.

I could tell that the jailers were escorting someone down...to my cell. I looked up to see a dark silhouette surrounded in light from the dull bulbs along the walkway. His presence filled up my room. I knew he was no angel, but even Lucifer had appeared as an angel of light before he fell from heaven. It was like heaven's gates had opened up in the midst of my hell. Of all the people I had expected to visit me in prison, Gavin certainly wasn't one of them.

He leaned up against the bars and wrapped his hands around them as he slid his face in between them to stare longingly at me. It was strange to see a vision as actual human flesh; none of my dreams had ever truly done him justice. All of my words eluded me, and I mentally drank up the hope he was providing to me just by being there.

I pinched myself to make sure I wasn't dreaming, and I was giddy to feel the pain that told me this was real. Neither of us spoke, and I wondered if he knew me or if it was possible he had ever dreamed about me, too.

I was afraid to say a word for fear he would disappear like a mirage. I was so embarrassed for anyone to see me in a jumpsuit—especially him. But when I looked into his eyes I could see how he gazed at me like I was the Mona Lisa, and he wanted to remember every last detail of my face.

"Addie, I'm Gavin," he introduced himself to me in a voice that was as smooth as velvet.

I was speechless and could not stop staring at him.

"It's nice to meet you," he tried again.

Silence on my part.

"I'm here to break you out. Are you ready to leave?" he asked gently.

"Am I ever?!" I blurted out. All it had taken were those few promising words from him for me to find my voice again. I noticed the corner of his mouth twitch up in a mischievous grin. He looked like hotness and hell on wheels personified.

"I came to put a ring on your finger."

"Say what?" I blurted out again being as awkward as I usually felt.

He pulled a ring of the warden's keys out of his pocket, which he held out dramatically towards me and asked in a teasing tone, "Would you do me the honor, my dear?"

"How were you able to pull this off?" I asked in a mixture of admiration and curiosity.

"I made a deal with the judge. He didn't want to set bail on you, so we made a trade instead."

"How were you able to convince him to do that?"

"Let's just say I can be very ... persuasive," he said softly. I mentally recalled the dream I had had of him where I consented to a business proposal from him without any idea as to what I was agreeing to.

"Then you'll have to work something out to help John, too."

"It's already been taken care of, my dear. We're headed to spring him now. Are you ready to go?" he teased as he swung the jailer's keys around his fingers. Those keys looked like the last glass jar of sweet tea on a muggy, Memphis day.

I grinned in excitement at him, and he grinned back. He started to open the door, and I immediately felt embarrassed about my appearance.

Then I remembered how lucky I was to still be alive, and I decided looking shabby for my first encounter with Gavin was better than being dead. He unlocked the door and made a sweeping gesture with his hand to indicate the walkway toward freedom was wide open.

I felt like I could breathe again just stepping out of that cell. Gavin whistled a haunting, eerie tune I was not familiar with as he led the way down the cold, white corridor past the cells stacked with prisoners, who all looked much more intimidating than myself. He turned past rows of bars toward a different area of the facility until I noticed the population of prisoners had shifted from female to male.

All of the convicts watched me with interest and reacted to Gavin in fear. Gavin ran into some wardens, who asked him a lot of questions about what he was doing with me and why I was out. He whispered in all of their ears, and whatever he said shocked and startled them.

To my amazement, they all apologized for having bothered him and permitted us through. I wondered what kind of spell he had cast on them, and I was immediately impressed.

It wasn't long before we walked up on John. The relief he displayed from catching a glimpse of my face was immediately replaced with a mixture of shock and fear when he saw Gavin.

"How are you out, and what the heck is he doing here?" John asked incredulously.

"We're breaking you out, jail bird," Gavin said smoothly.

"What mischief did you create to pull this off?" John inquired suspiciously.

"Do you want out or not, John?" Gavin questioned him as he showed him the keys to entice him to cooperate.

The temptation was effective, and John conceded, "All right, man. Get me out of here."

I didn't know how Gavin had pulled all of this off, but right now I was too relieved to care. After more whispering with the wardens, Gavin walked us to our boxes to retrieve our personal belongings. I was thrilled beyond relief to find the ring and pocket watch were still there. Maybe there was hope after all.

We walked out of the prison walls together when Gavin turned to me and asked, "Where to, my dear?"

"We've got to rescue Amber from her abductors," I said with determination and without any hesitation. "I bet the Skullbangerz have her."

"I agree we need to get her back, but I think you'll be surprised to know that she's not with who you think she is," Gavin said.

"What is that supposed to mean?" John snapped clearly as caught off guard about this new twist as I was.

"It means she is not in the company of that thug, Chris.," he said soberly. "She's being held by Hoodoo Helen the conjurer instead."

My heart dropped as the visual of the terrifying hoodoo witch doctor presented itself in my mind. I didn't know where she had gotten all of the bones she used for jewelry, but I hoped she didn't think Amber's were available for her collection.

If one hair was harmed on my cousin's head, I would be getting picked up for murder again soon, and this time the charges wouldn't be false.

Chapter 15

Getting broken out of prison from a guy I've been dreaming about my entire life? Strange. Finding out that Amber had been abducted by a conjure doctor, who has been following me around for weeks? Bizarre. Figuring out how to spring my favorite cousin from the clutches of a psychotic woman? Unbelievably challenging.

Gavin was driving John and me to Hoodoo Helen's in his vintage black ride. Being around him made me want to take a bite out of an apple, and after all the slop I had been turning down in jail, I was starving. He tossed to-go bags to John and me with take-out from town.

We opened them up to find catfish, black beans, and cucumber salad, which were to die for. After finishing off the food, I felt somewhat better. A shower would have made my day, but I was still relieved at Gavin's next announcement.

"I took the luxury of grabbing some clothes for you two. I figured you wouldn't want to break Amber out of captivity looking like jail breaks yourselves," Gavin announced before handing a pile of clothes to each of us.

I was taken off guard to see that he had pulled out the same pair of jeans, which was holding the Indian coin the garage intruder had left behind weeks ago. I wondered if this was deliberate or accidental, but I was not about to ask. I slid my hand in the pocket to find it was still there—almost like it had been waiting for me.

"I don't know how I feel about you going through my unmentionables," John sniffed a bit defensively.

"Oh, not to worry. Yours weren't anything to write home about. Yours, on the other hand," Gavin nodded to me, "were quite nice, I must say."

"How exactly did you manage to get a hold of my drawers anyway?" John snapped at him.

"Obviously I had to break into the house," Gavin said as if he had just remarked that the weather was sunny today.

"What gives you the right to go into my place?"

"Who said I broke into your house? She had plenty of your things at her home, so there was no need to go to yours," Gavin thumbed my direction. "And you, my dear, need to get your security system fixed. That thing doesn't work at all."

"You better drive not dish or dictate, devil man," I confronted Gavin behind narrow eyes.

He laughed evilly and put the car into high gear.

I was thankful for the clothes, the food, the presence of Grandma's ring and pocket watch, and I was surprised about the Indian coin. If we could only manage to spring Amber, the next two things on my to-do list were to check my mail and figure out how to use this ring and pocket watch to help our hazardous situation.

I turned on my cell phone, which began buzzing with messages. I saw one very important person's name pop up several times, so when Keisha started calling my phone at that exact moment, naturally I felt compelled to pick up.

"Keisha!" I exclaimed.

"Addie! What the heck is going on? Are you okay? How can I help?"

I hated to talk about everything with the two new men in my life sitting right beside me, but it would have been unfair to have kept her in the dark any longer.

"Everything is okay now, I promise. I don't need a thing."

"You don't need anything?! Well, I don't know who you think you're fooling, but it sure ain't me! You're all over the news for getting taken to jail, and Amber's been abducted right after she got run off the road. Your grandparents died less than a month ago, and even though we've been best friends since Pre-K, you barely call me back anymore. This is me you're talking to, so don't go telling me you don't need anything! What is wrong with you?"

Like me, Keisha's accent showed her true Southern roots when she got upset. I squirmed in my seat feeling uncomfortable by the blunt attacks, but I could not dispute the fact that all of her questions were founded. There was no doubt that my behavior had been completely out of character since my grandparents' deaths. So, I answered her as calmly and honestly as I could.

"Well, I got drunk at the concert with Will."

"You're back with Will?" she interrupted me.

"No, I'm not back with him ..." I said before Gavin interrupted me.

"Who are you not back with?" he snapped a little too defensively.

"Who is that?" Keisha asked.

"Oh, um, that's Gavin ..."

"The devil? Oh my word! Addie, where are you? I'm

coming to get you!"

"Whoa, hold on. Look, I'm trying to tell you I made a bad decision getting drunk in public the other day, and Chief Stamper showed up with his guys and arrested me on charges of murdering my grandparents and abducting Amber and . . ."

"What the heck? That's ridiculous! I knew you had gotten picked up, but I didn't know what was going on. My Dad's been trying like crazy to bust you out."

"Tell him I appreciate that—so much more than you know. But Gavin made a deal with the judge and got John and me out."

"John got locked up, too?!" she exclaimed.

"Yeah, for interfering with the cops when they were trying to pick me up."

"Well, he's a heck of a lot better than Will then," she said wryly. "As soon as you got picked up, he plastered the whole story on social media. Talk of your drunken arrest is all over campus. I think he was more interested in having interesting gossip than doing anything productive to get you out. Oh, Addie, you were right about him. I should have listened to you. I'm so sorry."

"Keisha, I owe you a huge apology. I have been so caught up in my own issues that I have been such a bad friend lately. I'm so sorry I've been so sorry. I promise to do better—I swear it."

"So, I want to know...are you dating this John guy?"

"What? No. He's like..." I cupped the phone trying unsuccessfully to be discreet as I struggled to explain my feelings for him. "He's like the overprotective, big brother

I never got to have."

"Who's your brother?" John asked curiously.

I snapped in irritation at both of them.

"Can I not have a conversation without the two of you butting in every five seconds?"

"Well, I'm not completely convinced he exists. Every time anybody else comes around, he disappears," Keisha noted wryly. She took a deep breath as if stopping herself from another flood of emotions before she proceeded more cautiously, "Addie, you promised me ... you promised you wouldn't keep me in the dark."

"And I won't," I promised even though I wasn't sure if that was a promise I could keep. "I've just been having a hard time handling things for myself, and it's been easier to let John take care of things for me'

It was a lame explanation for keeping my distance from her.

"Why you need him to take care of things for you?" Keisha interrupted me. "You got friends and family, who love you, and you're pushing all of us away. You don't even know this guy!"

My anger started to boil irrationally. Keisha didn't know anything about John, but the truth of the matter was that I certainly didn't know much about him either. Inside my head I counted to ten before responding.

"Keisha, I know my behavior has been confusing lately. I'm sorry I haven't been more present, but I've honestly been depressed," I confessed even though I was embarrassed for John and Gavin to overhear this admission. "You know I don't like asking for help from anybody—even from y'all. But John gives me help anyway and doesn't take 'no' for an answer. He's the executor of Grandma's and Pop's estate, and he's been a tremendous help. I need you to trust me on this one, okay?"

"Addie, I'm always here for you. You know that. Just please take care of yourself, or let one of us help you if you get to where you can't. That's all I'm saying …"

"I will. I promise." I nodded in consent, not that she could see me do that over the phone. I hung up and cleared my throat awkwardly. Gavin turned on the radio to try to cure the awkward silence, and a local blues band was playing. It was hard not to stare at him, but I controlled myself as best as I could.

"I hope you have a game plan for our escape," I said to Gavin.

"Oh, trust me. Hoodoo Helen has a good reason for having Amber, and the best thing about the conjurer is that she can always be bought with a price," Gavin said. "If she's got your cousin, it might actually be to keep her safe from other people since the two of you are quite valuable."

I reflected on this new possibility.

"So, let's say her having Amber is actually to protect her, and she's keeping her safe instead of kidnapping her. What if we could pay her to do an incantation to protect Amber and me? We're the only people being affected by this danger as far as we know. I feel like we're playing a game of Russian Roulette with all the people trying to murder the two of us. Or is that crazy since she might cast a spell to hurt us instead?"

"Hmmm ... very interesting idea. I'm surprised your grandparents never thought of doing this for the two of you."

"Maybe they did, and Grandma never told me about it." I stated.

I had had several dreams about the hoodoo lady, but I don't know what the outcome of those dreams were. Considering my recurrent dreams typically came true, it seemed inevitable that Helen and I were destined to meet whether I wanted to meet her or not.

Even if Helen was helping Amber, I would naturally have concerns about confiding in someone, who could be bought by the highest bidder. I stuffed the ring and pocket watch even deeper into my pants pocket to hide them from Helen, who sounded like the kind of person, who would exploit them in a Memphis minute.

"We could tell her that you need a spell of protection, because we suspect foul play in your grandparents' deaths and that Amber and you continue to experience threats," Gavin suggested.

"Addie, all that does is open the door for some hoodoo doctor to ask what those people are after and to start poking around to try to figure out why your family is so important," John pointed out.

We hemmed and hawed and talked back and forth about pros and cons. My dreams had showed me how powerful she was, so I felt strongly that she could offer us some form of immunity. Now that Amber had been threatened, it seemed that keeping everyone safe should be our top priority. We traveled quietly, and half an hour later with clean clothes and a full belly, we were almost to Hoodoo Helen's.

"Addie, are you okay?" John asked me.

"Shhh—I'm praying," I whispered.

"Why are you praying?"

"I'm praying every prayer of deliverance I have ever heard, and you should pray some, too."

"I believe in packing heat over prayer." he said somberly.

"Well, today, John, you need to pack *and* pray."

Gavin continued to drive far north of the city off into the country down a winding road. He turned onto a dirt road and crept slowly along the shaded, dusty path.

"We're here," I whispered.

"How do you know we're here?" Gavin asked.

I didn't answer him, because I was having a serious case of déjà vu. Everything looked exactly like I had dreamed. We drove outside of a rural town I had never visited before and pulled up at a decrepit, wooden house with crooked shutters, which swung and creaked in the wind.

"Whoa, seems like she could take a break from all of her hoodoo voodoo to do a little work around this place!" John said. "We better be careful going inside—it appears her porch is caving in. The steps are rotted, too; they look like they used to be painted gray, but they're so spotty, it's hard to tell."

"Watch out for that cat!" I warned John as he stepped out of the car. He narrowly missed stepping on a black cat, who was hissing at him.

"Whatever luck the hoodoo doctor was trying to secure by keeping that feline around has certainly not helped the aesthetics around this place."

"What kind of trees are those?" I asked.

"I don't know, but they are the biggest and oldest looking trees I've ever seen," John said wide eyed. "They're black as night and not a single leaf on any of them! This whole area looks like it got burned in a wildfire, and the witch doctor kept right on living here without even noticing."

We walked toward the dimly lit house wondering if we were about to meet a friend or a foe. As soon as we stepped onto the porch, her front door creaked open, and there stood Hoodoo Helen in the flesh.

Before I could prepare myself, she was sashaying towards us. She was a gaunt African American lady with hollowed, sunken eyes, and her flamboyant attire had a disturbing presentation despite the bright colors. I was confused since I didn't see Amber with her, and my surprise at her absence both elated and terrified me.

As I watched her approach, I had an impulse to slip on Grandma's ring and shake her hand. Just toying with the idea made me sweat, but I made a split second decision to leap before I looked. I toyed with the ring before sliding it on.

I put a fake smile on, tentatively introduced all of us, and reached out to shake her gnarled hand. She accepted my handshake cautiously, and then I was blown away to find myself sucked into a terrifying moment of Helen Harrison's life.

Black smoke was suffocating me as it wrapped around me like a python. On the fringe of a fire in the midst of the fog was young Hoodoo Helen transfixed on the face of her hoodoo mentor.

Animal blood was running off the hands of her mentor as she proclaimed to Helen, "After this you are a student no more."

She painted a skull and crossbones in animal blood on the conjurer's cheeks with a brush made of feathers and bones. Then Helen consumed the animal blood out of the carcass of a raccoon. After she drained it dry, she threw the remains into the flames, as its lifeblood ran out of the corners of her mouth. She raised her arms toward the heavens and looked up with eerily black eyes. I startled out of her significant moment to find her eyes peering curiously into mine.

"I'm sorry—what were you saying?" I stammered.

She eyed me suspiciously and remarked, "I was saying I've been trying to get your attention for weeks now. I believe I have something you want. Follow me," she hissed as she swayed and led us through her front door and down a corridor, which was decorated with bizarre tribal art. Branches of dried herbs, bones, and roots filled her doorways, and they made me shudder. As I followed her, John, Gavin, and I exchanged glances before she offered us chairs covered in animal print. I had just gingerly sat down when Amber popped into the room.

"Addie! You came for me just like she said you would!" Amber squealed and hugged me.

I was immediately sucked into Amber's most

significant moment to date, which was when she had been abducted by members of the Skullbangerz. She had been surprised to see that the Skullbangerz were being aided by people, who had seemed like "some of the good guys" to her, even though she didn't know who they were.

She had been terrified and tormented until Helen showed up. Helen had cast spells and thrown dirt at Amber's attackers before making off with Amber like a hoodooed bandit. Amber had been at Helen's Hollow every since, and her creepy house had been a surprising sanctuary from her abusive abductors.

"Oh my gosh, you're alive!" I exclaimed when I came out of her significant event. I slipped my hand into my pocket and slid the ring off. Spying on Helen had felt necessary; spying on Amber had felt intrusive.

"So, what exactly do you want from me?" Hoodoo Helen hissed. "Besides the girl, of course."

"Thank you for rescuing her. You don't know what that means to me." I said swallowing a lump in my throat as I clung tightly to Amber. I was surprised that the person I feared had been the one to save the person I loved.

"No thanks are needed. Your grandparents paid your debt long ago," she replied mysteriously.

"What's that supposed to mean?" I asked her.

She eyed me steadily as she ignored my question, and I watched her mouth wondering if a forked tongue would pop out at any moment.

"I see you've met the Man. It's not like you to get involved," she remarked to Gavin, and it almost sounded like a reprimand.

"It was part of the trade," Gavin sniffed stiffly as a clear indication this was information I was not supposed to be privy to.

"We're interested in hiring you to concoct a spell of protection." John suggested carefully.

"Is that what you want?" she asked me steadily in an abrupt dismissal of John.

I was having a difficult time looking at her, much less speaking to her, as the image of her gulping the coon's blood replayed over and over in my head.

"Yes, like John was saying, um, we want a spell of protection, and we can pay you," I said with my voice fading.

"What makes you think I can help you?" she asked.

"Well, we understand you know hoodoo." I spoke carefully and cautiously. "We are in need of protection, and we are taking a chance on you."

"Yes, but why me?" she persisted. "Surely there were others you could call. I sense there is something you are not telling me,"

She frowned and stared at me willing me to go on.

I was shaking like a leaf and quickly getting drawn into her seductive gaze; she sat as still as a statue leaning towards me like the Tower of Pisa. I snapped myself out of her hypnosis as I tried to shake off the heebie jeebies. I wanted to get this meeting over with as quickly as possible. The way her words slithered together made the hair on the back of my neck stand up, and I wanted to pull away before she got close enough to bite me.

"Can you help us or not?" I asked, growing impatient.

"Yes, I can. But at some point I expect you to tell me the whole story. I don't like to be lied to."

She looked like the snake in the Garden of Eden, so her lecture about honesty felt hypocritical to me, but I was too scared to engage her any further.

"I've been dreaming about you for a while, Addie Jackson. I saw you coming long before you arrived. Can you explain that to me?"

"No," I stammered, "But maybe that's because you're supposed to help me," as I gave her the answer I hoped was true. After a brief hesitation, she accepted my response only because I gave her no other option.

She had a pungent smell in her home which made me want to lurch out of the room. I noticed John shudder a little in spite of himself when he saw the claws and animal bones in jars and baskets surrounding us. I was afraid that all of the delicious soul food I had gulped down thanks to Gavin was about to come right back up.

She had countless bottles of all sizes, shapes, and shades lined up on shelves on every side of the room. We saw legs of animals, heads of critters, skeletons, roots, dirt, sand, plants, and smoking, bubbling liquids in the vials.

There were canisters of herbs, minerals, and incense, and baskets full of candles and floor washes. Everything was stacked around the room haphazardly, and the crooked rocking chair in the corner of her room had certainly seen better days.

"Oh my gosh, if those ants get out, I'm getting out, too," John muttered under his breath as we followed Helen to the back of the house to do Lord knows what.

"What ants?" I said nervously.

"Don't you see all the nests of live ants?"

"Holy smokes!" I felt sick. I was guessing she used them for spells, but I was not about to ask. Gavin looked as cool as a cucumber through all of this. John didn't scare easy, but all of this superstitious mumbo jumbo had him rattled. Gavin looked like he was in his element, and I wondered if there was anything in the world that could scare him.

"What are all those books for?" John inquired.

"What books? Ow!" as I stubbed my toe and cried out in pain. The dust from the books engulfed me, and I hopped around and had a hacking spell. Hoodoo Helen stepped over to us, ignoring my clumsiness.

"I am well versed in hoodoo, which is also known as conjure doctoring," she explained. "I am a two-headed woman, because I am guided by a spirit, who helps me to lay tricks on people."

I was trying to follow what she was saying, but I was distracted as Amber ran into a conjure altar covered in dripping candles while trying to keep up with her.

"I can act as a spiritual doctor by praying for you, or I can help you magically without laying tricks or putting jinxes on your enemies," she continued. "Laying tricks will cost you extra, of course."

"Um, no tricks or jinxes today, but thanks for the offer."

This woman scared me half to death just making a spell to shield us—I didn't think I could handle her jinxing and laying tricks on folks.

"Suit yourself, but I could always use magic foot powder on those enemies, who are after you." she tempted me as she watched me behind hollowed eyes.

"What's magic foot powder?" Amber asked.

"It's a powder to sprinkle around your enemy's doorway. It makes him leave his home to wander the world."

"We aren't completely sure who the enemies are or where they live," I admitted feeling embarrassed. I knew the Skullbangerz had attacked us, but that didn't explain all of the other attacks on my family through the years. The gang would have had to have been working around the clock to have been responsible for all of them, and I didn't find that likely.

"That's very peculiar. But when you find them, as I expect you will, it would be helpful to have ..." she retorted eerily. "Besides, they obviously took your cousin to get your attention. They clearly don't mind doing whatever they have to do to get what they want."

John and Gavin looked at me as if to say, "This is all you—it's whatever you want to do—we wash our hands of this."

"Fine. We'll take some." Amber agreed before I could speak. If I had just been abducted, I imagine I would have taken it, too.

"Excellent," Helen said. "You'll also need silver dimes and Devil's Shoe String twigs for your shoes and for around your ankles to keep you safe."

She fished around in her cracked pots with her yellowed, curled fingernails before producing some silver dimes and twigs for us. Curiosity overcame me, as it often did, so I pulled the Indian coin that the intruder had dropped out of my pocket.

"Does this Indian coin provide safekeeping the same way those silver dimes do?" I inquired.

"Where did you get this?" she hissed. Her eyes widened dramatically, as she snatched the Indian coin from my palm.

"Some guy tried to break into my garage and dropped it on his way out."

"In hoodoo, Indian coins are used for old-time law to keep away spells." she said.

"Come again?" I asked.

"The Indian is an Indian Scout, who keeps a look-out for law enforcement to make them stay away. He is also known as the Black Hawk." she continued.

"Why does he have a hole through him?" Amber inquired.

"You are supposed to nail these coins around door frames, and the more of them you use, the more effective the spell is in keeping the law away." Helen explained like this was the most obvious thing in the world.

"So, he must have just nailed some up wherever he was staying and then accidentally dropped this one when he left my place."

"That is highly doubtful. It's much more likely that he was sending you a message," Gavin jumped in, which made me wonder yet again if his selecting the jeans with the coin in the pocket had been intentional.

"What kind of a message?"

"That the cops can't help you, because they have been hoodooed to stay away from wherever they are, so the fuzz will be of no help in finding them for you."

John spoke as if a light bulb had just come on for him. It certainly explained the cops' lack of interest and attention to our case.

"Be discerning in using this only as I have instructed, or I can not guarantee what will happen," Hoodoo Helen cautioned me as she carefully filled a bottle with magic foot powder. "Now, Addie, I really need you to tell me more about what is wrong and what you need."

I looked to John for direction, but he was distracted examining candles of Orishas dressed up like Catholic saints; I noticed that images of them were on the incense and powders here, also.

He couldn't hear me anyway over the pendulum squeaking back and forth beside one of the rows of bottles.

"Well, we're under attack, and we need ongoing safety," I responded. I had seen her dark side with my own eyes—I wasn't about to divulge any more than necessary. She studied me strenuously as if trying to pick more details from my brain, but it was apparent that was all I was going to give her for now.

"Your elusiveness is your loss," she surrendered reluctantly. "Let's begin now."

Gavin, John, and Amber crowded around me. Gavin must have picked up on my anxiety, because he reached over and took my hand. It was the first time he had ever touched me in real life; his fingers were warm—almost as if he were running a temperature.

I reflected on the dream of him lighting a bonfire with his hands, and I hoped I wouldn't go up in flames. Hoodoo Helen narrowed her eyes and stared at our hands as if filing this away for future use, but whatever her thoughts might have been, she didn't volunteer them to me anymore than I had volunteered mine to her. I scowled, because she was more observant than I would have liked, and she was picking up on things I couldn't even explain to myself.

"You'll need to mix up salt and pepper and wear it in your shoes," she instructed John and Gavin. "And for you girls," she said pointing at Amber and me, "I'm making you nation sacks."

"What? Why just us girls?" Amber asked as if she were about to go on a feminist rant.

"Nation sacks are created for women; I'm putting Queen Elizabeth root in your sack—it helps with protecting ladies. Mojos or bojos are for men or women," Helen hissed as she began gathering ingredients for our potions.

"It's imperative for all of you to keep your mojos or nation sacks on you or for you to keep them on the doorknob in your bedrooms for this to work," she explained. "Don't let anyone else touch them, because that will make them lose their effectiveness. Hoodoo can give you all kinds of powers, you know. There are spells for getting the love of your life back, spells for gambling luck, spells for having peace in your household, and psychic vision spells to help you develop the gift of psychic dreams."

My ears perked up at the mention of the psychic

dream spell. For me, sleeping was like watching train wrecks coming all night long without knowing when they were going to hit and feeling powerless to prevent them, but I didn't trust her enough to reveal any of this.

"I'm adding five finger grass to your mojo and sacks, and I'm going to chant Psalms 37 over them with your names," she continued.

"Why are you doing that?" John asked.

"The Bible is the greatest conjure book in the world, and Psalms is a particularly powerful book. Personalizing your mojo and sacks will increase their effectiveness, so I need to know your favorite Bible verses, so we can include them."

"Well actually, my favorite passage in the Bible is Psalms 91 where it talks about God providing David with protection from his enemies," I remarked. I suddenly remembered Grandma doing a weird chanting ceremony using Psalms 91 when I was younger; it was strange that I had not considered her hoodoo habits until after her passing.

"That will work. John, what about you?" Helen asked.

"I've always like the third chapter of Exodus." John responded quietly.

Without another word, Helen ripped our specified chapters out of the Bible and stirred them into our individual concoctions. I was surprised how John was able to identify his favorite part of the Bible so quickly.

"What's the third chapter of Exodus?" I whispered to

him.

"It's the part about God commanding Moses to lead his people out of Egypt; Moses is scared, but God tells him that He is on his side."

"Why is that your favorite part?"

"I don't know, but for some reason it's always captured my attention," he shrugged, but something told me he wasn't being honest with me.

"What about you?" Helen asked Amber.

"Fine." Amber sighed an exaggerated groan. "It's 'Jesus wept.'"

"You can't be serious."

"What? I don't pay much attention in Sunday School—I'm usually checking out Jack Jamison. He is so fine!" she remarked with a grin. I shook my head but felt secretly relieved to find her acting like herself again.

"Well, then Jesus is definitely weeping now," Gavin teased lightly.

"Now what Bible verse does the Man want to use?" Helen asked looking at Gavin.

"Making a sack for me is completely unnecessary, Helen ... you know that," Gavin said wryly.

"And you know that it's good energy when everyone participates. So, go ahead and tell me," Helen persisted with him.

"Psalms 139:13-16," Gavin replied quietly after a brief hesitation, and I made a mental note to look up those verses later.

"Hey," Amber whispered not so discreetly. "What does everyone keep calling him the Man? Is he some sort of boss?" I shushed her as John fought to hide a smile.

So, Hoodoo Helen cast a spell with red dust and cat's eye shell. She blended in lemon verbena, lemon grass, rye, bay leaves, and rosemary.

"This is John the Conqueror root—keep it in your pockets," she advised after handing us roots. "I have a feeling you're going to be needing wisdom, so I am including King Solomon root in your sacks to guide you on your way. Master of the Woods will give you exceptional strength, so I'm empowering you with that also. Remember to keep your mojo and nation sacks hidden, because if someone else touches them, their luckiness will be killed. You will also need to keep them watered with a liquid personal to you."

"What do you mean about watering them?" Amber asked.

"You want to water them with your own body fluids or another fluid that is particularly significant to you to insure they keep working," she replied slowly, as if talking to a child.

"Whoa, lady, you're telling me we have to water our flannel sacks and mojo with our own body fluids?" John interrupted. "Yeah, if there's some way to get invulnerability without the body fluid part, I'd be real interested in that."

Helen did not take kindly to John joking about her hoodoo voodoo, so she graced him with her scariest look yet.

"If you will recall, you hired me to keep you safe. If you want to live, do exactly as I say. Personalizing your mojo increases its effectiveness, and watering it with something that comes from you is both intimate and effectual."

I didn't think there was anything intimate about urinating, but I wasn't about to tell her that—this lady could eat me for lunch and never look back. John composed himself and cleared his throat.

"Well, I like whiskey—it's my favorite drink," he announced.

"I like coffee," I answered.

"I really like a perfume that I have with me," Amber said as she grabbed some out of her purse.

"I like green tea," Gavin remarked, as we all turned to look at him in surprise. "What? It has antioxidants—you should try it."

Hoodoo Helen whipped out bottles of coffee and whiskey. She snatched the perfume from Amber before she made a pot of green tea. When she was finished, she poured the lone liquids into our separate sacks.

"Now spit in them," the hoodoo doctor ordered as she held the sacks under our mouths.

We reluctantly spit into them, as Helen nodded in stern support.

"Now you have to write down your personal requests for what you want the hoodoo to do for you, and then I'll include your messages in your concoctions."

I wasn't sure where in this creepy, chaotic cave I was supposed to find paper and a writing utensil, but Helen was too caught up in her root working to be bothered with practicalities like that.

So, we braved her home on our own and stumbled past jars of bat dung and crocodile bones before securing a tattered notebook with an old pencil that looked like it had been sharpened with a dull knife. We all gingerly wrote down different prayers of security before handing the crooked pencil and crumpled paper back to Helen.

"I've been practicing hoodoo for a long time. We had an Indian Grandma in my family; she was Native American, and her family's magic has been passed down for generations."

"How is Hoodoo different from voodoo?" asked Amber. "I find all this very confusing."

"Voodoo is its own religion, but hoodoo traces its roots back to Christianity."

"No way," said Amber. "How do you get that?"

"People believe it all started with Moses in the Old Testament. Slaves used it to protect themselves from mistreatment by their masters. It gets mistaken for voodoo a lot, but like I said they are not the same."

"Tell me this—how did people originally get the power to practice hoodoo?" John asked, causing Gavin to look uncomfortable for the first time. "It's not like you are licensed or anything."

"A long time ago some powerful hoodoo doctors got supernatural strengths by going down to the Crossroads." she said stealing a glance towards Gavin.

"The Crossroads?" Amber answered.

"Yes, they went down to a fork in the road and met with the Man. They made trades with him for the power of hoodoo. Isn't that right, Gavin?"

Amber and John looked fearfully at Gavin before he murmured fiercely, "That's enough, Helen."

"It's time now," she announced ominously.

None of us were prepared for what happened next.

Chapter 16

Some chef's made hash with herbs; apparently Helen made hers with her hoodoo from hell. We were at the conjurer's house when she started chanting and mumbling all kinds of hoodoo mumbo jumbo as she threw eye-in-hand amulets, cat's eye shells, and angelica roots into a pot. I felt like I was seeing the world's weirdest cooking show as I watched Hoodoo Helen make strange hand motions and chant intentions and Bible verses. The smell of sulfur grew strong, and black smoke began pouring out of her brew.

Helen cupped her hands around her herbs and hissed loudly, "I charge these sacred herbs from the earth with the properties of protection to repel any negative energies that come your way. This energy goes wherever you go!"

A Western wind started whipping past me as if a funnel cloud was churning up in the middle of her twisted house. The floor began vibrating underneath our feet, and the tremors grew increasingly more terrible as she continued chanting our Bible verses in conjunction with our names and rocking back and forth.

We stumbled and staggered around before finally hunkering down in a crooked corner as jars of guts and brains fell off the shelves and shattered around us. Gavin put his arms around me, and I put my arms over my head. The aroma of apples on him was intoxicating, and it was almost enough to overpower the funky smell in Helen's house as long as I stayed pressed against him.

I pulled my hands off of my head just long enough to

catch a glimpse of the conjurer, whose eyes had rolled back in her head. She picked up handfuls of red powder and threw them at all of us. She was chewing something that resembled a root and paid no mind to the juices, which were running out both sides of her mouth. She turned away from us with outstretched arms, and I closed my eyes tightly, helplessly willing this horror to go away.

After what seemed like an eternity, the whistling wind and tumultuous tremors abruptly ceased. The witch doctor's face held a hazy expression, and she looked satisfied and only slightly less horrifying. She lit a flame and put the sacks and mojos through the flame three times with her bare hands; there was no way humanly possible she couldn't have been burned, but she didn't even flinch.

"Come and see," she hissed wildly.

"What was that? What did you do? How did you do all of that?"

"I told you I knew hoodoo . . ."

The smoke began to clear, and we stepped over all of the broken odds and ends to join her; curiosity drew me to her like a moth to a flame. She rubbed oil on the nation sacks and mojo bag and talked to them as if they were friends, who were going to keep us safe. She tied the bags up with string and evil eye beads.

"Make sure you recharge your bags weekly by watering them, praying over them, or speaking words of intention over them," she wheezed. She gave us a potato sack and filled it with charm vials, flasks, horseshoes, and a protection powder for security. She included dragon's blood oil for good luck and eucalyptus to drive away evil.

"What were you doing when you were chewing on that root?" I inquired after I had gathered enough nerve.

"Intimidating your antagonists."

"How do we know this is going to work?" Amber asked, the worry showing on her face. "What if it doesn't, and people get hurt?"

"Let us see what we shall see."

She retrieved a tall candle shaped like a cylinder and placed it on her altar with ash and incense. She lit it with a taper candle and watched it closely. She hunched over and reached for some unbroken jars of alligator and badger bones and cast them onto the floor as she began swaying and chanting.

"I read the bones. The candle burns clear, and there's little wax left, and the smoke is transparent—pure white," she reported after some time, as if that explained everything.

I felt sick but pressed her anyway.

"So ... that's good?"

"Yes, that's very good—that's a blessing, which means your request will be answered," she said, sounding pleased.

"Okay, thank you for your help . . . do you need us to help you pick up your house?" John asked.

"No, I'm used to this—you never know what will happen when you use hoodoo. Besides I nailed my house down with railroad spikes a long time ago—that way no matter what happened, my home would stay put."

"What exactly happened today?" Amber asked, still feeling shaken.

"I believe we experienced a small earthquake and a funnel cloud."

"At the same time?" asked Amber.

"Yes," said Helen.

"How could we even have an earthquake in Memphis? I thought only people in California had those."

"Memphis in near the biggest fault line in the world—we just don't have noticeable activity very often."

"Are you telling me that hoodoo caused those quakes?" I asked in disbelief.

"We have funnel clouds or tornadoes around here every year, in case you haven't noticed. Hoodoo does some very peculiar things." she said cryptically. "Now take these Addling Ashes and put them in your car."

"Okay, but why?"

"When you need them, you'll know."

I couldn't wait to leave her house. I was so nervous I felt like my knees were going to give out at any moment, and I couldn't get into the car fast enough. All I could think about was the smoke, sulfur, animal dung, and the various hoodoo powders that were all over me.

I thanked her for her help, and she said she would be sure to request a favor in return sometime soon. I agreed to help her in the future, but her maniacal grin immediately made me regret being indebted to her.

When we finally left Hoodoo Helen's bizarre home, I sprayed a whole bottle of air freshener onto all of us. I kept praying out loud and thanking God for letting us get out of there alive; I said a private prayer asking God to keep any possum ghosts or hoodooed ants from plaguing our

288

houses. We rolled the windows all the way down trying to dry off and air out.

"Oh my word, Addie! I don't know what I was expecting, but it sure wasn't anything as freaky as that!" John shivered.

"I know! I was so scared I thought I was going to pee my pants!" Amber squeaked, and we all roared with laughter.

"That would have given you some personal body fluid to water your nation sack with!" Gavin joked.

"Oh my gosh, that's disgusting. But seriously though, what was up with the earthquake and the funnel cloud? Do you think hoodoo really caused all of that?" I asked still having a hard time wrapping my brain around all of it.

"I don't know, but if that woman is capable of controlling Mother Nature, I'd hate to think what else she was capable of," John said seriously.

"The road has gotten uneven – part of it looks like it's caving in." Gavin observed. "I guess that earthquake messed up the streets."

"Holy smokes! Looks like several trees are down. Wow, this is crazy!" Amber shook her head at all of it.

So, we snickered about what we had just been through—not because it was funny but because it was terrifying. It was the kind of nervous tither you do, however inappropriate it may be, because laughing seems easier than crying at the time. I sneezed on the hoodoo powder that had just fallen out of my hair onto my nose. I was not looking forward to leaking weird hoodoo goo everywhere I went from now on; we were all going to have to find some creative waterproof containers.

We escaped the ragged road and roughed up forest to head back towards Memphis when I told Gavin we needed to take a detour by Collierville so that I could check my mail. He headed East but asked no questions, and John and I did not elaborate. I wondered if the post office would even let me in with the way I stunk to high heaven. If Geena had been here, she would have pushed her way through for me like a bull in a China shop to demand I receive service. The odds were she was at a card table though, so as usual she would be of no help.

Amber started getting calls about the tornado and the earthquake. Her friends said the quake had caused damage as close to us as the outdoor shopping center. Businesses had closed for the day, and the public was panicking buying up bottled water, generators, and flashlights like it was Hurricane Christina all over again.

There were a lot of detours with the road conditions on the way to the post office, but with some creative maneuvering, Gavin finally got me there. The gang stayed in the car while I walked inside to check my mail. Upon opening my box, I was thrilled to find another long white envelope lying there waiting for me. I opened it and found bittersweet comfort in stroking Grandma's scrawling penmanship.

Dear Addie,
My child, I know what it feels like to lose the people you care about. Just before Moses and Zephorrah expired after a losing battle with Yellow Fever, they used their last bit of energy to cast a spell of protection over me.

Their hoodoo terrified me, but the intention of the incantation was to keep their secrets and me safe. Moses and Zephorrah said an invocation so that as long as the ring was in my possession, no unnatural death could ever come to me, my future spouse, my children, or my grandchildren. They said that the ring would have to be kept on me or in the building I was in at all times for the spell to provide safekeeping for my family and me.

Moses and Zephorrah gave me strict instructions to give the ring and watch to their only known living descendant, Mary Smith, who lived in Jackson, Mississippi. Their orders to me were that as soon as Mary reached the age of eighteen years I would contact her and reveal everything to her. At the point in time I was given these instructions, Mary was only nine years old, so I had to keep the ring and clock under my protection until Mary was old enough to take them.

They told me that until I was able to pass the ring and clock onto their descendant, if the ring and watch were to ever leave my possession or my home without me, my family would be an open target to those of ill intent, who wished to acquire the ring to abuse its power and exploit others. My experience with the pocket watch was that it seemed to be useless without the ring, but I could never be sure of this since the only people, who understood the capabilities of the pocket watch were deceased.

Keeping such a big enigma under wraps was a lot of responsibility for me to carry at such a young age. However, Moses and Zephorrah had confidence that I could handle it, and unfortunately for me, I was the only person nearby that they could trust. They told me they expected me to always use what they had entrusted to me for good and to keep those tools from evil. But ultimately, they hoped that their descendant could accomplish what they had been unable to – for the sake of their family and enslaved people everywhere.

Right after the spell was finished and this responsibility was assigned to me, Moses and Zephorrah passed away. I was left all alone with no one to confide in about this bizarre information that had been passed on to me. So, you and I are not so different, my child. I have had many fascinating experiences using the ring and watch over the years. I have always grieved losing my friends, but I have continued on with daily life as much as possible.

I grew older, and Mary Smith did, too. As promised, nine years after Moses and Zephorrah's deaths, I snuck out of my parents' house, and I hitchhiked all the way down to Jackson, Mississippi looking for their descendant. I knew the harsh consequences I could expect to receive from my father when I returned, so I fully intended to make that trip count. I tracked down the Goodwin family, who reportedly owned Moses and Zephorrah's only living blood line.

Naturally the Goodwins were wary and suspicious of a single girl from Tennessee, who had a peculiar interest in one of their slave girls. I explained that my family had owned some of Mary's family and that they had died, so I was trying to relay the sad news to her. I lied and said that I was in Mississippi visiting relatives. I told them that I was just trying to do the good Christian thing by passing on this bad news to the poor soul. The Goodwins scratched their heads a lot and assumed things must be handled much differently with slaves in Tennessee.

Unfortunately, Moses and Zephorrah's dying wishes never came to fruition, because the Goodwins told me that Mary had died in childbirth the previous year, so they would be unable to help me. I inquired about the child Mary had carried, but the Goodwins said that the baby had died in labor as well. I was devastated, because I knew that now this burden would stay on my shoulders forever, and it was one I had never wanted to carry. I felt like I had failed Moses and Zephorrah, and I had no idea what to do with the ring and the clock. I was afraid that everything Moses and Zephorrah had tried to accomplish would be for naught, and there was no one to ask for guidance with the next step.

So, I did the only thing I knew to do. I guarded the ring and watch carefully. I grew up, married, had children, and confided in no one but Pop about the ring and the clock. Time and time again evil people tried to steal them to do wrong with them, but each time they tried to, bad things would always happen to them. Everyone who tried to hurt my family ended up dead or harmed to the point that they were no longer a threat. The curse on the ring was so strong that not only did it protect our family from harm, it insured no danger would ever come to us from that source again.

I had one big slip up with the ring. It goes down as my greatest mistake in life. I had gone into a diabetic coma one time, and this required me to go into the hospital. Your Pop got my jewelry box with my pocket watch, so he thought my ring was in there with it. Unfortunately, Rosy's grandson, Billy, had gotten a hold of it and was playing with it, so it never made it to the hospital with me. Billy put it on, and then he went into Rosy's garage and took their car completely apart. Strangely enough, after separating the entire vehicle, Billy was able to put it back together without a single part out of place. Rosy was so flabbergasted that she grounded Billy for six months, because she didn't know how else to react. Rosy never stopped talking about that in all the years she and I have been neighbors. She thought God had blessed Billy with an unnatural inclination to work with cars, and she said she thought it was a sign that this was God's purpose in life for him. Naturally, I never told her any different.

While I was at the hospital in that diabetic coma, Pop was praying beside me unaware that the ring was with Billy. Addie, at that exact point in time, your baby sister, Amy, got run over by a hit-and-run driver and died.

Honey, I'm sorry for all of this. Your life ain't never going be the same again. The world will look totally different now. I know you hoped getting your questions answered would provide you with piece of mind, but there ain't no peace in any of this, child. This is why I always tried to warn you to be careful what you wish for...

I love you, Addie. I always will. I promise to write again soon. Please be safe.

Love,
Grandma

All I wanted to do was to go back to the way things were. Since that was impossible, I wanted to sleep until I didn't feel like my world had collapsed on top of itself. I had images of masked men carrying red flannel sacks full of coffin nails and graveyard dirt making threats against my life. There's nothing in this world I wouldn't give for just one more day with Grandma and Pop.

I hid the letter in my pocket and returned to Gavin's car where the crew was waiting on me.

"Well?" John asked curiously.

"I want to go home," I stated firmly.

John frowned, clearly frustrated that I was not letting

him in, but Gavin put his car into high gear and headed towards my house. Country music blared over his FM radio, and I was grateful for the distraction as the detours to get home with the road damage were significant.

Amber took phone calls the whole way there from people, who were worried about her, and to her credit, she gave us props for springing her out. After my recent arrest, I figured I could use all the positive public relations I could get. I was so worn out I just wanted to rest my head on Gavin's massive shoulder and go to sleep. However, considering I had not met him in real life prior to today, that seemed highly inappropriate, so I restrained myself.

We finally made it to my place, and I asked John to stay, because we had a lot to work on. Gavin offered to take Amber home, and with her being as boy crazy as she was, she grinned like a Cheshire cat about the possibility of riding in the front seat beside him.

Gavin walked me to the front door, promised to see me again soon, and carefully stroked my cheek just once before leaving. It wasn't much, but it made my heart stop for a moment.

When John and I got inside, I pulled the ring out, and I rolled it around in the palm of my hand. Every hair on my body stood up, and I looked at John who met my gaze solemnly. My hands had always looked so much like Grandma's, and today they did more so than ever.

"May I?" I asked John as I tentatively held out my hand for his.

He took a deep breath and gently placed his big, rough palm into mine.

I slipped on Grandma's ring, and immediately, I was watching him on the day that my grandparents had died. He was walking through my front door and glimpsing me for the first time. I surveyed myself as he saw me so slight and vulnerable, and he was overwhelmed with compassion and concern. He seemed as upset about the loss of them as I was. It was almost as if he was trying to share a burden with me and that this was a culminating point in his life. As soon as I dropped his hand, I was immediately back in my living room with him.

"How long was I gone?" I asked him.

"Five seconds...it's always five seconds..." he said.

"What did you see?" he asked, and his face held a furrowed brow. I shrugged and tucked my head to look down at my feet, which were twitching. He persisted in asking me until I finally told him.

"I went to when you first met me...to when you knew they had died. It was when you accepted your role in sharing this burden. I sincerely do appreciate the fact that I'm not in this alone, John, and I thank you for that."

His face held an expression that I just couldn't place, and then he leaned forward and held out his hand to me.

"May I?" he asked.

I was curious as to what he would see, and since I felt I had nothing to lose, I gave him the ring. He slipped it onto his pinky, and the fit was so tight that it would only go down to his first pinky joint. I nervously held out my palm to his, and he took it carefully. He stared off into space blankly as I counted to five, and then just like clockwork, he came back to the present.

Overwhelmed with curiosity, I blurted out, "Where did you go?"

"To when you found them ..." he spoke with sadness as his voice trailed off; he did not need to say anymore for me to know he was referring to the discovery of my dead grandparents. "Addie, I'm so sorry. I know how awful that was for you."

John was too close to my core for comfort, and he must have picked up on my uneasiness, because he changed the conversation as he said, "We know your Grandma talked about how it enhances natural abilities. So, what are your natural abilities? It would help you to know ..."

"My natural abilities?" I said. "Um, yeah...I don't think I have any."

"Of course you do, Addie. Everyone has natural abilities. Think about it. What are yours?" he asked.

I sighed and chewed on my bottom lip.

"Okay ... well...honestly, I have no idea."

"I think you're pretty perceptive, and I think you should pay a little more attention to your grand-parents ... focus on their dying ... and then tell me what you come up with."

I didn't like the idea of having to reflect on my deceased loved ones again. I felt sad enough about losing them without intentionally focusing on them. But I took a deep breath, put the ring on, and gave it my best shot.

I closed my eyes and watched a movie reel in my mind of my life with them. I saw them throughout every stage of my life—always present, even when they were in the background. I witnessed events I had never noticed in great detail before. I sensed Pop's protectiveness of me, Grandma's distrust for others, and the enormous amount of pride they held in who I was. How strange it was to have had so much go on with them that I had never noticed until now.

I forced myself to focus on them all the way through their death, the funeral, and the events surrounding all of that. And then I started to piece something together that I hadn't completely seen before. I perceived how healthy and happy they were on the day they died.

I was fully aware of how organized the house had looked. I noted how cold and lifeless they were when I had returned to find them dead. I realized that the house had been disheveled like someone had torn it apart as if his or her life depended upon it.

I understood the fear in Amber's eyes when she talked about how everything had been fine when she had left them—as if part of her thought something didn't add up either. Then suddenly I knew with absolute certainty what I had begun to suspect—that even though I had no evidence to back it up, their deaths had been no accident.

I was overflowing with emotions; I was enraged and distraught. I felt paranoid about who might have hurt them, and my heart ached at the thought of them having suffered for even a moment. I didn't understand how the police could have suspected me (the person who loved them most) and yet they had neglected looking into one of their many enemies. I couldn't comprehend how they had missed this and why they hadn't found whoever had done this to them—to us! I didn't know why the cops hadn't questioned me to try to help them locate the real killers after my release. I was incensed with rage, and I jerked the ring off my finger as I was overcome with a feeling of absolute authority.

"Somebody killed them. Somebody did this to them. Their deaths were intentional."

"I agree, and I wondered if you would come to believe that as well," he said sadly.

"I don't understand why they aren't searching for who could have poisoned them. I had just bought them a new carbon monoxide detector, and I changed the batteries right before I left with Keisha. It would have started beeping if there had been a problem. This doesn't make any sense. Why didn't Grandma pick up on the problem? Maybe the police messed with the batteries?" I scrunched up my face in confusion. "Maybe they were trying to see if it was working or why it wasn't operating correctly?"

"Addie, the cops were not interested in whether or not your carbon monoxide detector was working," he spoke gently. "The police wouldn't have tampered with it. But if what you're telling me is true, someone else did tamper with it, and sometime over the weekend your grandparents died of carbon monoxide poisoning. That's too strange to be a coincidence, don't you think?"

I had to admit that the odds of this being accidental were pretty far-fetched.

"Okay, so if it was intentional, who on earth would have done this to them? And how could this have happened—a death by natural causes if they had protection from the ring?"

"How do you think it could have happened to them?"

Then suddenly I knew. I saw their ransacked house. I remembered Geena's guilty face as she talked about stealing the ring to pawn it to pay her overdue bill. I glimpsed their own daughter taking the very thing that had protected our family for almost seventy years and then blaming them for her inability to manage her own life.

I visualized my poor grandparents tearing the house up looking for their protective burden. I pictured them feeling dizzy and light headed and laying down to rest. I watched them dying quietly in their sleep from carbon monoxide poisoning. I imagined myself strangling Geena, and I was consumed with rage.

"Addie, Geena didn't know. She's not all good, but she's not that low either," John said quietly. "She had even more to lose with their passing than you did. She hurt them plenty indirectly, but she would never do it on purpose."

John was much more understanding about Geena than I could ever be, because right now I was just seeing red. I had a lot to process, and I was not ready to argue with him, so I focused on the other dangerous individuals we would probably agree on more.

"John, I know how it happened. I see it now. I don't understand how anyone could have done something so cruel and inhumane to people as good as them."

"The thirst for power can drive men mad, Addie," he said hopelessly.

I had always been a peaceful person, but after today I was different. I wanted vengeance on whomever did it, and when the opportunity presented itself, I wanted to be the one to pull the trigger and put a bullet in his head. I knew I had to protect the ring and pocket watch, but right now the main thing I wanted to do was kill Geena.

"I'm not sure if the hoodoo on the ring will continue to provide you with any protection, Addie, but you know I'll look out for you as much as I can," John promised.

While I was grateful for his allegiance, neither one of us knew if the shield over the ring could keep me safe or not. The protection I had unknowingly enjoyed while Grandma was living was now gone, and I felt like I had a big target on my back.

"I'm not sure if my family heirlooms and insider info make me safe or make me a sitting duck. I don't know who to involve and who might be endangered if we do." I felt like a war veteran with PTSD, looking over my shoulder and running from invisible enemies. "I have no idea who killed my grandparents or who has been trying to steal from them, and everyone who attempted to harm them is either dead or unable to communicate with me, so those are all dead ends. I think we need to go see Nosy Rosy to try to get answers."

"Let's do it then," John announced as he stood up. "I'm sitting on go."

Something about the fact that she had recommended a repair man to Grandma and the fact that Grandma and Pop turned up dead the weekend he was supposed to work on their house has been bouncing around in my mind every since I put the ring on.

We walked to her house together, and her fluttering

curtain told me she saw us coming but would never admit it. We rang the door bell together, and she peeked through the blinds, pretending to be surprised to see us.

"Well, my stars!" she exclaimed as she opened the door. "Addie, you're a sight for sore eyes, child. It's so good to see you—look at you all grown-up and ladylike! I do declare you look more and more like your Grandma every day."

I swear she smelled like prune juice and moth balls, and she wasted no time before diving in to inquire about John.

"Well now, who is this?" she asked as if she had not been spying on him for weeks. She seemed torn between admiring him for his good looks, wondering if we were dating, and trying to decide exactly how scandalous it would be if we were.

"John, Mrs. Rosy. Mrs. Rosy, John. John is the executor of Grandma and Pop's estate."

To her credit, at least Rosy had the good graces to first tear up and talk about how much she was missing Grandma instead of grilling John.

"Addie, I just hate what happened to them. Who knew carbon monoxide was in your home? This world has just gotten so bad, and you can't trust nothing these days..." she fussed and then started as if she had forgotten her manners. "Well, forgive my rudeness, child. You two want to come in and sit down? I got some gingersnaps—just baked them today. They go down great with a cold glass of milk."

I thanked her, accepted the cookies, and started to eat

them; John took some but didn't touch them. He viewed everything as potential poison, even baked goods from the elderly were a possible threat in his opinion.

I think he accepted the cookies out of etiquette rather than hunger but would have starved before sampling them. After going through the polite social banter until I didn't think I could take it any longer, and after Rosy had expressed her condolences a thousand different ways, I asked her what we really wanted to know.

"Rosy, Amber and Geena said that you suggested Grandma contact a service man to install a security system in the house. Is that right?"

She bobbed her head and proceeded to cry, "God bless her soul. Your poor Grandma. Yes, I sent somebody over. She knew you was worried about all the break-in's, and I had just hired this guy by the name of Bill Thompson to do some work for me. He's a real nice guy—good Christian fellow." Then she waved away her tears and swooned, "I must admit ... that man's so hot I declare he could melt butter!"

I snorted my milk; it was almost impossible for John and I not to giggle while eighty seven year old Rosy rambled on about how cute the repairman's buttocks were.

Rosy, how do you know for sure that he was the one, who came out to our house?" I forced myself to stay on track.

"Well, because your Grandma called to tell me that he made it over there. She said she couldn't talk long, because she had lost her marbles—she was always saying stuff like that—you know how she was," as her eyes welled up again. "But she told me Bill was real nice and that he was helping her out a lot."

I had a pretty good idea as to what Grandma had lost, and it wasn't marbles.

"So, when did you talk to her next?"

Rosy's face filled with hurt and sadness.

"Now, Addie, you know that was the last time I spoke to her. It breaks my heart—it really does. The next thing I hear is that she and your Pop had died from the carbon monoxide poisoning. That stuff's supposed to be the silent killer – yep, that's what the experts say."

"Rosy, do you have this guy's contact information?" I asked, because by this point, I was really alarmed about this service man.

"Why, certainly, honey! What kind of neighbor do you think I am? He's legit, I promise. You want anything done, just give him a call – he'll come right out. He fixed a lot of stuff for me, and he had real reasonable prices," she advertised before she thumbed through some recipes, coupons, and a pile of receipts on the kitchen table looking for Bill Thompson's business card.

"Rosy, I have to admit ... this service man makes me a little nervous. He was the last person to see my grandparents alive."

"Why, here it is!" she beamed. "Y'all can have this one—I got an extra."

She produced a strange card with a black rooster on it and Psalms 91 in small letters at the bottom of it. Something told me the Bible verse didn't mean he was a friendly, Christian businessman any more than the black rooster was supposed to represent a simple, Southern symbol.

"Thanks, Rosy. Listen, please take care of yourself. It was good talking to you. I got to go now. I promise I'll see you soon, okay?"

"Oh, Addie, you're so sweet to be worried about this old, widow woman the way you are, but that man would never hurt a fly—you just don't know him like I do. When you get in touch with him, you tell him to ring me up, because I got a lot of jobs around here I would love to watch him do! Mr. John, it's sure nice to meet you (pronounced 'meetcha'). And next time you'll have to stay long enough to tell me all about yourself—I just love getting to know people!"

"Nice to meet you, too, ma'am." he responded agreeably with tongue in cheek as Nosy Rosy reached over to clasp my hand. I accepted her palm and was immediately sucked into her significant event.

She was opening her door while a game show played in the background. Her friendly service man was waiting on the front porch, and one look at him told me she had been hoodooed for sure. He was balding, sporting a pot belly, spoke in a high-pitched squeaky voice, had bad teeth, and a scruffy goatee.

I noted that his smile did not meet his eyes, which were cornered in by his thick eyebrows. However, the detail that was most interesting to me was the chain he wore around his neck, because a brass charm of lovebirds hung from it. If he was capable of casting a romance spell over Rosy, chances were that he was capable of using hoodoo to harm my grandparents, too.

Rosy doted on him, bringing him glasses of sweet tea while he worked on her water heater, her bathroom pipes, and her wobbly ceiling fans. Bill Thompson politely smiled and listened to her stories.

After Bill had spent a great deal of time listening to Rosy, he started asking questions about her neighbors and church members. He wanted to know who lived close by and if the neighbors looked out for each other much.

Rosy shared a lot of info about my family and me, and I was offended to hear her prattle on about how tragic it was that I was such an old maid to be single with no children at the ancient age of twenty.

Bill grew more attentive as Rosy discussed my family. Nosy Rosy told him how involved she was in looking out for us, and with the way she described her concern for everyone in the neighborhood, you would have thought she was a saint.

"I'm just so glad I got your advertisement on my door last week," she said before he left. "I'll have to call you again real soon."

"Well, ma'am, I really appreciate the business, and I would be more than happy to help out any of your other neighbors, who could benefit from my services."

"Well, June Jackson could sure use the help, but she's too proud and paranoid about strangers to ask for it."

"But, Miss Rosy, you can tell her that I'm not a stranger anymore since we're good friends now, aren't we?"

"Lord, you're the best looking friend I've had in a

long time!"

Rosy squealed and giggled like a school girl.

He kissed her hand after he shook it, which sealed the deal with Rosy, because after he left, she closed the door, leaned against it, and swooned before she picked up the phone to tell Grandma all about it. The strangest thing of all was that when she started talking to Grandma, I realized that at the time of this call, I had been home. I distantly remembered hearing the other end of the phone conversation while eating breakfast with Pop; Grandma had rolled her eyes at me as Rosy rambled on and on.

Then instantly I was back in the present as if I had never left. I felt completely exhausted. The way Bill Thompson so easily used Rosy to hurt my family had chilled me to the core. I had just spied on the murderer, who had killed the people I loved most, yet I had not been able to do anything to stop him.

Rosy was as unobservant and talkative in the present as she had been in the past, so I felt free to let my mind wander. I thought about how even though I had a visual on my grandparents' killer, I still didn't know how I could relay this information to law enforcement in a way lin which they would believe me.

We thanked Rosy for her time and left her house. John and I walked quietly until we were certain we were out of Rosy's range, and then John asked for the business card. He used his cell to call the number on the card, but a recording from the operator answered and stated an automated message saying, "We're sorry, but your call can not be completed as dialed. Please check the number and dial again. This number is no longer in service."

"It's on Poplar Avenue, and that address sounds familiar," John muttered while staring at the address on the business card. "Let's go," he instructed as he herded me towards the truck, and off we went down Poplar.

So, off we sped, and with every mile I felt like I was racing closer and closer to my impending doom.

Chapter 17

After we arrived at the address, we were surprised to be staring at a restaurant. Most people went to Tennessee Tate's for some of the best barbecue in the South, but John and I went there to face down my family's killer.

"Well, now we know with certainty that the serviceman is not legitimate," he said soberly.

"I think we already knew that, but maybe there's some reason he chose this address. Maybe he works here, or maybe someone employed here knows him."

"I suppose we could go in to inquire about him as long as we don't disclose anything to them," John said.

I headed inside with him not far behind me. As soon as I opened the door, the sweet smell of barbeque and the sound of a guitar playing overwhelmed me.

I had slipped on Grandma's ring on the way over; I used my intuition to take in the staff at the barbeque joint. I felt drawn to the female bartender, who had just turned on the Shelby College basketball game for the patrons. When she reached to change the channel, I noted a black cat tattoo on her forearm, and then I took an empty bar stool and motioned for John to do the same.

"What can I do you for?" she asked while drying the bar mugs.

"I'll take a sweet tea. John, what do you want?"

"I'll have the same." he agreed.

"All right, two sweet teas coming right up." the waitress announced.

Her name tag said, "Brenda" on it. I was torn between

asking her directly about Bill Thompson or figuring out a way to make contact with her so I could see her most significant event.

For some reason, I couldn't take my eyes off of her tattoo, so I remarked, "I like your tattoo; what does it mean?"

She looked down at it and seemed a bit taken aback but cautiously explained, "Oh, you know black cats are supposed to be good luck; at least that's what people, who practice hoodoo say. I got it to help me when I go to the casinos in Tunica to play craps."

"Does it work?" I asked.

"I do okay for myself. Putting Peter's Perfume on before I go seems to help better than anything though," she answered me but withdrew a bit. "What's it to you?"

"Oh, it's nothing to me. It just caught my eye, and I was wondering what it meant."

"Do I know you from somewhere?" she quizzed me.

"No, I don't think so, but I am looking for someone. I was trying to hire a guy to do some work for me, and he listed this address as his business location. His name is Bill Thompson; he doesn't happen to work here, does he?"

Her face went cold before she lied, "Nope, can't say that he does."

"That's strange … I wonder why he put this down as his business address."

"Probably because he used to shack up at my place before I kicked him to the curb." There was a tone of bitterness in her voice.

"Oh, so you were his girlfriend?" I inquired.

"I guess you could say that, but that was before he got too weird for me," she leaned over and whispered almost as if she were glad to confess this to someone.

"Too weird for you?"

"Yeah, I thought he was the cat's meow for a while—I couldn't get enough of him. But then one day I woke up and wasn't attracted to him at all anymore—it was the weirdest thing. It was like I finally saw him for what he really was – a master manipulator."

"How was he a master manipulator?" I asked. Something about the way she described her attraction to him reminded me of the way I felt drawn to Gavin; for the first time I kicked myself for not considering the fact that maybe I was being hoodooed by the hoodoo man.

"He got into some kind of black magic—creepy stuff. I liked the white magic part of hoodoo, but then he got into gray magic. And once he stepped into the black magic … well, that was too much for me. He started trying to command spirits and other scary stuff I don't believe in using it for."

"Does black magic have anything to do with why he put a black rooster on his business card?"

"So you thought that seemed a bit off, too, huh? Clever girl. Yeah, the black rooster is how the Man presents himself sometimes when you go to the Crossroads to bargain with him for what you want."

"Good grief! Why didn't you go to the police about him?" I asked feeling more and more hopeless by the minute.

"If I didn't know any better, I would think you were

drinking something besides iced tea to ask me a crazy question like that," she laughed. "What was I supposed to do? Go tell the cops that my ex-boyfriend, who is in an unknown location, has been practicing magic to try to cast spells on people? There's no way to prove he did anything to anybody, and that's the scariest part about hoodoo, because it's powerful, but most people don't even believe in it. Listen, lady, I don't know why you're looking for him, but I'd forget about him if I were you. That man is nothing but trouble, and I wouldn't trust him to fix nothing for me."

I felt sick, but I had to ask, "Don't you have any idea where he might be?"

"Ma'am, I don't know, and I don't care. But if you do stumble upon him, you had better run."

A crowd of customers poured into the bar, and she excused herself to wait on them. I tried to shake her hand to spy on her, but she didn't give me the opportunity to make physical contact.

John quietly steered me to the car, and once we both got inside with the doors securely shut, I said, "I don't know if it would do any good or not, but I feel like at this point, we just need to go to the police to file a report on this guy. I'm tired of them dragging their feet, and I don't care if they're under a spell or not. We need some help fast."

"Addie, I don't trust them," he argued.

"I can't say I'm crazy about talking to them either, but I feel like we've got to do something. You heard what Brenda said about this guy—he's extremely dangerous. My grandparents deserve justice, and I want to take whatever measures necessary to get it for them." I stated with determination.

"If my memory's not failing me, we've done this dog and pony show more than once, and they've consistently blown us off."

"Yeah, because they were hoodooed, and that's not their fault." I fussed.

"So, now you think the spell has been broken? I don't understand your train of thought, because best I recall, there are still bad people, who have themselves barricaded somewhere inside a fortress nailed up with Indian Scout head coins."

"You're not listening to me—we're going to report Bill Thompson and then figure out a way to get him out of his hoodooed house, so the cops can capture him."

"Okay, now I'm listening. Then what comes next?" he asked clearly hoping there was more to this plan than that.

"That's all I've got right now."

John sighed, shook his head at me, and reluctantly drove to the police station. I figured the two of us were still traumatized about getting locked up, so voluntarily showing up there was probably one of the stupidest things we would ever do.

Apparently, my concerns that the cops would be overly attentive to me were irrelevant. When we arrived, we were greeted by a handful of law enforcement officers, who attended our church and simply wanted to express their condolences again. I was happy we didn't see any of the men, who had arrested us. We asked to speak to the police chief, and with some raised eyebrows, they escorted us back.

The chief lumbered out and seemed shocked to see us there again, and he said, "Good to see you here when you're not being interrogated for murder, young lady. I heard you helped rescue your cousin from her abductors though, so I have to commend you on your bravery for that. I'm real sorry about you losing your grandparents, Ms. Jackson; everyone knows they were right good people. I have to admit I am more than a little curious about what is so important that you would show up here again."

The chief leaned back into his rolling chair, which groaned under his weight, as he waited for us to explain what we wanted from him.

"We appreciate the sympathies, but we are here, because an unknown service man came by to do some work on my grandparents' house the weekend they died. It was not until after he left that the house appeared completely ransacked.

"I know the cause of their deaths was carbon monoxide, but before I left for the weekend their carbon monoxide detector was in working order. Yet when your officers came to inspect the house after my grandparents had passed, the batteries in the detector were dead.

"We tried to reach the service man, but his phone was disconnected, and the address he gave was to Tennessee Tate's Barbecue. We met his ex-girlfriend there, and she said to stay away from him, because he's into dark magic."

Chief Stamper cut me off.

"Ms. Jackson, what exactly are you implying?"

"I am merely stating that I think your suspicion that my grandparents' deaths were from foul play was correct. Obviously, I didn't do it, but I really believe someone else did. I want this sketchy fix-it man tracked down and questioned."

He leaned back even further into his chair, although I didn't see how that was possible. I expected that any moment the creaky, old seat would start begging for mercy under the cop's weight. He folded his hands on top of his big belly and exhaled.

"Ms. Jackson, it is perfectly normal to want somebody to blame when someone you love dies; we see this all the time in our line of work," he lectured me. "However, after further investigation, we have determined that there is no reason to suspect foul play in their passing."

"But, sir ... with all due respect....don't you think it's suspicious that some stranger went into their house – an unknown person with fake contact information—and now they're both gone?"

"Ms. Jackson, I see your point; it's a strange circumstance, but that doesn't change the cause of death. If they were shot, poisoned, or strangled ... forgive my crude descriptions ... that would make the idea that they were murdered much more logical. Young lady, I know you've been under a lot of stress. I'm sorry our department contributed to that when we pulled you in here for questioning. However, I'm afraid that not having a working carbon monoxide detector is extremely common; people have their homes burn down with inactive smoke alarms every day…"

"But, Chief Stamper, our carbon monoxide detector was working when I left, and this service guy needs to be investigated."

"Ms. Jackson, if we had some way to contact him, I suppose we could question him, if it would put your mind at ease. But seeing as how you got no address and no working phone number, and all you got is some crazy ex-girlfriend, who said he's some loony magician, I really don't know how we're supposed to find him. I sure hate it for you, Ms. Jackson. Tragic situation, really it is. But I just don't think we can be of anymore help to you at this time. Now if y'all will excuse me, I've got a meeting to go to."

He stood up to indicate that this conversation was clearly over, and I wanted to ask him if the meeting was a donut eating contest, but I restrained myself.

"No, I'm sorry, but I can't do that yet," I firmly planted myself in his office. "I will sketch you a picture of what Bill Thompson looks like right now. I am worn out and fed up from waiting for your men to protect my family. Both my grandparents have been murdered, and I told you about the prime suspect, and now you want to blow me off. And while we're at it, you need to look at the Skullbangerz, because they've been after my family for months. If you won't help me, I'll go over your head to find someone else to do your job for you."

John's mouth fell open wide, and he stared at me

aghast.

"Now hold on there, Missy," the chief guffawed. "There ain't no need in you getting your panties in a wad."

I eyeballed him good.

"Chief Stamper, I've got two witnesses—my neighbor and Bill Thompson's ex-girlfriend. So, are you going to help me, or are you going to force me to go above your head?"

His face turned beet red, and he huffed and puffed before he bellowed, "Now you just wait a cotton picking minute! I don't want you or nobody else in this here community thinking they got to go above my head to get things done. And strangely enough, it seems you ain't the only one that thinks there was some kind of funny business around their deaths."

"What do you mean?"

"Some man named Gavin, who was dressed all in black, came by today. He was adamant that I needed to look deeper into this case. He is some sort of specialist in strange sightings—he communicates with the dead, ghosts, and does a lot of other stuff that creeps me out. He's an odd duck for sure, but I have to admit that what he said made sense. Listen, little lady, you draw me a picture, and I'll post it to try to find this guy. If we see him, we'll ask him to come in for questioning, but, Addie, I can't make you no promises. Maybe the man moved. Maybe he went out of business. Heck, I don't know where he is—I ain't in the business of looking for service men—especially one who done a good job and didn't swindle nobody."

He puffed as he sweated more bullets than he

probably carried in his gun.

I grabbed a pen and paper and sketched him the best drawing I could, and he accepted it and committed to do what he could to find him.

"Thank you," I said sincerely, and after John and I said goodbye, I walked out feeling like the queen of the world.

We headed back to my house, and I was finally feeling hopeful for a change, so I should have known Geena would be laid out snoring on my couch, just waiting to ruin my day. A pile of casino tokens was on the table, I didn't know what I was supposed to do with her.

I shouldn't have been so hard on how my grandparents dealt with her, especially since thus far, I certainly had not done any better. She woke up, stretched, and wiped slobber off the side of her face. I stared at her trying to figure out how to handle the situation.

"Well, if it isn't my favorite niece!"

I had the good graces to refrain from pointing out that I was her only living niece left.

"Somebody tried to break into your place last night. The jerk got the lock cut halfway through, but I opened the screen door and gave him the evil eye, so he ran off."

My aunt did crazy better than anyone I had ever met, so if someone had tried to break in, I didn't doubt that one psycho stare from Geena would have been enough to send an intruder packing.

"You would think that with a brand, new security system, I wouldn't have to worry about this kind of stuff so much."

"Addie, it's funny how you're always underestimating these people," Geena said bluntly. "They ain't scared of much of nothing."

"Well, they were scared enough of you to run off."

"That's because I done had dealings with them before, and they know I'm crazy. That's the part I worry about with you."

"Which part?" I asked.

"You're too sane to be mixed up in all of this. Sanity is predictable, and that makes you vulnerable."

She stated just as simply as if she had said it was going to rain today. I felt chills go down my spine and thought I probably needed an alarm system for every area of my life.

If only that were possible.

"I can't figure you out. You act like this good girl all the time, yet you hang out with a murderer everyday."

"What are you talking about?" I asked aghast as Geena cast an angry stare toward John, who looked like he was about to come unglued.

"Geena, you need to quit making up stories and picking on John! Leave him alone already," I wagged my finger at her.

"Come on now, Addie. You're a smart girl. You can't actually believe that hoodoo was the sole cause of the people, who've attacked our family dying all these years now, do you?"

"What are you insinuating?" I asked as John squirmed in the corner.

"I ain't insinuating nothing. I'm telling you that John

319

Hamilton has murdered more people than I care to count. I can't believe you fraternize with him much less let him sleep on your couch. My Dad was a dang fool for giving him as much power as he did—I just got scared of how much dirt he had on him that he turned everything over to him when he died, because he was too afraid of him not to," he bellowed.

"You're lying."

"The time of truth is coming, man. What is done in the dark will always come into the light," Geena roared at John before addressing me and saying, "You not believing me don't change that it's true. Do you really think he's been honest with you about everything so far? I guarantee you he hasn't."

My head was swimming; I remembered John expressing his concern that Geena would try to turn me against him, but I wasn't sure who was manipulating me anymore – Geena or John or both.

"Did he explain why my dad never let you go into the attic? Did he show you everything that was in the safe?" Geena grilled me before taking my silence as confirmation for her assumptions. "Did it ever occur to you that he might have good reasons for keeping you in the dark? He who knows the most has the most power - now wouldn't you agree?"

I couldn't take the drama anymore. I whirled away from John and Geena, stormed off, and locked myself in my room. I toyed with the locket John had given me that I had been fortunate enough not to need thus far. I ignored John's knocks on my door.

Finally he left after Geena dragged herself into the guest bedroom to sleep. I reflected on my grandparents' death and my Grandma's bizarre history, which all seemed like some kind of twisted jigsaw puzzle. I had put some of the pieces together, but I still believed that if I could just find a few more corner and edge pieces, the overall picture might finally start to fall into place.

Living in my grandparents' creepy house for one more night might kill me, but I'm too emotionally invested in them to leave. I had always thought that one glorious, distant day I would move away from Memphis and live somewhere peaceful—far away from my grandparents' scary neighborhood. However, now that they were gone, I felt like their house was my last connection to them.

I was also starting to suspect that their house held more evidence than FBI headquarters and that part of their decision to will everything to me was to keep all of their skeletons in the family. It had also begun to seem more likely that John played a more important role in this hoodoo game that just some guy Grandma trusted enough to look after me.

I was living with my grandparents' riddles even though I had been trying to avoid them since their deaths. I thought I wanted to know everything. I thought I wanted in on their ruse, but the more I learned, the more dangerous it got for me. I was wrong to think my life would make more sense if I could understand my history better. Increased awareness had only made me feel permanently screwed up.

I have circled their house of secrets every day since

they died. I have passed the couch that hides the trapdoor, and I have walked under the attic pull that my grandparents ordered me to stay away from. I recall how my Pop never even let me into his tomato garden, which seems particularly unsettling now. I check the pocket watch every hour and twirl the ring around on my finger constantly, and I remember how adamantly Grandma warned me against using the pocket watch in her letters.

I now fully understand the expression, "Curiosity killed the cat." I am trying not to be an officious feline, but this house gnaws and claws at me teasing me to open Pandora's box. The faucet in the kitchen drips loudly, and the old mantel clock chimes to taunt me.

I am turning into my grandmother and losing myself, and I don't like it one bit. I haven't checked the mail this week. The recurrent dreams by themselves are already enough to make anyone go nuts.

It's not that I don't have questions; it's just that I don't want to become so terrified by the answers that I go completely mad.

Chapter 18

When your insomniac bodyguard who never takes a day off is unreachable, you know you have problems. I had been calling John all morning, and despite blowing up his phone, I had not gotten a single response from him. I even used the locket he gave me to page him for the first time ever, but he still didn't show. Gavin called, and when I told him what was going on, he was worried, too, so he came right over so we could figure out what was going on.

As soon as he arrived, we hopped into his ride to head over to John's house to check out the situation, and I tried not to bite my nails on the ride over. After arriving, I was relieved to find his car in the driveway, but I was puzzled when he didn't respond to our knocks on the door. Gavin and I went around to the back entrance, but he didn't answer there either.

When I had just about decided he was intentionally ignoring me, the door creaked open indicating it was unlocked and ajar. As vigilant and paranoid as John was, I knew now something had to be very wrong.

Gavin's face went dark, as I cautiously whispered, "John, are you there? Are you all right?"

Only silence answered me. His house was so dark and quiet that it took a minute for my senses to focus on what we had found. After my eyes adjusted, I saw John tied up in a chair with layers and layers of rope. His mouth was sealed with duct tape, and his eyes were wide open silently pleading for us for help.

I leaped forward to assist him when two figures

stepped out of the darkness and approached us. I immediately and very clearly saw that they were dressed like the Man from hoodoo history. Their faces were uncovered today, and the fact that they weren't worried about us seeing them made me feel very frightened that they probably didn't figure we would live to identify them.

"Well, Clint, she finally showed up," Jaydon Swisher said coldly. Fear gripped my heart at the sight of the gang leader, who had been trying to kill me.

"And not a moment too soon. I was getting kind of tired of torturing him," Clint responded.I blinked after catching a glimpse of his face. He might not have been in uniform, but I clearly recognized him as one of the police officers, who had paid a visit or two to my house. "Maybe we can work on her next."

"Who do you think you are? Hey, check it out. He's dressed up like the Man." Jaydon poked fun and his finger at Gavin. I waited for Gavin to light them on fire, but he was clearly sizing up the situation and trying to determine which approach to take. While the dangerous duo eyed us, I had the foresight to fumble with my cell phone and start recording the audio of what was going on in case I lived to testify about any of this.

"You don't get to touch me," Gavin said in a menacing voice, after Jaydon poked him. They continued to talk a big game, but even they had the God given sense to inch away from him a bit.

"It's so nice of you to join the party, Addie," Clint said slyly.

"What are you guys doing together, and what do you

want from us?"

"She knows exactly what we want. If she gives us the ring and the pocket watch, no one gets hurt. If she refuses, you all die, and Mr. Hamilton gets to watch us kill you slowly and live with knowing he was responsible for your deaths," Jaydon calmly explained as if he had ordered French fries as the side dish with our last meal.

"Nobody gets hurts, huh? If all you're concerned about is the ring and the clock, and you don't have any interest in hurting anybody, then why did you kill my grandparents?"

I confronted them with clenched fists as they grinned back to taunt me.

"We didn't kill June and Louie personally, but they brought their deaths upon themselves by not being more…cooperative," Clint said callously.

"Cooperative … meaning they didn't just roll over and give you what you wanted from them?" Gavin clarified.

"They were a hard-headed old couple, and they really never had any business having the ring and the watch in the first place, so they were simply in the way."

"So, you guys just kill anybody, who gets in your way—is that how it is?" I asked, shaking.

"The two of us weren't responsible for their deaths, but one of our men saw an opportunity to end them and took it. You see, Miss Jackson, we represent a calling higher than you would ever understand. The loss of your grandparents was a small sacrifice for a better future. And if you are smarter than your grandparents and cooperate, this will be the last you will ever see of our men." Clint spoke as if he really thought I would negotiate with him.

"We can't believe anything you say. How do we know that if she gives you the ring and the watch, you won't still kill us both?" Gavin said lightly, but his eyes were tight.

"Oh, Mr. Hamilton here is quite valuable to us. You have merely been a pawn to bring him to us. We knew he would always be close to you, so if we kept close tabs on you, he wouldn't be far behind." Jaydon explained.

"Why is John so important to you?" I asked, feeling confused.

"You really don't know?"

Clint looked back and forth between Jaydon and me like he was enjoying their having inside information I didn't share. The amusement Jaydon and Clint seemed to share by my confusion made me want to punch them to wipe the arrogance off their faces.

"Oh, Mr. Hamilton is a complicated man; I suppose I'm not surprised he hasn't told you yet," Jaydon whispered in John's ear as he twisted his arm, and John winced in pain.

I looked at John, willing him to break free and explain everything to me, as he gazed helplessly back at me.

"John is the last living descendant of Moses and Zephorrah. He is Mary Smith's great grandson." Clint said with no small amount of satisfaction at the shock on my face.

"But that's impossible…" I blurted out.

"Isn't it? I guess you won't live to know for sure."

Clint cocked a gun and pointed it at my head. Gavin inched slowly closer to the two of us.

"Listen, murdering her won't help you, because you still need the ring and the watch." Gavin said.

"Keep talking," Jaydon ordered him.

"We can get them for you, but they're not here," Gavin lied. He knew I never went anywhere without the ring and watch; right now they were hiding deep inside my pockets.

"So, where are they?" Clint barked in his best bad cop voice.

"You'll need to take John's duct tape off so he can tell you." Gavin suggested as he crept stealthily ever closer to them.

"You're full of it, and you know it! Your family has kept that ring and watch for years, and John has never been responsible for them."

Jaydon swore in anger as if he was starting to feel like we were messing with them.

"Well, the burden has been too hard on me since my grandparents died, so I put John in charge of taking care of them. Ask him."

I chimed in as if it were painful for me to admit weakness in front of them. John's voice was muffled behind the tape, so Jaydon roughly ripped the sticky substance off of his mouth. I noticed for the first time how bruised and bloodied he was, and I fought back tears at the realization that they had tortured him.

"Addie, I've been telling them where the ring and watch are, but they don't believe me," John's hoarse voice cracked. My new least favorite cop punched his mouth, and blood and spit ran out the sides of it.

"Of course we don't believe you!" he yelled in his face. "You're trying to tell us they're in some special safe that only you can access with your finger prints. Do you honestly expect us to just let you go to the bank and trust that you'll come back to give them to us?"

"It's true about the safe!" I corroborated with John. "He is the only living person, who can open it. You could take us to the bank, we'll let you into the safe, and you can walk right out with the goods."

Clint snickered as he kicked John before he snarled, "Why don't you take him to the bank and leave me here with the Southern belle? She ain't from no significant blood line, but I'm sure I could find something fun to do with her while you're gone."

He gave me a look that made me feel naked, and Gavin and John's faces darkened.

"I don't think I'll kill her just yet," he continued, as he watched her with a predatory eye. "A bullet in her back will be the icing on the cake—after I get her on her back, of course."

"I'll kill you, man. You better not even think about touching her," John threatened Clint before he spit in his torturer's face.

One look at John's face made it evident that he had had all he could take. At that moment, his antagonist began punching the daylights out of him when Gavin snapped his fingers and opened his hand up to reveal a fireball.

The flames were just enough to distract Clint into

dropping his gun. I lunged for the weapon, but Jaydon pinned me to the floor. Fortunately, I was able to at least kick the pistol under the couch.

In a surreal out of body experience, it occurred to me how poorly prepared I had been to deal with this situation, but my adrenaline kicked in, and the desire to live and survive was bigger than my limitations. Before I had time to process what I was about to do, I grabbed the first thing I could—John's baseball bat—before I began beating the mess out of the man.

It wasn't that I had much to live for, and it wasn't that my life was all that important. I wasn't afraid of dying anymore, but if it was my time to go, I was determined to die with dignity—not after this psychopath had had his sick fun with me.

When the time came for me to leave this world, it would have to be a sacrifice I made to serve the greater purpose of others. I remembered Geena's remarks that they would stay away from you if you acted like you were crazy, so I figured that the more unstable they thought I was, the better off I'd be.

So, I started howling like a wild banshee and clobbering the crook for every bad thing that had ever happened to my family and me.

Clint had gotten close enough to John's face for John to bite him, so apparently he and I had both paid attention to Geena's lesson on having an insanity strategy. John stood up attached to the chair he was tied to, and he used the seat to back over Clint and slammed him into the wall repeatedly. Gavin used the fire to burn through the ropes, and before long John's arms commenced to coming free.

"You crazy witch!" Clint screamed at me in my screwy state. "What are you doing to him?"

"I'll kill him," I screamed. "I swear I will!"

Gavin and John started towards me to assist me, but I hollered, "Don't take this from me! This guy is mine!" as I kicked Jaydon in the groin. "If you take one more step, I'll smash his head in so hard he'll never speak again."

All I was seeing was red. Gavin looked at me with concern before he snapped his fingers on both of his hands, produced two new fire balls, and lit both of the crooks's shoes on fire. John's mouth fell open, and I was furious Gavin had taken my revenge from me.

"Whenever you two fellas get settled down enough to sit in those kitchen chairs, I'll put out the fire on your feet," Gavin shrugged nonchalantly.

John's ropes had burned through, and the remnants had fallen to the floor, so he took advantage of the opportunity Gavin had given him and retrieved the gun from behind the couch.

"I'll execute every member of your family myself," Jaydon tried to talk a big game while hopping back and forth from one foot to the other wincing in pain.

Gavin's eyes glittered as he whispered in a sing song voice, "I'm waiting. It can always get hotter, you know."

The heat must have gotten to them, because they begrudgingly sat down in the two kitchen chairs while they kicked their feet and screamed. John slipped up behind them with the part of the rope that had been untouched by the flames. He tied Clint's hands and body to the chair, and

I did the same with Jaydon.

I exhaled in relief as my rage began to subside and the adrenaline wore off just before uncontrollable shaking set in. As promised, Gavin filled a bucket full of water and poured it on their feet to put out the flames. Despite my hatred for them, the compassionate side of me was secretly glad the flames had not burned through their shoes to hurt their feet. I was impressed Gavin had been able to pull that off.

"We've got questions, and you'd better give us some answers," I demanded.

Clint and Jaydon were unhappy about the seats they were in and clearly did not like the way the tables had turned. They ignored the questions I shot at them like a firing squad. Gavin rolled his eyes at them and pulled out some red pepper and poured it into their mouths.

"What are you doing?" I asked.

"Getting the truth out of them," John responded smugly as he folded his arms and waited.

"I'll never answer your questions!" Clint spit at me before he began howling in pain that his tongue hurt.

"Tell the truth, and the pain will stop," Gavin said.

"We aren't going to tell you anything!" Jaydon said, screaming from the hot pepper as it heated his mouth up more and more with each lie.

"Who are you people?"

"You wouldn't believe us if we told you." Jaydon cried, and I wondered how macho his band of hoodlums would think he was if they could see him now.

"Try us." I said.

The heat must have reached epic proportions for the two, because Clint finally broke down and admitted, "We're working for a special division of P.E.A.C.E." He immediately looked relieved when his tongue didn't burn at this omission.

"We've heard weirder." Gavin said. I knew my Grandma had had trouble with this charity before, but to hear they were behind all of the attacks and terrible tortures my family had endured was still unbelievable.

"The organization that represents minorities and advocates for equal rights? They're the ones who ordered the church break-in's, kidnapped my cousin, and killed my grandparents?!"

"Yeah, the powers-that-be discovered that waiting for things to work out didn't always get them what they wanted, so from time to time, they take matters into their own hands. The ring your family possesses was never meant to be yours. It was designed to right the wrongs of slavery and to end the abuse of African Americans, so we are going to use it to get justice for them." Jaydon spilled his explanation as he stopped screaming while the heat subsided with each truth he told.

"Keep talking," I conceded.

Clint continued: "The ring is very valuable. We're planning to use it to blackmail corrupt people into giving us funding and control, so we can utilize their resources to assist underprivileged minorities."

"That's the most messed up Robin Hood story I've ever heard. So, your division does whatever it has to do to keep P.E.A.C.E. afloat – even if it involves killing, blackmailing, and exploiting others? And it's all done under the pretense of promoting peace, love, and happiness and all that other crap?!" John sneered in disgust.

"For someone like you, who doesn't serve a greater purpose in life, I'm sure this is too much for you to comprehend," Clint shrugged in his sneering, condescending tone.

"I had a purpose in life until your people killed them," I said coldly. Massacring them seemed mighty appealing to me right about now, but Gavin put his warm hands on my shoulders and pulled me away from the murderers.

"How did you know about Addie's family?" Gavin demanded.

"Oh, we've been keeping tabs on them for years, but we never had the opportunity to get close to the ring until recently. We weren't sure what was keeping us away. Of course, we assumed you had something to do with that."

"What do you mean?" I asked.

"I mean that your brave defender here has quite a brutal history with our people; if he weren't so important to the cause, we would have buried him long ago." Jaydon said seriously. John's eyes were hollow, and his face was swollen. He looked like a man, who had been in several bad fights and lost all of them.

"Addie..." John started, but I didn't let him finish.

"So, you're a criminal and a killer? Is that what you're telling me? You were hired by my grandparents to kill people?! So, Geena was right about you ... is that what I'm hearing?!"

I burst into tears.

"No, no, it's not like that!" John swore under his breath.

My eyes welled up with tears as I persisted, "What do you mean it's not like that? John, I feel like I don't even know you anymore."

"Addie, please ... now is not the time for this conversation," Gavin pleaded as Clint and Jaydon looked us up and down like they were eying their next meal. The two troublemakers cussed at us for binding them and demanded to be set free.

"Now you fellas ought to know better than to use that kind of language in front of a lady," Gavin said. "We ought to wash your mouth out with soap for talking so dirty!"

Right about then a light bulb came on in my head.

"That's it! Y'all watch these two. I'll be right back."

"Okay, but don't run off for long." John said seeming confused. I hurried to my car and pulled the Addling Ashes out of my trunk before I headed back inside. I figured if Jaydon and Clint were inebriated, it would be a lot easier to maintain control over them.

"I think John's right—you two need to clean up your act, and we're going to help you do it. We'll cool off your feet too with a nice soak in the tub. John and Gavin, let's give these two a bath."

"You got it," Gavin complied as Clint and Jaydon gave each other very perplexed looks. I ran a bath and loaded it down with the ashes, as John proceeded to sit both of them into the tub fully clothed facing each other.

"Y'all are mighty strange," Jaydon remarked, as I smiled back at him.

"This here is the best bath I ever got," Clint remarked in no time. "We should stay at this hotel more often."

"Who are you, and why are you talking to me?"

"Now, now, you know who I am—I'm your big brother come to take you home to see Mama. You've always been such a kidder."

"Oh, right! I did that on purpose now, didn't I?" Clint snickered, and they laughed like they had just told the funniest joke in the world.

"The best part is we've got the whole thing on tape," I told John and Gavin.

"Addie, you are pure genius," John said.

"Well, now that they're pleasantly perplexed, what do we do with them?" Gavin asked.

"How about we blackmail the blackmailers?" John asked.

"How do we blackmail people, who have developed dementia?" I inquired.

"We need to speak to whoever runs P.E.A.C.E."

John and I got on the Internet while Gavin kept a watchful eye on Jaydon and Clint, who were singing nursery rhymes to each other.

"It looks like Ruth Sistrunk is the CEO over there; I wonder if there's a way to reach her directly rather than calling a general toll free number."

"Maybe Clint or Jaydon have a cell phone with her info in it." I rummaged in their jacket pockets, which were strewn on the kitchen table to find a cell phone, which listed Ruth Sistrunk's cell number in its contacts.

"So, what exactly do you want to demand of her?" Gavin asked.

I thought about this intently before responding.

"We tell her we've turned the tables on her," I said. "We know she sent these men over to kidnap you and kill me, but we know everything about what they have been up to, and we've got the whole thing on tape. We demand that she tell us everything she knows about Bill Thompson and that she leave all of us alone. We inform her that the minute her guys start messing with us again, we'll publish the tapes."

"That might actually work, because P.E.A.C.E. survives off of donations. If we leaked to the public what they were really doing, it would be the end of them, and they'd all go to jail," John agreed. "The odds are she is probably cutthroat enough to sacrifice a few of her men to save the organization. It would also send a message to other power hungry people out there that they better not mess with us again."

"Yeah, and then after Ruth tells us how to find the service man, we have these guys and him arrested to send a message to their whole, evil division." I said angrily. "They will have to guarantee they won't bother our friends and family again and give up on trying to steal the watch and the ring forever. The moment we suspect they're breaking their end of the bargain, we turn all of them over to the authorities. And if the police won't listen to us, we go straight to the FBI."

"You know, this probably sounds crazy, but I can't

help but feel that they were able to finally hurt us today, because I forgot to water my nation sack," John said. "I think I may have accidentally 'killed' it, so it's not working anymore. Do you think that's nuts?"

"No, that makes perfect sense," Gavin said. "Trust me. I'd know."

I was not about to question the authority of the Man on a hoodoo matter.

"So, are you ready to call Ruth?" Gavin asked.

"Yeah, let's see how reasonable she can be," John said.

We used Clint's cell phone and dialed her number while I kept a watchful eye on our bathing buffoons. A female voice came through.

"Clint, what's the status? Please tell me you have John and that the girl is dead. I'm so tired of you guys mucking this up." Ruth complained.

"Ruth! It's so good to hear your voice. Long time, no speak. Listen, plans have changed," I said probably enjoying this a little too much.

"Who is this?" she said in surprise. Clearly hearing my voice on the line had shaken her.

"Why, this is Addie Jackson, and I'm sitting here with John Hamilton. John, would you like to say 'Hello?'" I taunted her and left Gavin out of the introduction. He had not been a target for her, and I didn't want him to become one by exposing his involvement.

"Hello," John said smartly.

Ruth's voice dropped to a pressured whisper as she hissed, "What do you want?"

"Well, actually I want some peace and quiet from your peaceful organization, but we realize your charity has been responsible for a lot of lost lives and suffering here as of late. Now we're reasonable people, Mrs. Sistrunk, and we understand you just want my Grandma's ring and clock, but we're here to tell you that's not going to happen—not today, not ever. See, we've taped your men trying to kidnap and kill us, and we've also taped their admission that your organization kills people at will, so it seems to me it's high time you started negotiating with us."

"You have my attention." she whispered.

"Either your people leave our family, friends, and us alone and give up on trying to steal the ring and watch, or we expose your company for what it really is to the entire world."

"I can't concede to that; the ring and the pocket watch are far too valuable," she said stiffly as she clearly sensed she was at a significant disadvantage with us.

"They are valuable, but they weren't entrusted to you, so they're not yours to take, and we're not negotiating with you. Your men are soaked and sitting in the bathtub high as a kite off of Addling Ashes. They can float here until Kingdom Come for all I care, and it would truly give us great pleasure to run your organization into the ground. So, you decide. Are you going to be reasonable, or are you going to be ruined, Ruth?"

"The ring and the watch would be nothing without the charity to use it, so I'll agree to your terms." Ruth said clearly miffed that we had thwarted her plans.

"So, if anybody affiliated with P.E.A.C.E. ever gets anywhere near us again, your whole organization goes down in flames. Do we make ourselves clear?"

"Crystal," she quietly replied.

"So, we have a deal?"

"Yes, we will stay away from y'all, and all of our involvements remain confidential. And you can do what you want with those two—it doesn't matter to me. I will uphold our agreement," Ruth said callously, which confirmed to me that her heart was as frozen as we had feared.

"There's one more thing we want from you to keep our mouths shut."

"What now, Miss Jackson?" she asked tersely as Jaydon and Clint continued singing in the bathtub.

We want your guy, who dressed up like a service man and killed the Jacksons."

"Fine. He lives in Cordova,"

She gave me the address. Then just like that, Ruth Sistrunk hung up the phone.

"Wow, she is one cold character," John whistled.

"What are we going to do with our bath tub buddies? We can't leave them here—they might drown, not that I would cry, I suppose…"

"We keep them tied up and transport them with us when we go see Bill Thompson," Gavin said as if it were obvious.

"You must be joking!"

"Nah, let's have some fun with them. They're high as kites, and they won't be coming back down to Earth anytime soon. Besides, it will send a message to Bill Thompson about how mixed up you will be if you try to mess with us."

So, we put both of the tied up, slap happy, soaked men in John's car. They sang nursery rhymes while we tried to figure out how to get to Bill's house. Clint kept giving me the world's goofiest grin while we rode down the road.

"John, all of this ends tonight. I'm not resting until Bill Thompson is behind bars," I said firmly. I was tired of living in fear and ready for all of this to be over.

"Agreed."

We drove through a dark subdivision way out past Germantown Parkway to Bill Thompson's house where Indian Scout coins gleamed off of his house in the moonlight.

John quietly cut the car off and then asked, "What's our plan?"

"We lure him out of his house so he's not hidden in his hoodooed haven anymore," Gavin suggested.

"Yes, but how are we going to do that?"

"With a little bit of magic. We'll put the magic foot powder that Hoodoo Helen gave us all around the doors of his home."

"And how exactly would that help us?" John asked.

"It will cause him to walk out of his home and wander the world his whole life."

"So, if he wanders away from his home, the police will be able to pick him up."

"Exactly. I'm liking how y'all's minds are working." I

grinned at them and tried to tune out Jaydon and Clint. "He'll wander aimlessly away from us, too, so he won't have time to stop to hurt anybody."

I grabbed the magic foot powder and hopped out of the car.

"Addie, we need to formulate this plan better!" John said. "Get back in the car! Are you crazy?"

"A little bit!" I said before I reached the back door and began sprinkling magic foot powder all around it before working on the front door as well. Gavin followed me around while John sat in the car and shushed Jaydon and Clint. I finished up as fast as possible and jumped back into the car with Gavin right behind me.

"Addie, I swear you're about to give me a heart attack," John said, adding "I say we call the cops now."

"But you hate the fuzz!" I said in shock.

"Addie, you and I almost died tonight. I'm not willing to take anymore chances on your life than we already have."

"I agree," Gavin said before motioning to us to be still. "Shhhh! Look! Somebody's opening the door," he whispered as all three of us laid down in the seats and pushed Clint and Jaydon's heads down, too.

"Cut it out! That tickles!" Jaydon giggled.

"You're a real purdy lady."

Clint flirted at me with a goofy grin.

"Would you two shut up already?" I hissed back at them, and they kept giggling, but at least they quit talking.

"Oh my gosh, he's coming out of the house!"

I peeked up through the car window.

Bill Thompson came out on his porch, scratched his head, strolled down his steps, and kept right on moving down the street; he looked like he was sleep walking, and I could not have been more entertained. He was barefoot in his bathrobe and looked really rattled.

"Let's call the cops to come pick him up before he walks all the way to Arkansas." Gavin suggested before John pulled out his phone and called 911.

"911, where is your emergency?" a female voice answered the line, and John rattled off the address to her.

"Sir, what exactly is your emergency?"

"Ma'am, the man, who murdered the Jackson family is walking down the street in front of us. We've got two other men, who tried to kill Addie Jackson and me, tied up in my vehicle. We need some officers to come and pick these guys up right away."

"Did you just say you've got some men tied up in your car?"

"Yes, ma'am, but only because they tried to murder us," John explained, as if things like this happened every day. "They confessed to obstruction of justice and named Bill Thompson as the murderer of Louie and June Jackson as well. If you could just send some officers out, we'd be much obliged."

"They're on their way. Just sit tight," the dispatcher stammered again.

When John hung up, we looked at each other in amazement.

"Who use hoodoo? We do, that's who!" I sang just as the officers in blue pulled up with firefighters and ambulances in tow. I was ecstatic to see Mr. Kane and Keisha arrive just behind the cops as Amber and Geena trailed close behind in Amber's vehicle. Bill Thompson kept walking like a blind man as his bathrobe completely fell off. He was obviously oblivious to this fact, but the funny sight of him didn't go unnoticed by Jaydon and Clint.

"Hee hee! Look at that fella! He's so funny!" Jaydon howled before some officers cautiously approached our vehicle.

"Well, hi there! Hey, I know you!" Clint pointed at the cops, who started to pale and back away from the car. "You guys gave the Skullbangerz all the cash to help hide the murders! How y'all doing tonight?" Clint grinned at them before their denials began.

"You're drunk. I don't know what you're talking about."

"Oh yeah, man! I remember you! You got some more money for me? I want to buy some more of these ashes. They some good stuff! You going to give me some cash again today?" Jaydon asked hopefully while Chief Stamper listened to this conversation with his mouth wide open.

Down the street the other cops, who weren't listening to our conversation, were hesitant about even approaching, much less trying to arrest, a nude man. So, naturally they stalled a little while trying to understand why they needed to approach him as he walked further and further away.

My impression was that they were more concerned about who was going to get the short end of the stick and

343

have to handcuff him than whether or not my story was legitimate.

Chief Stamper grabbed the two corrupt officers, who were trying to back away and slip off. Mr. Kane chewed them out while the chief handcuffed them and roughly shoved them into his cop car. Then they snatched up Jaydon and Clint who sang like fools while they had their rights read to them before they were pushed into the other police car. For the first time in a long time, I immediately began to feel a weight starting to lift from my shoulders.

One of the officers took our statements, and John claimed that Bill Thompson had attacked him to explain his banged up condition. Gavin claimed Jaydon and Clint had walked into a fire to explain their burned shoes.

By the time we had finished giving our accounts, the service man was in custody. The police kept yelling at him to stand still and to quit walking, but he wouldn't or couldn't do it. They threw a blanket around him and stuffed him into the back of their cop car, but he kept moving his feet and legs trying to wander the world the whole time.

"It's a shame how nuts some people are nowadays," one of the men in blue remarked. "The poor man must be on drugs. Maybe we can get him into a program at the prison to help with that."

"I think that's a nice idea, officer," Gavin said with tongue in cheek as he slipped his arm around my waist.

After we gave our statements a million different ways, Jaydon and Clint began to come out of their confusion. As soon as they started to sober up, they really began to cut up. They yelled at me from the back seat of the cop car, and they blamed me for their situation.

All of us ignored them; they had already taken enough from me, and I was not about to give them anymore attention. Keisha and Mr. Kane hugged me. Amber squealed and engulfed me, and even Geena gruffly made a point to tell me how glad he was that I was okay.

"Addie, I'm afraid I owe you an apology," Chief Stamper announced as he approached me. "I should have taken your claims more seriously. It seems we may have had some corruption in the ranks, so only time will tell what we will find after we get to the bottom of that," he said grimly referencing the officers sitting in the back of his patrol car. The reasons they had missed all the clues gleamed in the gold coins on Bill Thompson's house, but I didn't tell the chief anything about that.

"Well, I'm just glad your men arrested them," I said, shaking the chief's hand.

After answering a zillion questions, John, Gavin, and I were finally released. We used some hoodoo herbs to help treat and nurse John's wounds, since he refused to go to the hospital for them. I hoped that P.E.A.C.E. would uphold their end of the bargain and that the arrest of the Skullbangerz leader and the corrupt cops would give us some peace for a while.

John was relieved to be alive, but his shoulders were heavy. I felt sorry for him, because I felt like he was probably the only person I knew who had to carry around more secrets than I did.

That night after I finally crawled into my bed, I was

surprised to find that for the first time since my grandparents had died, I slept soundly the whole night through.

Chapter 19

Over the next few days, the excitement was all over the news. The local media had labeled Bill Thompson "The Walking Wacko." The magic foot powder was so effective that he continued wandering in circles in his jail cell day in and day out while awaiting his court date. He was like a man possessed, and we all speculated that his lawyers would plead insanity to avoid him getting the death penalty.

After Clint's arrest, rumors of more corruption within the ranks of law enforcement started to swirl. Even Jaydon's minions went underground as the Skullbangerz's criminal activities declined without the direction of their captain to lead them.

P.E.A.C.E. was still running their tolerant, uplifting commercials on television, and I usually threw whatever object was closest to me at the TV whenever they came on. Our attacks from men dressed in black had subsided, and for the first time in a long time, no one tried to break into my church or my house.

John remained private about his history and changed the subject whenever I tried to bring it up. However, he remained committed to keeping me safe, and he never gave me any reason not to trust him.

Even the strained relationship I had with Geena began to change. I never talked to her about how her theft of Grandma's ring had led to their deaths. Despite the fact that she had always been my enemy, in many ways she had now become my unexpected hoodoo ally.

I knew she had her flaws, but I also knew she was the only person in my life, who had loved my grandparents almost as much as I did. She had begun letting John and me in on some tricks of the trade to stay safe, and I appreciated the helpfulness she hid under herd tough exterior.

Hoodoo became my alternative security system. I buried boxes of red root under the house and put a devil pod over the front door. I applied patchouli oil on my doorknobs to protect people I loved when they were inside.

I planted some sedum plants known as "hens and chicks" to provide protection from theft. I had even written out a petition for safekeeping, anointed it with Fiery Wall of Protection, added the Blessed Thistle herb to it, and buried all of it together with some dirt from my grandparents' grave site.

However, despite the arrest of my grandparents's killer, the feeling of unfinished business with them still resonated deeply within me. Even though we had arrested their murderer and the crooks, who had aided them, their story had been cut short much too soon.

Despite my fear about using the pocket watch because of its unpredictable tendencies, I was resolved now more than ever to go back in time to bring them back from the dead. I decided that even though I always dreamed of having an adventure away from Memphis, there seemed to be plenty of adventures waiting for me in the Bluff City. So to keep from missing out on the excitement, I figured I'd stick around to see what was just around the corner for me here.

While I realized that protecting the ring and the watch from people, who would have exploited their powers, had been the right thing to do, I didn't know what I was supposed to do with them next. All of the pieces to my family's twisted puzzle swam around in my head, as I stared off into space trying to put them together. Today I was taking the day off from my hoodoo responsibilities, but tomorrow I would be getting back into the saddle again. I was overdue in checking the mail from Grandma, and if I could get my nerve worked up, I figured maybe I'd try out time traveling with the pocket watch next week.

Keisha called to check on me, and I was glad I could honestly tell her that I was feeling better than I had in months. Even though I knew I had other enemies lurking around, the key problems were currently caged, and I finally felt like justice could be served.

After we discussed all of the hoodoo happenings, Keisha told me that Will had expressed worry to her for me, and I rolled my eyes over the phone. Will certainly hadn't been concerned enough to stop gossiping about me or to visit me when I had been in jail, so for now at least, he was of no concern to me.

Keisha, being a much nicer person than I would ever be, argued, "Addie, Will wasn't a complete jerk. He was just clueless. It ain't his fault you're secretive and don't let people know how to help you."

I winced at the truth in her words, but as usual, my stubbornness trumped my reason. So, I held my line and my grudge against him.

"He crossed the line. There's no going back from it."

"No going back from what?" she asked sounding confused since she had always been more forgiving than I had ever been.

"He talked about my family, and that's a deal breaker. I haven't got much, but what I've got, I won't have taken from me—especially not from somebody, who's had the world handed to him on a silver platter."

"That ain't his fault either," she pointed out.

"I never said it was," I conceded. "But it changes nothing for me."

Keisha expressed understanding but still confessed, "I guess I just hoped you'd like him enough to forget about the Man."

"Gavin. His name is Gavin. And you're not being fair. You don't know him yet."

"Oh, trust me—the memory I have of meeting him the other night is burned into my brain forever. I can see why he would have a lasting impact on you."

My door bell rang and startled me enough to get me off of the phone. I was surprised to see how late it was, but I was elated to see Gavin's gorgeous face behind the glass.

"I came by to check on you to see if you were all right," Gavin said softly after I let him in. His voice was as smooth as velvet. "I got you something that I thought would be helpful," he explained tentatively before he pulled a chocolate Labrador Retriever out of his arms and handed her to me. She was beautiful, and I accepted her as she crawled up onto my shoulder and nuzzled my neck.

"I've never had a pet before. I don't know what to do

with her," I admitted feeling embarrassed as I cuddled her.

"I brought supplies for her. I know you're used to taking care of your folks, so I thought it might help for you to have some company to look after over here. Besides, she's...special," he toyed with the word as if he were holding back a lot about my new pet. "I wanted to get you a big, ferocious guard dog for safety reasons, but somehow I think she's going to be just the right fit for you."

"I don't think she's likely to scare anybody."

"The two of you are evidence that good things come in small packages which should not be underestimated," he said gently as I set her down on the floor to explore her new home.

"I'm surprised you brought me a chocolate dog with green eyes. I thought black was your signature color."

"Yes, but let's just say I have a thing for green eyed brunettes," he said looking at me earnestly, and I smiled in spite of myself.

We followed her around the house while she growled and attacked the pages of a magazine advertising for P.E.A.C.E. She continued to pad around until she wiggled under my Grandma's bed and pulled out her pink bunny ear shoes. My new puppy dragged them over into the corner of the room, circled around seven times, laid down, and went to sleep on top of those ragged, old house shoes. I teared up, and Gavin put his arm around me for support.

"I've been wondering something since our run-in with Clint and Jaydon at John's place the other night," I said tentatively. "I really wanted to bash their skulls in, but you wouldn't let me."

"When an individual invites revenge into his world, it becomes a toxic, consuming force. If you let it fuel your life, it will poison everything important enough for you to live for. Revenge clouds your judgment and warps you into somebody you don't want to be. You're better than that, and if I'm being perfectly honest, I can't let negative energy consume you, Addie, because I need you to stay good." he explained candidly.

"What makes you say that?" I asked.

"You make me want to be a better person. You inspire me and give me hope, and it's been a long time since anyone has had that effect on me. You're going to make a positive difference in this world," he said as my face conveyed disbelief about his predictions to him. "Just wait—you'll see."

"I don't know why they thought I was cut out for all of this," I confessed to him. I did not feel as sure of myself as he seemed to. "I never wanted any of it."

"That's why they gave it to you. They knew you wouldn't abuse the powers they entrusted to you, and they realized that when it became possible, you'd figure out how to do something good with it, Addie," he stated as if it were so obvious. I shivered at the way he said my name, and my heart skipped a beat. "The people, who don't want to be in power are the very individuals who need to be."

"But I don't know what I'm doing," I sighed.

"Don't you think they belieed you were competent enough to figure it out?"

I didn't know if he was right or not, but it was nice of him to say so.

"I've been meaning to ask if you would mind if I took you out to dinner this weekend." he asked tentatively as he swallowed hard like he was afraid I might say no. The nervousness in his face caught my attention. He scared plenty of people but didn't scare easily himself.

My father was an alcoholic, my mother was a workaholic, my aunt was a troubled gambler, my sister was autistic, my grandparents were adrenaline addicts, and I had already developed panic attacks from all of it.

I had pretty much concluded that I had more issues than a magazine subscription. There was a much greater chance that I would lose my mind than that my life would have a happy ending. I certainly didn't want him to hang all of his hopes onto me when my plight was surely cursed.

So, with a heavy heart I told him candidly, "Listen, you don't want to get mixed up with me. I'm ... genetically predisposed for tragedy. I would never be able to put you first, and you'd grow tired of that, and I couldn't blame you. Honestly I'm going to feel like a jealous harpy whenever I see you out with someone else, but the truth is, I'd rather you have all the good you deserve from someone else than have you stay with me while every day I would have to live with the guilt of knowing you would always go without. I care about you too much to deprive you of anything...even if that means I lose you."

Yet at the moment I confessed that I wanted him, his eyes lit up, and he stepped towards me and kissed me so intensely that I quickly forgot what my argument against being with him had been.

He overrode the guilt I felt about the burdens he would bear from getting involved with me, and in spite of everything difficult I would face in my world, the temptation of being with him was enough...it was so much more than enough.

When he pulled himself away from me he said, "Let's try this one more time. Addie Marie Jackson, would you mind going on a date with me?"

"I would only have minded if you hadn't asked," I admitted feeling thankful that he had given me the opportunity to offer him a better answer. Then we grinned at each other before he gave me another real, honest to goodness, earth shattering kiss.

He finally stopped kissing me reluctantly as he admitted, "I have to go to work."

I checked the time and remarked aghast, "But it's almost 10PM!"

He shrugged. "You know I work the graveyard shift, and there will always be someone who wants something waiting for me."

"Just don't forget that I'll be waiting for you, too," I said sincerely as he hugged me tight before he departed.

The delicious aroma of apples lingered behind him long after he left, and I reflected on how John had called him forbidden fruit. He must have seriously been underestimating my stubborn, curious streak in ever advising me to refrain from having him.

I had an unintended flash back to Amber being under the love struck spell for Chris, and I quickly pushed back the fear I held that maybe I had been hoodooed, too.

That night Keisha and Amber sent me some sweet text messages checking on me, and John insisted on staying at my house to keep guard for me. Even Geena made up a lame excuse to swing by to grab Pop's shovel when both of us knew she was just making sure I was all right. Most of my family might have died, but that didn't mean I didn't still have a lot of people in my life, who loved me.

Maybe Gavin was right. Maybe there was hope after all. Maybe I could make things better. Maybe I could fulfill the legacy that had been cut short for them.

Then there in the middle of my musings, I recalled the warmth of his mouth on mine, and the memory was almost as hot as the reality had been.

When I went to sleep that night for the first time in a long time I dreamed about the future. In my dream the city had healed from the earthquake and the tornado. I was finally able to attend all of my classes like a normal college student. No one was trying to kill my loved ones and me, and for the first time in my life I was not afraid. I was free of my panic attacks, and I had poured the last of my liquor down the drain. Keisha's worries had lifted, and John was finally sleeping soundly again.

Amber had found a nice boyfriend, who even Geena approved of. Of course there were obstacles and hardships ahead, as there would always be, but I was and had always been equipped with everything I needed to get through them.

My lab and I continued to dream peacefully curled up in my bed, and I was thinking that she and I were going to get along just fine. At last there were no intruders trying to break down my world, and despite my puppy's youth, I think she would have gone down fighting to try to protect me even if they had. I believed that even if someone tried to break in to hurt me, I was more prepared to deal with that than I had ever been in my life.

For no matter what I was going to go through, I would overcome it. I would always persevere, because I was, after all, my grandmother's child.

Acknowledgements

Special thanks to Memphis, Tennessee, and Jackson, Mississippi, for which the fictional Jackson family was named. I appreciate Anthony, my best friend and husband, for his support throughout this lengthy writing process. Since I hold his opinion in high regard, his critiques were critical to the creation of this tale. I was blessed by James Dickerson of Sartoris Literary Group, for without his advice and encouragement to keep writing, this book might not have been.

I am indebted to Jill McCarty for her valuable literary perspective, her genuine faith in me as a person, and her honest voice. I appreciate Sarah Pederson-Garrison, who assessed various versions of this novel and whose perspective I trusted. I am obliged to Kimberly Creekmore Witter for suggesting the title, loving this novel long before it was worth reading, and cheering me on until the story was polished.

I am grateful to Jennifer Pennington who shared her valuable perspective as an avid reader with me. I appreciate Stephanie and Rebekah Britt who gave me their feedback to tweak the opening chapter. I thank Katie Rogers and Betsy Martin for their keen literary eyes and their emotional support. I am grateful to everyone I confided in about my writing since each of them responded positively. While there is not enough room to recognize everybody, each individual held up a lantern to illuminate my path, and I am forever indebted to each of them for that.

Made in the USA
Charleston, SC
10 October 2015